Around the time symptoms of Huntington's Disease began to appear in their lives, Hugh and Cathie Marriott sold their house, bought a sailing boat, and embarked on what was to become a nine-year voyage of discovery. By the time Cathie could no longer get in or out of their small dinghy or safely clamber on board their boat, they had visited 40 countries and sailed almost the whole way around the world.

After moving ashore again Hugh settled down to write about the most significant aspect of the voyage: coming to terms with someone in the grip of a debilitating disease. In *The Selfish Pig's Guide to Caring* he tries to put his finger on the advice he would like to have been given while he was struggling to learn new skills and find his way in an unfamiliar role.

THE SELFISH PIG'S GUIDE TO CARING

Hugh Marriott

Illustrations by David Lock

TIME WARNER
BOOKS

TIME WARNER BOOKS

First published in Great Britain in 2003 by Polperro Heritage Press
Reprinted in 2003, 2004
This paperback edition published in May 2006 by Time Warner Books

ISBN 0 7515 3709 8

Typeset in Baskerville by M Rules
Printed and bound in Great Britain by
Clays Ltd, St Ives plc

Time Warner Books
An imprint of
Time Warner Book Group UK
Brettenham House
Lancaster Place
London WC2E 7EN

www.twbg.co.uk

To everyone else in the farmyard

The Selfish Pig's Guide to Caring

> Pig: a term of abuse; esp. a disagreeable, obstinate or unpleasant person.
>
> The New Shorter Oxford English Dictionary

There are people who cheerfully sacrifice time and freedom to care for another human being. They eagerly embrace the onerous task of caring, and are never known to complain about their lot. These people are saints, and this book is not for them.

There are others who are paid to care. Their job is hard and the money not always very generous. Even so, it *is* a job, and therefore something which can be walked away from at the end of every day. Dedicated workers they may be, but this book is not for them either.

There are others of us who have come reluctantly to caring. We feel bad about our unwillingness, and secretly think of ourselves as selfish pigs. Like pigs in nature, we can be of either sex. Also like real pigs, we are not necessarily, or at least always, disagreeable and unpleasant. But we're certainly obstinate. This book is for us.

Contents

Preface

Looking after another human being who can't survive without you can be hard. It may well be harder than anything you have ever done before.

There is a long list of reasons why this should be so. But the most compelling are our secret thoughts. And these are universal.

So wherever in the world you live, there should be something in this book that makes you think: yes, that's me.

But there may also be words and expressions which need to be translated, and perhaps whole sections which don't apply. In North America you'll be a caregiver, not a carer, so even the title of the book will need translating. Then there are differences in the amount and nature of the help (if any) you can expect from statutory or charitable sources.

This paperback edition is going to need editing to make it fit your latitude and longitude, and you're going to have to do it yourself. I hoped the publishers might take it on, but they pointed out that it would necessitate printing multiple versions of the book.

It's bad enough that you need to read a book on this subject at all, without being asked to edit and translate it as you go. You'll manage, though. You're a carer (or maybe a caregiver). So you're resourceful, and all too accustomed to doing a difficult job for nothing.

CHAPTER 1

Warning

What this book is not

It isn't politically correct
It isn't a medical textbook
It isn't a guide to benefits and grants
It doesn't supply a foolproof method of turning
    you into an angel of mercy
It isn't a how-to-care manual

What this book *is*

It's about you

Who's the author?

Why's he written it?

How to use the book

Keep it in the downstairs loo or by the bed
Or turn to a specific chapter
Or you can read it like a novel

Warning

You may have acquired this book under false pretences.

You *think* you're a selfish pig. But that's because

- you never expected to find yourself in the role of carer

- you're pissed off about it

- you feel guilty about your reaction.

Well, what I know, and you don't, is this: everybody who gets lumbered with the job of caring for somebody else goes round and round in the same emotional whirlpool. And there are millions of us carers. If you don't believe me, have a look at pages 50-1.

We didn't apply for the job. Most of us don't have a vocation for it. We've had no training. We're certain we aren't much good at it. Plus, and this is the nub of the matter, we've got our own life to lead. Are we expected to throw that away because of somebody else's disability? We've got things to do, places to go. And now it looks as if we might not be able to.

But aren't we just as important as they are? Why are we expected to sacrifice ourselves for somebody else? And yes, I mean sacrifice. We're not talking about giving up five minutes of time once or twice a week. Or putting off a holiday from this year to next. We're talking about changing our entire way of life. The old one wasn't perfect, but it was the best we could do. This new one isn't even ours. It's somebody else's life. And it's one that doesn't suit us at all.

It isn't fair!

Sure, sure, sure. I'm not going to argue with you. All I'm going to say is that none of this makes you a selfish pig. You're reading the book, aren't you? Well, you've got this far, anyway. That probably means that you're caring for someone. Or thinking about caring for someone. Selfish pigs don't do that. They get somebody else to do their dirty work. Or they just turn their backs on the problem and walk away.

So what are you, if you're not a selfish pig? A reluctant carer?

No, you're just the average carer. The reason you aren't aware that you're walking down a well-trodden path is because carers don't get much publicity. Or attention. When someone pushes a wheelchair through a crowd, it's the wheelchair that attracts the sideways glances. Or which causes passers-by to look politely away. In either case, the person who's doing the pushing is invisible. Those people in the crowd don't spare the carer a thought. Be fair, did you ever, before you became a carer?

No. So what goes on in the minds and deep dark despairing souls of the carers is a complete unknown. Except to other carers. They know. They've been there.

Did you really think all those other carers were doing it because it's what they always aspired to? Maybe they won the big prize in a competition? Or saved up for years so that finally they could take up this glamorous way of life?

And do you somehow believe they're better at it than you?

Hang on, I know what you think. You've convinced yourself that they're better than you, full stop. That someone who cares for another human being, long-term, is a better person than you are.

Well, all I can say to that is Ha! The only difference between them and you is that they're a bit further ahead, that's all. They kept walking down the path that you're just starting out on, and along the way they discovered things. They didn't have any training or vocation or special ability. They aren't more capable of loving. They most decidedly are NOT less selfish. They're exactly the same as you. Just more experienced at being carers, that's all.

So there you are. Whether the title of this book is a good one or not, the book may have some stuff in it that you'll find a use for. I have no plans to try to turn you into somebody else. Change your nature, and so on. Endow you with limitless patience and goodwill. All I'm proposing to do is walk with you down the path, pointing out a few things as we go. You'd stroll down it perfectly well without me. But together, we might go a little faster. And who knows, we might even have a laugh on the way.

> Remember that crack of John Lennon's? The one about life being something that happens to you while you're busy making other plans?

What this book is not

It isn't politically correct

I haven't got time to go through the manuscript changing 'he' to 's/he' in a high-minded attempt not to be gender specific. I might say 'they', if I remember. Or 'she' even, particularly when I'm thinking of my wife.

Oh, and I probably won't use the proper word for the person you're caring for. I don't even know what the proper word is.

'Patient'

'Cared-for Person'

'Loved One'

'Disabled Person'

or even just 'Person'.

In fact, now I come to think of it, I don't believe there is a sensible word. I'd better invent one.

'**P**erson **I G**ive **L**ove and **E**ndless **T**herapy to'

Which is terrible, I know, but at least you can shorten it to Piglet.

It isn't a medical textbook

People can be piglets for hundreds of different reasons: old age; some past illness like polio or a disaster like a motorcycle accident which results in a lifelong disability; autism, epilepsy, Down's Syndrome, Huntington's, MS, Alzheimer's. Whatever. Disabilities can be physical, mental, or both. Piglets can be young or old.

Every illness and disability has its own symptoms and sets its own agenda. A book could be written, and hundreds probably have been, on each one. It's quite likely that you're already an expert on the one that affects your piglet. If you aren't yet, you will be. You'll have to be.

You'll acquire this specialist knowledge and expertise partly by direct experience, and partly by studying all the source material that's available to you. It'll come to you via the doctor, or the support group you attend, or the internet or library or bookshop. And it'll keep coming. You probably won't ever stop learning about it.

'People sometimes ask me what it is like being a carer, and I can honestly say that for me caring for my demented mother in law was utterly different from caring for my physically disabled husband. Carers are different and need different information and support from us.'

Alison Ryan, Chief Executive, The Princess Royal Trust for Carers

If this book tried to cover all these conditions, you'd never get it through the front door let alone into the downstairs toilet or on to your bedside table.

It isn't a guide to benefits and grants

When you become a carer, you suddenly find yourself in a new socio-economic bracket. This is because you almost certainly won't be able to earn as much as you could if you weren't a carer. Or as much as you need. On the other hand, there may be a variety of State benefits to offset the discrepancy – well, let's not be ridiculous, the State isn't going to make up the difference; just toss you a few crumbs. But anything is better than nothing – so you're going to want to become an expert on this aspect of caring.

The trouble is

- benefits change every time the government sneezes, so if I tried to detail them here (which would be a daft thing to do because not even the officials who administer them understand them) the book would be out of date already

- they vary not only from country to country, but within counties or states or even sub-divisions of those.

So this book isn't going to dish out specific advice on how you should get your hands on whatever financial help is available. What it does do, though, is suggest a few ways of dealing with this problem, in Chapter 7.

It doesn't supply a foolproof method of turning you into an angel of mercy

It would take more than a book to change your personality, let's face it. In any case, what I know and you don't is that you're not so bad, and probably don't really need changing. Much.

It isn't a how-to-care manual

There's plenty of advice flying around about diets, and cheering piglets up when they're down, or distracting them when they're being difficult. Some carers can do all this naturally. Others, like us, have to learn the hard way.

There's a certain amount (not much) about topics of that kind later on in the book. But all that stuff is really about the piglets. Whereas what this book is about is:

you.

What this book *is*

It's about you

In it, the piglet takes second place. This is only partly because you're a selfish pig. It's also because:

- If the carer falls down on the job, the piglet is the one who suffers. And who's doing the job? You are

- In considering any other kind of job or career, you'd take into account things like prospects, holidays, lifestyle, earnings. Even teachers are concerned about what they themselves are going to get out of teaching. I've heard it whispered that doctors are no different, either. Well, this is a job, too, and it's an important one. Lives are at stake here. Admittedly you may not get paid very well, or at all. And you may not actually have applied for the job in the first place. Never mind. You're in a job, like it or not. So what this book does is look at the job from your point of view

- Other books about caring, and lots of conventional wisdom, put the piglet first. If you're lucky they might accord you equal status. But not here. In this book the piglet takes second place, and you're Number One. There are going to be plenty of moments as a carer when you're not, so you may as well enjoy it in these pages.

Who's the author?

Not a social worker. Not a doctor. Not a psychologist, or occupational therapist, or any other kind of professional specialising in either disability or caring. My qualification is that I was, and still am, an incorrigible SP (Selfish Pig).

My piglet has Huntington's Disease. It's caused by a faulty gene which damages nerve cells in some areas of the brain, and leads to gradual physical, mental and emotional changes. It usually comes on in middle age, and symptoms include uncontrollable muscular movements, lack of concentration, and mood swings. Some people, and my piglet is one of them, have trouble swallowing and making themselves understood.

One of the characteristics of Huntington's, at any rate in our case, is that its progress is very slow. A piglet with Huntington's can go on for decades, gradually becoming more and more dependent. The effect on this SP is that there has been plenty of time to savour all the conflicting and painful emotional difficulties of coming to terms with caring.

I kept a log of what happened to both of us. And I compared notes with other carers. Even so, it took me years to discover that my experience was by no means unique. What I learned was that carers are like lovers. They're convinced that they're the only people in the world, in the whole of time, who've ever felt like this.

Why's he written it?

When I was at school, I thought I'd like to be a journalist. I learned to type when I was 15, and started in on shorthand a year later. At university I worked on the students' newspaper. My first paid job was with a provincial daily newspaper. I was an indentured (a word I still haven't looked up) trainee, and once a week my fellow junior reporters and I were despatched to the local technical college to sit a journalism course. Its syllabus included subjects like printing, typography, and the law of libel.

But I didn't write this book because I'm a trained journalist. I wrote it because I'm an *untrained* carer. Most of the lessons I learned about caring I learned the hard way. Of course, in the process I got practically everything wrong. As a result my piglet suffered. And so did I.

After I'd discovered that carers are expected to learn their trade all by themselves as they go along – an illogical, inefficient, and thoroughly UNCARING policy – it seemed to me that there were a number of things I could do about this:

- Congratulate myself on having become better at the job with the passing of time

- Try to help other carers by lobbying for a training programme to be put in place

- Initiate a training programme myself.

I did do a bit of the first, I suppose. Sorry about that. I did absolutely nothing about the other two. My excuse is that, by the time I thought of it, I was too busy being a full-time carer. There was no way I could take time off for meetings away from home. And in any case it seemed to me that you could lobby your heart out for years on end without getting anywhere.

But it eventually dawned on me that there was another option:

- Write a book about it.

Once I'd thought of it, I could immediately see several advantages in this course of action. For one thing, I'd already done a lot of the research, and by chance I'd kept all the notes. For another, I could do the work in moments when my piglet didn't need me. In fact, clattering away at my keyboard would be a positive pleasure, and would qualify as respite care.

What would I put in the book? Simple: all the things I wished I'd been told. I started to jot them down.

Then, an uneasy thought. If I *had* been told any of this stuff years before, would I have paid any attention? Would it have changed the way I felt? Would I have responded and acted differently as a result?

Hmmmm. No, probably not.

The great advantage of learning in the school of hard knocks is that when something creeps up and whacks you over the head, you're somehow ready for it. After that, you do respond and act differently. But there's a proper time for everything, and you can't beat the clock.

All right, then, I thought. I'll do the book in such a way that when people are ready to take on board this particular thought, or that specific piece of information, they'll be able to find it. Easily.

So that's what I've tried to do.

How to use the book

Keep it in the downstairs loo or by the bed

Or somewhere where you might be tempted to pick it up and glance inside from time to time. Please don't put it on a book-shelf just yet. Once a book gets in there, it's curtains.

Or turn to a specific chapter

Like the one entitled 'Pushing Them Down The Stairs'. Hopefully you'll be able to see from the contents page which bit you're curious about. Or, more likely, seething about. If you can't find it, try looking at the subheadings listed at the beginning of each chapter. Or in the index at the back.

Or you can read it like a novel

ie, from start to finish. I haven't tried that, so I don't know if it'll work.

CHAPTER 2

Why care at all?

Love

Money

Guilt

Obligation

Expectations of others

Relatives

Religion

Don't know?

Why care at all?

Ever asked yourself the question: What the hell am I doing this for?

Ever allowed your mind to contemplate what your life could be like if you weren't being a carer?

Perhaps you're one of the rare people who don't torture themselves with thoughts like these.

But if you're not – ie, if you're like the rest of us SPs – you'll find yourself examining your motives in times of stress. And questioning them.

You may know precisely why you're a carer. If so, you may derive renewed strength every time you remind yourself why you're doing the job. But it's more likely that there isn't just one reason. There could be several. You might be hard put to identify them all, or to decide which are the important ones. It can be a complicated business.

Does it matter? Maybe the only thing that really matters is that you *are* caring. *Why* you're caring is perhaps irrelevant.

Well, that's a point of view. But the thing is this: the reason why you're a carer might affect the way you care. And even more important for the purposes of this book, it could affect the way you feel about yourself. And this in turn can have a bearing on your physical health and your mental well-being. We'll get to all that in Chapter 10. Meantime, it's worth taking a look at some of the possible reasons which might lie behind your caring role.

Love

Love is the public reason why we care for our piglets. And it may even be the real reason. In fact, there's quite a good chance that love, or what we take for granted as love, is our first motive. But there's very often more to it than that.

You see, the trouble is that the piglet may not have had this

17

disability when you first loved them. And the disability, if it came later, probably changed them. So now they're different. And to be totally honest about it, they may not be quite as loveable as they were. They may not be loveable at all. There may even be times when they're absolutely, undeniably, bloody well IMPOSSIBLE to love.

But you won't want to admit this. Not even to yourself. After all, why else would you be doing this ridiculous caring job? If it wasn't because you loved them, you'd be off doing something else with your life. It's got to be love. Hasn't it?

Duet from *Fiddler on the Roof*

Tevye	Do you love me?
Golde	Do I what?
Tevye	Do you love me?
Golde	Do I love him?
	With our daughters getting married,
	And this trouble in the town,
	You're upset, you're worn out.
	Go inside, go lie down.
	Maybe it's indigestion.
Tevye	No. Golde, I'm asking you a question:
	Do you love me?
Golde	You're a fool.
Tevye	I know. But, do you love me?
Golde	Do I love you?
Tevye	Well?
Golde	For 25 years I've washed your clothes,
	Cooked your meals, cleaned your house,
	Given you children, milked the cow.
	After 25 years why talk about love right now?
Tevye	Golde: The first time I met you was on our wedding day.
	I was scared.

Golde	I was shy.
Tevye	I was nervous.
Golde	So was I.
Tevye	But my father and my mother Said we'd learn to love each other And now I'm asking: Golde, do you love me?
Golde	I'm your wife.
Tevye	I know. But do you love me?
Golde	Do I love him?
Tevye	Well?
Golde	For 25 years I've lived with him, Fought with him, starved with him. 25 years my bed is his. If that's not love, what is?
Tevye	Then you love me.
Golde	I suppose I do.
Tevye	And I suppose I love you too.
Both	It doesn't change a thing, but even so, After 25 years it's nice to know.

It's not just you who makes this assumption. It's as if everybody does. 'I can see that you really love your piglet,' they say. (Except that they don't use the word 'piglet'.) They never seem to ask whether you do, in fact, love them. They just seem to know it, whether or not you're entirely sure yourself.

There's quite a lot of taking for granted going on around here. Even the word 'care' kind of assumes love. When you care about someone, you love them.

> *Girl I care about you*
> *I'm there for you*
> *So why don't you care for me*
> *Like I care about you*
>
> *I'm all you've got*
> *Sometimes I'm not sure if you love me or not*
> *One thing I know*
> *Girl I care for you*
> *And the one thing that I want is that you care for me too*

Lyrics of song by Babyface

Well, fair enough. I'm not saying you don't love your piglet. All I'm saying is that the person you care *about* may be a bit different from the one you care *for*.

Lots of us carers experience sudden onsets of unexplained misery. It descends out of nowhere, and won't be shifted. What's that all about, then? I haven't a clue. But it's just possible that it's got something to do with doubt. Something inside you wants to know what the hell you're doing in this situation. And it isn't satisfied with the usual assumption that you're there because, and only because, you love your piglet.

Now, you can't very well say to your piglet: 'I have no idea why I'm looking after you, and sometimes I don't even know whether I love you or not.' It's hard to voice these doubts to anyone at all, let alone yourself and especially to your piglet.

You probably do love them, all right. In a *Fiddler on the Roof* kind of way. But other factors could be joggling around in there as well.

Money

Well, obviously you're not in it for the money. At least, not unless you're hovering by the bedside of some ancient and wealthy person who might, with a bit of encouragement, leave you an enormous fortune. I somehow think, though, that if this was your cunning plan you wouldn't be bothering to read this book.

On the other hand, money does have a habit of poking its nose in everywhere, particularly where it doesn't belong. And you'll certainly have given it some thought.

It's perfectly possible you'll have considered handing the caring job over to somebody else, but reluctantly decided it would all be too expensive. If your piglet is your spouse, and let's say you were tempted for a moment there to walk out, you'd quickly have bumped your head against some uncomfortable calculations about splitting your assets.

Even more ludicrously, you might be thinking about the benefits you've eventually been able to squeeze out of an unwilling government. They aren't exactly megabucks, but they are money. Walk away, and you get nothing. You haven't even considered the money aspect? Well, good for you. Lots of us have, is all I'm saying. And if you have too, however briefly, all I'm saying is that it goes with the job. You'll have had to come to grips with some financial considerations – extra costs of care, and special equipment, on one side of the balance sheet; disability benefits, special grants, on the other.

At the end of the day, you might conclude that money is one of several reasons why you're caring for your piglet. Does that mean you're mercenary? Nah. Just that you live in the real world.

Guilt

Here's the theory:

Your piglet has this disability. You haven't. You feel bad about that, and this is your way of making amends.

Do you buy that?

No, neither do I.

Obligation

Your piglet is a . . .

- parent? – well, they looked after you when you were small, so you feel it's only fair that you should look after them now

- spouse? – maybe you said those words about sticking together for better or worse, in sickness and in health, and now you're stuck with the consequence

- child? – no parent ever totally backs away from the responsibility to look after their child. But a child with a serious disability imposes huge strains. This makes the obligation that much more binding, but it doesn't make it any easier to cope with

- sibling? – blood is thicker than water, charity begins at home, and so on

- neighbour? – and they don't seem to have anyone else able or willing to look after them, so you don't see quite how it can be right for you not to pop round? Only popping round has somehow turned into being there most of the time, so now you've got no time left for yourself.

Expectations of others

Even if you don't feel, deep down, that you have a moral obligation to look after your piglet, you may suspect that other people do. You'd probably be wrong, mind you. Even if you're right, and the lady next door is keeping a beady eye on you to make sure you're doing the right thing, is this really a good reason for you to decide how to shape your life?

No, it isn't. But it might form part of the complex argument that resulted in your becoming a carer. And if it does, you might as well look it in the eye.

Relatives

Chinese proverb:
The old father is so sick and frail that he can no longer help man the fishing boat or mend the nets. His son sadly prepares the traditional wicker cage, bows farewell to his father in the time-honoured manner, and beckons him to step inside.

The old man does so, and his son begins to lace up the cage so that there will be no escape. The old man folds his arms across his chest, resigned to his fate.

The young man hoists the laden cage into the boat, and readies himself to row out to sea, to lower it over the side.

'Son,' says the fisherman, 'I'm no longer any use to my family or to the community, and what you do now is a fitting thing. But one word of advice.'

'Yes, father?'

'After I'm dead, raise the cage to the surface, take it back to the shore, and keep it there in good condition. Then, when your time comes, your son will not have the labour of making a new cage for you.'

In some societies – not yours – family members look after one another for purely practical reasons: when it's your turn to need looking after, your family will do it. That's how the system used to work before nanny states came into being. It's how it still works in communities that run extended family systems. It's highly practical, and there's nothing wrong with it at all. In many respects, it's a better system than the nanny state version, because the caring gets to be shared among several family members, instead of devolving upon just one of them.

In our society, there may be another aspect to family caring. Let's say Grandad has Alzheimer's, and Granny's got the job of looking after him. The rest of the family are watchful bystanders. They do what they can, of course, but they can't relieve Granny of the main task because of jobs and school and distance. Nevertheless, they see what's she's doing, and they're affected by it. In time, when a similar responsibility descends on the shoulders of one of the grandchildren, they may be more willing and more capable of taking on the job as a result of what they've learned from watching Granny, in her time, do the same thing. But what if she couldn't manage it?

In that case, even though the rest of the family would have understood and forgiven her, there's the possibility that some of them might have felt in some degree diminished. It's just the opposite of the strength they drew from the other example, that's all. So when Granny is trying to stay sane in the midst of the growing trauma of looking after Grandad's ever madder and more maddening behaviour, one of her motivating factors, besides her love or past love for Grandad, may possibly be this awareness of how the rest of the family will react to what she does.

Families are communities in which each member is affected by what happens to each of the others. If you're a member of a family, whether it's an extended one or not, and you're struggling to cope with a caring role, you could be conscious of the eyes of other family members on you.

This awareness could give you strength and joy. It could

equally well increase the burden of responsibility. Or sometimes the one, and sometimes the other.

There's no need to form a judgement about this. But if you lift your own eyes from the task in hand and gaze back into those other watching eyes, you might see what's going on, and be better able to cope with it as a result.

Religion

It may be that as far as you're concerned you don't really have a choice as to whether you take up a caring role or not. God expects it of you, and that's the end of that. Fair enough. Faith can be a great comfort, and a source of strength. It can also impose a lot of pressure. And that can have the opposite effect.

Don't know?

You've been flipping through these headings in the hopes that you might get a few clues about why you're caring? And you're none the wiser?

Understanding your own motives is always fraught. I'm not suggesting here that it's essential to understand what's going on behind the scenes. But I suspect it can be helpful, when you run up against the 'What the hell am I doing this for?' syndrome to recognise that:

- It's complicated

- To be unsure from time to time doesn't make you any more of an SP than anybody else

- Most people probably don't know. They do it just the same. Then, by the time they've found out how hard it can be, it's too late.

Considering how many sound reasons there are for being a carer, anyone would think that we'd feel really good about ourselves for doing this valuable and worthwhile job. Yet the fact is that most of us experience periods in which we despise ourselves for doing it, hate the piglet for being the cause of our troubles, and yearn for escape. We get ill, lose our tempers, and sometimes harbour secret thoughts about pushing our piglet down the stairs.

We're suffering from stress brought on by caring, and no amount of love or guilt or money or religion or approval by our neighbours and relations can ease the pain.

This is a big subject, and we'll get to it later on (in Chapter 11). You can go there now if you want. But if you prefer to wait, here's a quick thought to leave with you: maybe one or more of these motives for caring (love etc), is actually producing the stress. Or if not producing it, then making it harder to deal with.

CHAPTER 3

What if you didn't care?

Maybe you shouldn't even consider being a carer

Or would you go bonkers if you didn't?

Who would do it if you didn't?

Care-workers paid by you
Relatives
Neighbours
Charitable organisation
The State

Who would suffer?

What if you didn't care?

What if you decided not to do it? Not to take on the job of caring, or, if you *are* doing it already, not to do it any more?

What if you said:

- 'I'm not strong enough to do this.'

- Or: 'It isn't what I'm good at; I'd be the wrong person for the job; it wouldn't be fair on my piglet; we'll have to get someone in who has more patience; someone who's trained.'

- Or: 'I've got my own life to lead; I'm not getting any younger, and by the time I was released from the caring I'd be so old I'd be in need of caring myself.'

Or what if you simply said: 'I've tried as hard as I could, but I can't go on any longer; my life is in tatters; if I carry on I'll end up by committing suicide.'

It happens. I don't mean the suicide, though that probably happens sometimes as well. I mean that there are carers who feel they can't carry on. And there are people who can't bear to shoulder the responsibility in the first place. They're not criminals, or failures, or people with no sense of morality or obligation. They're just people. You wouldn't be the only one.

There's a difference – at least, I *think* there is – between refusing to do something and just not being able to do it. You could love someone as much as anybody could love anyone else yet, with the best will in the world, be incapable of caring for them. We all have our limitations, and if yours stop you short of being a carer, there's no point in trying to push yourself beyond the point of what you can do. Try, and it wouldn't work anyway, probably.

Maybe you shouldn't even consider being a carer

It's not as if it's a job you always wanted. What happened was that you suddenly found yourself in this position, and couldn't see any alternative. But it may not look that way to other people. They may think you're crazy to be doing it.

A friend of mine asked me how things were. I said: 'Fine.'

He said: 'No, I don't mean for both of you. I mean for *you*. How are you coping?'

I replied: 'OK. I think.'

He shrugged his shoulders. 'As long as it makes you happy.'

At the time I found this exchange vaguely unsatisfactory, but couldn't quite put my finger on why. I re-ran the conversation over the course of the next couple of days, and decided that what he had meant was that *he* wouldn't do it, and that I was a bit odd to want to do it. He probably thought I had some ulterior motive which he couldn't understand. Then he mentally made that face where you push out your lower lip and raise your eyebrows, meaning: 'Funny decision, but if it makes sense to you then it's fine by me.'

For some time afterwards I was unsettled, and went about wondering whether I was somehow doing something stupid and unnecessary, in caring for my piglet. It seemed to me that perhaps it wasn't inevitable, or the right thing to do, after all. I started to believe that there must be another, far more intelligent, course of action open to me.

The only problem was, I couldn't think of one.

Or would you go bonkers if you didn't?

Perhaps it's the other way round, and instead of being mad to do it, you'd *go* mad if you didn't.

A woman I met is caring not only for her aged mother but also for her mother's aged sister.

She had asked herself the usual question ('What on earth am I doing this for?') and had come up with an answer.

She had concluded that all her life her family had been the most important thing in the world to her. It wasn't just that she loved all her relations (she thought she probably didn't, really, all that much). It was more that family values, in her view, were the values that mattered. According to her, the family was the bedrock of a civilised society.

She thought: 'If I didn't care for my own family when they needed it, then I wouldn't be the person I'd always thought I was.'

Talking to yourself isn't the first sign of madness. Not knowing who you are is.

Who would do it if you didn't?

Let's say you belong to the group of people who just cannot do it. Maybe you

- feel you ought to, but can't bring yourself to

- want to, deep down, but can't face all the consequences

- have tried, for as long as you could, but can't go on any longer.

In fact, whatever the circumstances, let's say caring just isn't for you.

Who, then? Who'll take over the care of your piglet? Because somebody's got to.

Care-workers paid by you

Are you nice and rich, and easily able to make problems vanish by throwing money at them? Oh, good. In that case, what you might want to do is build a new wing on your house, fit it out like a high-tech nursing home, install a staff of care-workers in white coats, deposit your piglet inside, and go about your business secure in the knowledge that you've taken care of this particular problem in the way you know best.

Another version of this scenario is to pay for your piglet to go into a nursing home for as long as it takes. Given the costs of residential care, this is likely to set you back about as much as the solution in the previous paragraph. All right, not quite as much, but a helluva lot more than I can afford.

If on the other hand your level of wealth equates more closely with mine, neither of these two will be an option. In that case, you'll find yourself turning to other members of the family.

Relatives

Assuming there are any, that is. There are? Then how come you're the one that's doing the caring now? Or if you're not yet doing it, how come you're the one who stands to be left holding the baby?

Perhaps you're the closest relative. In which case it may not have occurred to you or any of the rest of them that anyone but you could do it. Or, if there are others of equal status, you could be the one who seems best qualified, perhaps because of where you live or what you do.

Then again, have they ever offered? Would they? Have you ever asked them? It could be that they've hung back because you're doing it, relieved that you are, but would step in, albeit reluctantly, if you pulled out. Alternatively, you might have asked before and got nowhere. But that doesn't mean they wouldn't step in if you baldly announced: 'I'm out of here.'

Of course, it's possible that you couldn't ask them. I'm not so much thinking of relations you haven't spoken to for years, ever since that row about who gave what to whom for Christmas. I'm thinking more about cases in which the piglet has a genetic disorder which other members of the family are in danger of inheriting. Family members at risk can't in all fairness be asked to assume responsibility in the same way as those who aren't, you might think. How could it be right to invite them to live with a disease twice – once with the piglet, and again later when they get it themselves?

Anyway, if you're unable to do such caring as needs to be done, and if there's not enough money available to buy that caring, the family will almost certainly be the first place where you look for help.

Failing them, there are the neighbours.

Neighbours

Neighbours care for neighbours, all over the world. Maybe not in horrible housing estates where graffiti disfigure the walls, or crowded inner-city ghettos in which people don't know who else lives on the same floor, let alone in the buildings on either side or the flats above and below. Nevertheless, neighbours are good and conscientious carers in the most surprising places. BUT:

- They usually do it of their own volition, and might not be so keen if a perfectly good relation was on hand who said they'd rather not

- Neighbours aren't really a long-term solution. They might move

- They can't be expected to provide the necessary funds.

All in all, neighbours might well do some caring, but they're more of a stopgap measure. Whereas you'd probably be willing to carry on with it yourself if you could see an end to it.

Charitable organisation

There might be one that would take your piglet on for as long as necessary. There are charities specialising in looking after ex-soldiers, actors, priests. There could be one that would assume responsibility for looking after your piglet.

It's possible. But it's very unlikely.

What's more likely is that you'll have no option but to turn to the State.

The State

Ah yes, the State. That's the entity that represents the combined strength of all of us. It's the mechanism by which we look after one other. We furnish it with money and people so that this can happen. When we hand over our hard-earned cash to the State, we tend to resent it a bit. But then, when we need it, we trust it to come up with the goods.

Will it? When the chips are down, does the State take care of its own? The answer seems to be that it does, but only if it absolutely has to. Ask it to take over the care of your piglet, and it'll kick and bite and struggle, and do everything it can think of to wriggle out of it.

If it can't get out of it, it will shoulder the responsibility of the care, but it'll try to make you pay. It'll peer at your worldly goods through a magnifying glass (it will find them even if you've secreted them away somewhere). Then it will almost literally blackmail you into keeping the caring in-house. Or in-family, anyway.

Before you write in to complain about my unfairness or cynicism, let me assure you that I'm not criticising or campaigning here. It's not the job of this book to change the way things are. Its job is to tell you what to expect. And what you can expect, if you're unable either to take care of your piglet yourself or find another individual to do it, is that the State would not allow the piglet to die. But it would try not to pick up the bill.

Faced with doing the caring itself, it would probably put the piglet into a nursing home; not the best, or the most comfortable, but somewhere. The care-workers there almost certainly wouldn't be as good as you. They might be the sort who keep the inmates sedated because this makes their job easier. Or the kind who don't keep them clean, or make any attempt to keep them happy, because again, it makes their job easier. But to be fair, the State will point all this out to you. It's part of the blackmail – sorry, pressure.

Nevertheless, if there is nobody else to take care of a piglet, and the piglet simply can't be left to do it for themselves, the State will step in. Should that happen, who would suffer?

Who would suffer?

Well, the sad fact is that if you opted out, despite the pressure not to, the worst wouldn't happen. Your piglet would be cared for.

So, why is that a sad fact? Not for the piglet, obviously. But maybe, a bit, for you. The thing is, it's common for carers to feel they're not valued enough. Well, this would devalue you even further. You were doing something, or faced with doing something, appallingly difficult, but you balked at it; whereupon somebody else waded in and did it. Where does that leave you? Not indispensable, after all. Less important than you thought.

You can live with that, so long as you don't have to do the caring? Okay, but there's more.

- You actually *are* strong enough to do it. Once you've discovered this, you'll be grateful you found out something about yourself you hadn't known. It'll come in handy for other parts of your life. If you hadn't become a carer, you'd never have learned this

- Although it's true that you haven't had any proper training, you *are* learning how to do the job. It's just that you're learning the hard way, and too slowly for comfort. By the

CARE|R E

time you're finished, you'll be an expert. I don't know why it is, but acquiring new skills is one of the most exciting and rewarding experiences going

- Then again, the fact that you're learning your trade will make it increasingly easy for you to cope with it. Aspects of caring which once frightened or disgusted or maddened you, you'll be able to take in your stride. Not only will you get better at the job, but it's going to become less and less of a strain

- By caring for your piglet, you're doing it in a way which nobody else could. So you are, as it turns out, kind of indispensable after all.

Feel resentful about not being able to sail round the world, start that business that would have made you a fortune, or go to all those wild parties? Yeah. This can be the hard part. Still, remember John Lennon (page 6). And think what could have gone wrong while you were sailing round the world, struggling to make the business pay, or attending one of those parties. Again, think what happened to him.

So, rewinding to the top of this section: what if you didn't take on the role of carer?

That's okay. But your piglet might not be the only one to lose out.

CHAPTER 4

You're on your own

Wishful thinking

Part of the job

Nobody knows you're in there

But you have your piglet for company

With friends like this, who needs enemies?

The need to communicate

Asking politely . . .
. . . Shouting loudly

You're on your own in good company

You're on your own

It isn't what you want to hear. That you're on your own in this caring business. It may be what you suspect, and it may be what you fear. But it certainly isn't what everybody out there tells you.

'Remember we're here to help,' is what they smilingly say. And you long to believe them. It's so comforting, reassuring, and untrue.

Or rather, it's only half true. There *are* lots of well-meaning, and in many cases lovely, people out there:

- Friends

- Neighbours

- Relations

- Agencies

- Services

- Support groups

- Charitable organisations.

And they may provide a degree of support. There's more on the positive side of all this in the second half of the book, in Chapter 17.

But what this chapter is about is the awareness that sneaks up on most of us in the early days of caring, that we're on our own. Talk to anyone who's been at it for a long time, and you'll hear the same story.

> Wendy, who's quiet, gentle, and diplomatic: 'I think you have to learn to be quite independent as a carer.'

> Bruce, who's capable, committed, and angry: 'You're on your tod. There are a lot of promises made, and they're always broken. In the end, everything is down to you.'

Bit of a bleak prospect? If this is the way it seems to you, then it's one area where you certainly are *not* alone. Most carers get bogged down by feelings of neglect and loneliness – until they understand what's going on. Which is that we're all sold the idea there's going to be a lot more help than there actually will be. There is some. It's just that there isn't as much as we're led to expect.

What's so hard to take is not the reality of having to be self-reliant. There's a lot of satisfaction in that. It's the failure of expectations which catches you out. It's like reaching for a banister on the stairs, discovering there isn't one, and almost falling over the side. If you knew there wasn't a banister in the first place, you wouldn't have had any trouble climbing the stairs.

The point of this section of the book is to make it clear that, though there is a banister, it's unreliable.

Incidentally, feelings of dreadful isolation are so commonplace among carers that I haven't been able to deal with all the aspects in this one section. So when you've finished here, skip to Chapters 10 or 11. Maybe there'll be something in one or the other that'll help you find a way through this emotional minefield.

Wishful thinking

A favourite phrase of well-wishers is: 'You only have to ask.' And yet Officialdom admits this is not so much well-wishing as wishful-thinking.

> 'The quality and type of support that carers receive remains a matter of chance. Support depends far more on where carers live and who they are in contact with in Social Services than on what they need.'
>
> *Social Services Inspectorate report*

It's the middle of the night and your piglet has first messed the bed, then spread it liberally about the bedclothes, pillow, and their body. After that, in an attempt either to cover it up or clean it up, the piglet tried to get out of bed but fell on the floor, breaking the bedside light in the process. That's what woke you up. The piglet is uninjured, but cross, uncooperative, and on the floor. It's 3 am, and you feel the same. You can either wade in to clean up and restore normality, or you can pick up the phone and say: 'Remember you told me I only had to ask? Well, now I am.'

Yeah, right. That's the trouble with offers of support. They give more comfort to the person doing the offering than help to you. In many cases they're not even intended to be taken seriously. 'Let me know if there's anything I can do' is only a figure of speech. You're not supposed to take them up on it.

In any case, you yourself know you probably won't. When you really need help you'll be fully occupied trying to cope. Making telephone calls and listening to excuses and apologies are the last things you need. Even if you do ask, and even if some sort of support is, miraculously, forthcoming, it will almost certainly be the moral kind. Tea and sympathy, as opposed to a solution to the problem. You'll still have to carry the load.

It's like struggling with a sack of sand. Other people may stop to talk to you from time to time and give you advice, or even take your elbow when you stumble. But the one thing they never seem to do is pick up the sack and carry it themselves.

Part of the job

Caring is bound to be more or less isolated because of the nature of the job. Most non-carers work in crowded environments. Or if not exactly crowded, at least places where other human beings are always coming and going. Very few workplaces are what you might call lonely.

True, there's a growing tendency for some people to work from home. These are usually the ones who stare at computer screens all day long, in which case they conduct their business in a kind of cyber workplace, which can be quite crowded in its own way. Or they're the ones who go out and about visiting. For them, home is more of a base than a full-time workplace. Either way, people in jobs like these get to do a fair bit of inter-relating with other human beings.

Carers are different. Our workplace, the one where we do our caring, is usually the place where our piglet lives. And if we live there too, we may find ourselves spending 24 hours of every day there. It can be a truly lonely place. You could go mad in there, and no-one would take any notice if you did. Or so you get to thinking.

This doesn't apply to all carers. Parents looking after a disabled child have each other (though all that really means is that they're alone together). Someone juggling a paid job in an office with the caring tasks at home will have their office colleagues for company. But most carers face an existence in which they feel or are in fact largely cut off from the rest of humanity.

Well, let me remind you of something. Isolation is a technique of torture. Recalcitrant prisoners used to be locked away in solitary confinement (they still are, under brutal regimes), not so much to prevent them from doing whatever it was they were doing, but as a severe punishment.

It's psychologically wounding to be deprived of company. In Germany they have a word for it: '*Isolationsfolter*' (isolation torture).

You knew that, of course – not the word, but that it's a sort of torture. But maybe you failed to relate the experiences of POWs in Colditz, or convicts on Alcatraz, to your situation. Think about it, though. Are you surprised that being stuck with your piglet day in day out, away from more usual company, makes you feel you're going mad?

'Isolation detention is truly "white" torture; it leaves no visible scars behind. Years of continued isolation detention destroys prisoners both physically and psychologically.

'The use of solitary confinement in U.S. prisons began in 1829, based on the early Quaker religious philosophy that solitary introspection would lead to penitence and reform. It soon became clear that people in isolation often suffer mental breakdown, so the general practice of isolation was abandoned.'

Solitary Confinement Torture in the US *by Bonnie Kerness, Associate Director of the American Friends Service Committee Criminal Justice Program in New Jersey and the National Coordinator of the National Campaign to Stop Control Unit Prisons*

All right, so it's a bit extreme to link the day-to-day life of a carer to dungeons, iron bars and jailors with masks over their eyes. Nevertheless, this is the effect it can have. A feeling of isolation is the biggest single complaint that carers identify. And mental breakdowns brought on by the stress of caring are often attributed to loneliness.

Nobody knows you're in there

It's bad enough being in solitary confinement. If nobody realises you're there, it's a helluva lot worse. And they don't. In a survey carried out on behalf of The Princess Royal Trust for Carers in the UK, people were asked which organisations they would support in the future, either by giving money, or offering voluntary help. They unhesitatingly put carer organisations at the bottom of the list.

I don't think this is because they know we're on our own but don't give a stuff. It may be the old invisibility trick, as I've said before: nobody knows we're there. Or it could be that they're vaguely aware of us, and are confident that we're doing okay. Help? Why should we need any help? We're the ones who *give* help, to our piglets. We shouldn't need help ourselves – what would be the point?

Whatever the reason, we remain stuck in solitary, unnoticed, and with very little prospect of remission.

But you have your piglet for company

People who haven't done any caring might well be saying right now (if they were reading this book, which they won't be): 'But you're not alone; you're with your piglet all the time. So what's all this whingeing about isolation?'

Well, if the piglet has any emotional or mental impairment, conversations you have with them won't be the kind that bring you much consolation, let alone stimulation. Even if their disability is purely physical, and your verbal exchanges are as sharp as the script of a Tom Stoppard play, they're still your piglet. They're your work. Or even if you refuse to admit that your caring constitutes work, your piglet is still your full-time preoccupation. They're what you need to get away from occasionally. They're what you need to talk about, let your hair down about.

Other people, in the course of an average day, get to talk with their co-workers. They can swap notes about the latest movie when things aren't frantically busy, and talk about everybody behind their backs. Even when there isn't time for that, they're in the company of people who understand their job. Sooner or later they know they'll be able to talk about their work problems, ask questions, sound off, debrief.

Carers get to do a bit of this. But not enough. Meetings of the support group only happen periodically. When the social worker comes round, the piglet is in on the meeting. And as for friends . . .

With friends like this, who needs enemies?

Friends who pop in (if any of them ever do) have a knack of saying things that make it clear they haven't a clue what's going on.

Cheery comments made to carers by well-meaning friends:

- 'We had a lovely time. Shame you weren't there.'

- 'Why don't you try and get away for a few days?'

- 'Have you thought about getting a job to give you something to do?'

- 'I can't think why you put up with it.'

- 'You really ought to go out more.'

Eventually they leave, congratulating themselves on having been helpful and supportive. And all you feel is the aching vacuum of the comprehension gap. You know how pleasing it is when you share a thought with someone you know very well just by exchanging a glance? No words need pass between you, but you can tell they're thinking exactly the same thing as you. It's somehow deeply satisfying, and it brings you even closer together. Well, when it's clear that someone you know does *not* appreciate what's going on in your mind or your life, it has the opposite effect. It drives you apart, and makes you feel even more alone.

It's hard to say exactly why some friends* are so useless when you're a carer. It's almost as if they think it's kind to pretend that there's nothing going on. That you're just like them, or exactly the same as you used to be before everything changed and you became a carer. To be fair, they don't do it to hurt. They may even behave like this out of praiseworthy motives, like loyalty to your piglet. Most likely it's out of a mixed bag of motives, some of which are ignorance and fear.

---

* Not all. My piglet and I have always been luckier than we deserve in our friends. But still, there are others. Luckily, they have no idea who they are, or what they did, so I can say what I like about them.

The need to communicate

What causes loneliness is not being alone, it's being unable to communicate with the people all around. The more people, the lonelier it is.

When I sailed across the Indian Ocean from Thailand to Sri Lanka, I was totally alone for eleven days. I didn't even begin to feel lonely – not once, not at all, not even a bit. I talked a lot, mind you. I discussed our progress with the boat, I invited the sky to tell me what the weather was going to do, and I had a long involved conversation with a fish I was trying to bring aboard.

It's true I also talked with people, on the radio. Not every day, but once in a while. This was nice but it wasn't that important. They were too far away for that. In fact, they were too far removed from my private reality to have any power to make me lonely.

Caring isn't as simple as single-handed ocean sailing. We carers are surrounded by other people, yet establishing communications is exceedingly difficult. So it's easy, and common, to be lonely. But the thing to remember is, if other people fail to communicate with us, it may not be entirely their fault. Somebody's got to start, after all, and it might be harder for them than it is for us.

Maybe we shouldn't always wait for somebody else to make the first move. Maybe we should jump in first, either by murmuring politely, or failing that by shouting, roaring and banging the table.

Asking politely . . .

Here's what happened when I took my piglet to the cinema one rainy Monday afternoon. It started by her refusing to go in the wheelchair in case anyone saw and thought she was disabled. By the time we had slowly staggered to Screen 2, the ads had started and the house lights were down. Neither of us could see a thing when the outer door swung shut behind us. I kept a firm hold of my piglet's arm while I waited for our eyes to adjust. Eventually mine did, and I saw a row of four empty seats within lunging distance. My piglet was still disoriented by the dark, but I thought I ought to be able to steer her towards the seats, so we headed erratically in their direction.

When we got there I could dimly see that the seats were folded up to allow people to pass more easily. Hanging on to my piglet with one hand, I reached out with the other to fold the seat down. But it was spring-loaded, and as soon as I let go it sprang back up. I tried again, and this time managed to get my knee on it to hold it down. But manoeuvring my confused piglet backwards, hampered as I was by having one foot on the ground and the other one airborne, proved too ambitious, and she landed on an adjacent seat. This one was in the up position, which meant that there was nothing for her to sit on, and she subsided to the floor, now even more confused than before.

Heaving her to her feet took longer than usual, and was quite noisy. My eyes had adjusted to the low light by now, and I could plainly see the occupants of the row behind. Their attention was held by the Levi Jeans commercial, which they were watching by craning their necks round our flailing bodies. They seemed to be able to hear the soundtrack perfectly well above the sounds of my grunting and my piglet's angry instructions to leave her alone and allow her to get up by herself. She did, too, with only a certain amount of applied leverage, and remained upright long enough for us to try again. But it was the backing towards the seat which undid us both this time round as well. We nearly managed it, mind you. She landed on the arm between two seats. The people in the row behind had to lean sideways to see past her, but not for long, because my piglet slowly keeled over like a capsising ferry.

On the third attempt I got her, only slightly askew, on to a seat. Although breathless, I thought of apologising to the people in the row behind, but by now there was an ad for Smirnoff Vodka on the screen, and I could tell that they didn't want to be distracted.

The first time this kind of thing happens to you, you can't believe that people don't willingly spring forward to lend a hand. There's no way they haven't noticed your struggle. It's easy to feel resentful at their lack of interest.

Then later you get to recognise what's going on. It's not that they think you're drunk, and are politely looking the other way. It's not that they're so goddam self-centred that they can't even be bothered to help for half a minute. It's not that they're concentrating so hard on something else that they haven't spotted you. No, what it is is that they're scared.

Scared? Are you kidding?

No. It's true. They're not carers (YET; some of them will be, later, and then they'll react differently). So they don't know what to do, and the unknown is scary. Getting involved, even to the extent of murmuring: 'Can I help?' could lead to something seriously embarrassing, possibly even a rejection. So they sit tight, and look the other way.

If I could re-run the cinema sequence, but introduce a change at the point where my piglet is sitting on the floor and I'm trying to heave her to her feet – if I were to direct a quick 'Do you think one of you could help me?' – there'd be someone on their feet and at my side at once, stretching out their hands, and the piglet would be up and on her seat in a flash.

The helper from the row behind would feel good about having been of assistance. My back wouldn't have been put out again. And we'd all have been quite pleased with ourselves. Except the piglet, of course. She'd have been cross, and would have told me later: 'I don't know why you make such a fuss. I could have done it on my own if you'd only left me alone.'

. . . Shouting loudly

Asking politely doesn't always work.

Hang on, maybe I should re-phrase that. Asking politely only works when you're not dealing with Officialdom. In the case of

Officialdom you have to insist, insist again, carry on insisting more and more loudly, bang the table and stamp your feet. It may be something you can do easily, something that's completely in character. Or it may be the kind of thing you'd sooner die than do.

Whichever, it's almost certainly something you're going to have to get used to doing. There's almost nothing more likely to make you feel alone and isolated than attempting to communicate with a government department. So for your own protection, it's best to develop a thicker skin. And for the sake of your piglet, ie if you want to get help for them, you're going to be a more effective carer if you really concentrate on being a shameless, practised, determined, strong-minded, and utterly SELFISH PIG. There'll be more on this in Chapter 7.

You're on your own in good company

Just as you can be lonely in a crowd, you can equally well be in good company when you thought you were alone. And that's precisely how it is for us carers. You are on your own inasmuch as you're the only person who can get your caring job done. And you may well feel virtually cut off from the rest of humanity. But there are millions of people in exactly the same situation as you. Millions! All grappling with the same difficulties. All assailed, from time to time, by guilt and doubt and loneliness and despair. All doing something that is necessary, worthwhile and, dammit, wonderful.

Have a quick look at that survey I mentioned up there just now. According to it, in the UK alone, there are 6 million carers. (The survey defined a carer as someone who, without payment, provides help and support to a friend, neighbour or relative who couldn't manage otherwise because of frailty, illness or disability.) By 2011, there are going to be 13 million in the UK. In the USA there are 50 million caregivers right now.

Everyone has a three-in-five chance of becoming a carer. By 2037 the odds in favour of anyone between the ages of 30 and 54 becoming a carer for someone older could increase by 88%.

Of today's carers, 42% are men, and 58% are women. 54% are aged between 35 and 59; 19% are under 35. 56% of carers are the chief income earner for the household, and 50% of carers are in employment other than caring, though only 20% are in full-time employment.

67% of piglets are over 64, but more hours were devoted to caring for people with mental or physical disabilities than for problems relating to old age.

There are 175,000 children and young people with caring responsibilities.

If every carer stopped caring it would cost the UK £57 billion a year.

33% of carers say that they haven't had a break in the last two years.

Carers in the survey identified three priority areas where they most needed support.

The main need was for information and advice. Equal second were:

- Help in dealing with health professionals, and

- Help with time off from caring.

There. I've rushed through the statistics because this book, as I said very loudly at the outset, is about YOU, not about all those others. Nevertheless, you need to remember, when the going gets/stays tough, that you're on your own in good company. And I mean good.

CHAPTER 5

Are you the one who needs looking after?

The world is full of piglets

Friends
Strangers
Professional care-workers
Doctors and specialists

Your case is more urgent

Help or hindrance?

Having your special needs assessed

What your assessors will try to find out
How they decide
What help you'll get
Unofficial support

Carers' rights

Be your own carer

Are you the one who needs looking after?

Before you started looking through this book, you may not have seen yourself as a carer, even, let alone as somebody in need of care yourself.

Now that you *are* reading the book, you may still harbour a secret suspicion that titles like carers and piglets are irrelevant anyway. Just words, and not particularly important or helpful.

Yes? Well, it's understandable. When you're used to being invisible, and hardened to getting by without outside assistance, job descriptions *are* pretty much irrelevant. Any time spent on that sort of nonsense is time wasted.

Then again, your piglet is probably someone close to you, and what you're doing for them is only what any right-thinking person would do. Are mums carers, you reason? Are they special cases, who need special care themselves? Well then.

Finally there's the 'caring is like being in love' syndrome. Being a carer can be such an intense experience, and so all-absorbing, that it's almost as if no-one else counts outside your micro-sphere of existence. All that matters is your piglet, and you.

So you stumble on until, inevitably, sooner or later and probably sooner, you become dimly aware that you *do* have needs that are different from other people's. This awareness dawns when you realise that your needs aren't being met.

No sooner have you arrived at this conclusion than you realise that nobody else seems to be aware of it. You're amazed that other people fail to appreciate your uniqueness. How can they possibly not see it? By now your predicament is so significant to you that you're convinced it should be obvious to everybody else. Yet they insist on treating you as if you're just like them, as if nothing had happened to you.

For a time you're really irritated. Their lack of recognition is inexcusable. Their uncaring attitude, their neglect, are little short of criminal. How are you supposed to do this thing on your own?

Aha! You're thinking of yourself as someone with special needs. You've become pigletised. But stay, as Shakespeare would say. Before you get too angry, spare a quick thought for all those really, really selfish pigs out there who can't see you properly because they're not looking.

The world is full of piglets

The world is full of piglets. The fact is, practically everyone you know is a piglet in one way or another. And it's not that they haven't been paying enough attention to you; it's the other way round. While you've been concentrating on your own business, you haven't been noticing theirs. For example:

Friends

Your friends are almost all piglets. Take a look at them.

- She's feeling wretched because she thinks she's unloved

- He feels crippled by lack of money

- That one over there is so anxious about his job that he's virtually frozen solid

- She's got so little self-confidence that she's no longer sure who she is or what she's for.

This is what's prevented them from leaping to your aid. It's not because they're blind or selfish. They're not bad friends. In fact, most of them think it's YOU who've been neglecting THEM. They believe you should have been leaping to their aid, not the other way round.

Strangers

Most strangers turn out to be piglets too. I'm talking about the ones who fail to hold doors open for you when you're trying to manoeuvre the wheelchair through. Who sigh and shuffle impatiently when you delay them by taking much longer to do something than it would have taken them.

Selfish pigs? No, what it is is this:

- That one, a teenager, is paralysed by worry about what her peer group thinks of her. It's so totally painfully desperately excruciatingly crucial to her that she hasn't got time for anything else

- He's discovered a lump in his groin and is convinced he's about to die.

Professional care-workers

All those professionals you see in connection with your own piglet's disability – if you do – they're piglets, too.

- This one took the job so that she could help you and your piglet only now she finds she can't do any good for reasons outside her control, like a budget that's too small, stupid legal restrictions, and inadequate staffing. It's making her feel helpless and bitter

- That one suddenly finds himself worn down by constantly trying to deal with other people's problems. Things have got on top of him. He doesn't know it, but he's close to burnout.

Doctors and specialists

Even your doctor is a piglet. There's only one of her, and she's being stretched to breaking point. Plus, she's got a private life too, and it's all gone wrong. But she can't talk to anyone about the torture she's going through.

Your case is more urgent

If everyone else has special problems and needs, it would be strange if you didn't as well. And, of course, you do. In your case, though, your needs arise absolutely directly from your piglet's disability. And that's what makes you a bit different from non-carers. And your case more urgent.

You see, your piglet isn't coping single-handedly with their disability. They've got you. You're sharing it with them. In a way, the disability has spread to you. It's the disability which is forcing you to live the way you do, making you think those thoughts you have, preventing you from doing all those things you would have been doing if life had worked out differently for both of you. So, if a disability is having these drastic effects on your life, I reckon it's fair to say you're a classic piglet.

Rubbish? Self-pitying claptrap? Well, according to British law, a disabled person is someone who is blind, deaf or dumb, or who suffers from a mental disorder (defined as mental illness, arrested or incomplete development of mind, psychopathic disorder and any other disorder or disability of mind). Okay, despite the fact that your caring sometimes drives you mad, you can see and you're neither deaf nor dumb. So this means you don't qualify?

But a disabled person is also, in law, anyone who is substantially and permanently handicapped by illness, injury or congenital deformity or such other disabilities as may be prescribed by the Secretary of State. *Now* we're getting somewhere. Are you substantially handicapped by your piglet's disability? And is this handicap a permanent one, so long as your piglet is disabled?

What it comes down to is that the person you care for has special needs, and therefore you do too. The government recognises this, even though it doesn't do quite enough about it. You may as well recognise it yourself.

Help or hindrance?

It's hard enough being a carer, without having to adjust your thinking to see yourself as a co-piglet. And even if you did, might it not be a touch counterproductive? You'd like some outside assistance, but what you need is to be empowered, not pitied.

Hmmm. That may be what you think today. But wait till you go down with flu, or badly strain your back. If you weren't a carer, something like that would merely be a pain and a bloody nuisance. But you *are* a carer, and that fact of life can turn a nuisance into a logistical nightmare. Suppose you become really incapacitated, as opposed to just feeling ill. You'll probably have to get help in. This is easy enough to write, but really hard to do when your head's thumping, your whole body aches, and all you want to do is lie still with your eyes closed. It's harder still when your back has locked solid so that you're as rigid as a garden rake.

In reality, you'll probably find that the easiest course when you're ill is to carry on regardless.

But okay, so you're not ill right now. And there's nothing wrong with your back. What's more, you're never ill, and you've never strained your back. So what's the point of worrying about these eventualities, which may never happen? You think: 'I'll come to that bridge when I cross it,' as my old boss used to say.

Now, it's true that self-pity doesn't do any good. You've found that out the hard way already. Strength is a must-have characteristic for a carer. Start feeling sorry for yourself, and you may as well give up altogether.

But think, for a moment, about what you do for your piglet. You have to

- recognise their disability

- deal with it day by day

- plan ahead for what might happen next.

Since your piglet's going to be in trouble if you're unable to care for them, you're pretty much bound to apply the same logic to yourself. You have to

- recognise that you're a special case

- look after yourself from day to day

- plan ahead for when something goes wrong.

I know, you're altogether too busy for all this malarkey. And as for planning ahead, how do you do that? Ring up your friends and say: 'If I go down with flu three weeks next Wednesday, do you mind dropping everything to come here and take over?' Yeah, right.

But you're forgetting that this is really quite important. It really is. And to prove it, the government thinks it's important too. Actually, let's not begin to speculate what the government *thinks*. It may not be a pretty sight. But what they've decreed is that all carers have the right to ask for an assessment by the local authority. They've also decreed that the local authority must carry out the assessment.*

There you go: it's your right. I'll come back to carers' rights in a minute. For the moment, though, get your head round the fact that your country recognises that you have special needs, just as much as your piglet does, and they they're ready and willing to find out what these are.

Having your special needs assessed

You may think you know what your needs are, even if the State doesn't. That you need a break, for example. So why put up

---

* Just to spoil the effect slightly, the government has stopped short of insisting that the local authority should do anything for you following the assessment. So if the authority says it would like to but can't due to lack of funds, that's just tough. Still, it's the thought that counts.

with the hassle of being interrogated in order to come up with the obvious?

Well, it's just as likely that you feel you could do with a bit of support in other areas as well, but you're not totally certain what form that support could take. For instance, you can tell you're being stretched in too many directions at the same time, but it's hard to put your finger on what anybody could do to help out.

What's more, there could well be some assistance which is available but which you haven't even thought of. It's one of the problems with working on your own – you don't have the benefit of feedback from others in the same situation. But Social Services do. They've encountered hundreds of people in your situation. Whether or not they end up actually doing anything for you, the very process of checking out your needs could well prove useful.

What your assessors will try to find out

- First they'll want to discover how you feel about your situation. This is when you run straight up against the difficulty of coming clean. What you probably feel like is a selfish pig, and this is precisely what you won't want to tell them. You'll find yourself saying that you're getting along fine most of the time, but just occasionally things are hard to bear. DON'T do that. Don't pussyfoot around. Tell it the way it is.

- They'll want to know exactly what you do for your piglet, and what impact this has on you

- Whether you need help with any of these tasks

- How many of your family, friends and neighbours help out, and in what way

- How you're bearing up, mentally and physically

- How willing you are to go on providing care. How able you are to do it

- What conflicts you have. For example, do you have another job which you need because of the money it brings in, but which gets in the way of your caring? Do you have other family commitments which you're finding it hard to fulfil as a result of your caring

- How clued up you are about your piglet's disability and its likely/possible development

- How good or bad a carer you are. What are your strengths? How are you coping

- Which parts of caring cause the most stress.

The assessment is a two-way business. From your point of view, you're lifting your head up from the task that's under your nose day in, day out, and inspecting it from a bit further away. You're trying to find out whether you should be a carer at all, or whether you're totally unsuited to it and doing more harm than good. You're also trying to get a feel for what help might be forthcoming.

Your assessors, for their part, are keen to establish whether you want, and are able, to carry on caring. If not, they're going to have to take your piglet off your hands, so they'd rather decide yes. In that case, they want to work out what support and assistance you need.

How they decide

Who knows? In the end, it depends on where you live. Local authorities all have their own eligibility criteria for deciding who qualifies for help.

Your job is to do your best to convince them. So don't even think about hiding your fears, or burying your desires.

If you want help, you tell 'em.

I don't know why it is, but asking for help is one of the most difficult things in the world to do. It's also probably the single most crucially important thing a carer needs to do.

Luckily, there's a technique. Apart from sinking your finer feelings, the trick is to sort out in your own mind what you want different people to do for you.

So try thinking of specific jobs you'd like taken off your shoulders. Like

- help with the toilet
- help with bathing, dressing, feeding, or lifting
- more information
- practical help with medication
- help with money
- help with disability aids like a stairlift, wheelchair ramp, glideabout, or handrails
- help with understanding the impossible, like the benefits system

- regular time off each week
- a holiday
- help with adapting your home or finding somewhere more suitable to live
- someone to come in each day and to help with cooking and housework
- help with transport
- someone to talk to.

What help you'll get

Again, who knows? You may be surprised at the amount of help that's on offer. Or more likely you'll be dismayed by how little there is. Assuming *any* is available, the next thing to find out is whether it'll come free of charge or whether you'll be expected to pay for it. Again, you could be pleasantly surprised.

There are all sorts of rules and guidelines about this, but they're incredibly complex and they're all liable to change. It's not the function of this book to go into them. To find out the current situation, you have to ask people who are up-to-speed on the subject in your area, at the time you need the help. I'm prepared to bet you won't get the information from just one person. For example, you'll probably get some of it from your social worker, some from your doctor, and more from your support group (see Chapter 17).

Unofficial support

We seem to have accepted that you're in the same position as your piglet: ie, that you have special needs. But that doesn't mean that you ought only to look for support from official sources. There are still those friends, relations and neighbours. They may not have come up trumps so far, but it's just as important to ask them in the right way as it is to ask Social Services in the right way. Saying 'I need help' just isn't going to work. If you're lucky it'll elicit clucks of sympathy, and possibly a squeeze of the hand or even a hug. And then you'll be on your own again.

You have to think of a job, earmark someone to do it, then sell the idea to them. As in any selling job, you'll meet your share of rejections. But there'll be somebody out there who'll say yes. There may even be somebody out there who's really keen to be asked.

So do it. This is not about asking favours. You have special needs, and you have as much right to seek support from those around you as your piglet has the right to be cared for by you. But hang on a minute. What is a right?

Carers' rights

A right is an entitlement under law. It isn't something you feel you somehow automatically ought to have, but which can be disputed. It's something that the State says you're entitled to, and must be given. It's all been debated and agreed. Laws have been passed. There isn't any argument.

So there's nothing demeaning about asking for our rights, just as there's nothing generous about the State's providing for them. But the weird thing is, thousands of us have no idea that we're entitled to anything. And thousands more who know about our rights nevertheless refuse to ask. 'All I'm doing is looking after Mum the way she looked after me when I was small.'

Am I in danger of getting a bit militant here? I hope not, because it's not my style. But I tell you what: sooner or later carers' unions are going to emerge. Perhaps by the time this book hits the high street shops there'll already be one. There are certainly enough carers, all struggling away as individuals, to warrant one. Did you know that there are more people caring for relatives at home than there are mothers staying at home looking after small children?

I'll give you some more statistics, if you like.

- One in three carers has a problem paying the bills
- One in five is cutting back on food
- Six out of ten believe the worry of caring has affected their health
- More than half have had to give up paid work to care.

But there's a problem with seeing yourself as a State piglet that the State is neglecting. What that does is turn you into a victim. It conjures up a sense of powerlessness. Apart from urging you to feel sorry for yourself, it could well make you less effective as a carer.

You're not a victim any more than I am. If it's true that we're not being cared for quite as much as we ought to be, then the way forward is for us to be our own carers.

Be your own carer

This is really what the book is all about. You're doing a good job caring for your piglet. You've probably been doing a bloody awful job caring for yourself.

Well, now I'm giving you a second piglet to care for: yourself. Be as conscientious with this new one as you've become with the first.

It may not be a right, but it's the professional approach.

CHAPTER 6

Remember you're a professional

You are, you know

Don't want to be?

How it can help

Self-esteem
Strength to fight
Sense of purpose
Down with wearing down

Trouble is, according to other people, you're not

No box for carers
There *are* professional carers, but they're different
  Friends refuse to think of you as a professional carer
  What, doing your own shopping?
  Lady of leisure

In fact, you're more than professional

For them, it's just a job
Part timers
Qualifications
Pay

How to acquire a professional mindset

Time to yourself
Say: 'I'm a carer'
Training
Attitude to pay

Remember you're a professional

You are, you know

You're doing a specialist job that requires specialist skills. Which society at large needs you to do. If you didn't, it wouldn't just be a shame; it would be a disaster. Somebody else would have to be found to take over, and that would be both difficult and hugely more expensive.

Compare your job as a carer with mine as the writer of this book. If I'd thrown in the towel and walked away from the book while I was writing it, in no way would it have been a disaster – though naturally I like to think it would have been a shame (don't worry, I won't ask for your opinion).

Now imagine what would happen if *all* carers threw up their hands and turned over to the government the responsibility of caring for their piglets. Not only would the bill be truly enormous, stupendous and mind-boggling, but the practical fallout would be that the government couldn't cope. There wouldn't be enough infrastructure in the form of care homes, social workers and nurses to make up the shortfall. Everybody's lives would be affected. Civilised life as we know it would virtually grind to a halt. People would die.

Oh, you're a professional, all right.

Don't want to be?

You don't like the idea of being a professional? You think it sounds cold and mercenary? You'd rather be just an ordinary person doing what's right? You feel that labelling yourself as a professional would in some way detract from your love, lessen your loyalty, weaken your sense of moral obligation?

I suspect what you feel is this: that when a mother cuddles her sick child, she does it because it's her child, not because it's her job.

71

And she does it more effectively because of this. A professional doing the same thing would merely do it efficiently, which to the child would not be the same thing at all. The professional's cuddling would be a trick of the trade, not a manifestation of love.

Is that the way it seems to you? You'd rather be a real carer, like the mother, than a professional one? If so, I honour you for it, even though it could turn out to be a hard path to tread later on. And whether you're right or wrong, ie whether you really are a professional or not, the one thing that's absolutely clear is that you are NOT an SP. You shouldn't really be reading this book. Even so, I'd like you to stick with me for a bit. I don't mind if you still disagree by the end of the chapter, and prefer to stay proudly non-professional. But you might find (I did, and plenty of others do as well) that your caring is enhanced when you recognise that what you're doing is a job, and that it's a valuable and skilful one.

How it can help

Self-esteem

There's something about the label 'professional' which suggests expertise, high standards, experience, and worth. Which implies that, if you're *not* professional, you're probably not very good at what you're doing, that your standards are low or non-existent, that you're inexperienced, and that on the whole you're a fairly insignificant sort of person.

Doesn't that make you feel just terrific?

No, probably not. And that's the trouble. Being perceived as an amateur, or seeing yourself as one, can erode your self-esteem.

And when that starts to happen, you could easily start to become less able to care for your piglet. Next thing you know, this feeling of inadequacy could begin to edge you towards depression, and closer to burnout.

It's incredibly easy for any of us carers to think this way. There's no aura about the job description. If you were an airline pilot, or a surgeon, or the manager of a rock band, it would be different. But you aren't. Maybe you were, once. Now you belong to a group which, though it does important and challenging work, has no glamour and receives practically no public acknowledgement. Refuse collectors get more recognition than we do.

People have nowadays more or less stopped saying things like 'I'm just a secretary,' or 'She's just a housewife.' Oh well, all right, they haven't stopped completely. But there's general agreement about the unfairness of that little word 'just'.

However, if you run across someone who looks after a family member full-time, and ask them what they do, chances are they'll say 'Nothing much,' or 'I don't really have enough time to work these days.' They haven't even got as far as saying 'I'm just a carer,' let alone announcing with pride: '*I'm a carer.*'

The word carer as a job description is virtually non-existent (except to describe those ones who draw a salary).

That's the way things are at the moment. I know you know what I'm talking about. Maybe you don't mind too much. But what if, for example,

- you've had a career which has been disrupted by the need to care for your piglet

- this whole caring thing has been sprung on you, and you haven't had time to adjust

- you don't like to admit it but you resent, a bit, the hand that fate has dealt you

- you're desperate to be getting on with something else but you can't because of the necessity to care?

If any of those conditions apply to you, then maybe you do get a bit pissed off that you seem to be so little regarded. What would perk you up amazingly is for just one person to say: 'Oh, you're a *carer*. Wow!' and shake you by the hand.

Strength to fight

Carers have been described as a forgotten army. (But only by other carers, or people who work with carers or look after carers when we run into trouble.) And it's true. We *are* forgotten.

Actually, no it's not. We were never noticed in the first place. We're not forgotten, we're invisible.

Which might not matter all that much. There's a lot to be said for not sticking your head above the parapet and getting missiles chucked at you. But the trouble is, we need to get things done. We have to do tough stuff like organising financial bene- fits for our piglets, arranging for them to get whatever gadgets (like wheelchairs and bath lifts) they need, liaising with doctors and specialists, fighting on their behalf for this and that.

And this takes more than time. It takes energy and determi- nation. It takes strength, tenacity, and willpower. Lots and lots of it. On an ongoing basis

Someone who's a bit downtrodden and under-confident is not going to be able to do it very well. Someone like that is going to be pushed to the back of the queue, or have the door shut in their face.

Invisible carers who don't think much of themselves are just not going to be very good at this side of things. Whereas carers who think of themselves as 'professional', who have a clear pic- ture of what needs to be done and a strong sense of the rightness of what they're doing, stand a much better chance of making things happen.

Sense of purpose

Carers who think of themselves as valued professionals are much less vulnerable than those who see themselves simply as relations or good neighbours.

If you're professional, you're protected from some of those wounding self-doubts. There's a bit of distance between you and some of the harder-to-bear aspects of caring. And when you itch to be doing another job, or living another life, then reflecting on the importance of the one you've been landed with may help your frame of mind. There's nothing like a strong sense of purpose for keeping burnout at arm's length.

Down with wearing down

Thinking of yourself in this new light will do the opposite of turning you into a cold fish. Far from downgrading the job, it'll raise it to a higher level. What you do, day in day out, will be more likely to fulfil you than wear you down. In short, you'll be better at the job, and happier doing it.

Trouble is, according to other people, you're not

No box for carers

'Would you mind taking a minute to complete this form?'

Oh lord, here you go again. And once again, before you even look at the first question on the form, you know very well that when you come to the part headed 'Occupation' you're not going to be able to tick a box marked 'Carer'. There won't be one. The closest to it is the box down at the bottom, marked 'Other'.

My friend Ruth is a carer. And when her new motor insurance certificate arrived through the letter box, here's how she found herself described:

> Principal occupation: carer (non-professional)
> Employment status: household duties.

It was the phrase 'household duties' which irritated her more than the 'non-professional' bit. Now she knew what her job looked like to people working in an office. Have a look at the panel to see just one of the things which she actually did and which was presumably nothing more than a household duty.

But it's all nonsense. There are 31 million carers in the USA and UK. Not people employed by Social Services or those who do it for a living. I'm talking about people like us. 31 million! All solemnly carrying out household duties non-professionally.

Well, if they haven't come up with a proper job description for us, that's their tough luck.

What you know, and they don't, is that everyone has a three-in-five chance (60%) of becoming a carer. And that by the year 2037 the chance of anyone between the ages of 30 and 54 becoming a carer for someone older could increase by 88%.* So whoever writes these forms stands a fair chance of having to tick the box marked 'Other' themselves one of these days.

> ### Ruth's household duties
>
> She had to admit that she felt it *was* her duty to care for Les. She certainly didn't know of anybody else who'd do it. And

---

* According to a survey carried out on behalf of Carers UK in 2001

it was correct that almost all of her tasks were household ones, in that she carried them out in the home. Of course she did. He was virtually housebound, and it was hardly ever possible for them to go out. Which meant that *she* hardly ever went out. So perhaps it was wrong of her to argue with the word 'household'. Nevertheless, she found it upsetting. She wondered why. Then she got to thinking that the phrase sounded a bit like 'household chores'. Well, she did those, all right. Cleaning, ironing, shopping. But what about the rest of what she did? She took a few minutes to run through what she'd done the previous morning.

She'd given Les a bath. They were still awaiting the bath lift which Occupational Therapy had promised them six months before but which hadn't arrived or even shown any sign of doing so. So after running the bath, she'd helped Les climb in and sit down on the plastic chair which she'd placed there. It wasn't a specialist chair like the non-existent bath lift. But it had rubber feet, it was strong (which meant it needed to be), and its biggest advantage was that its price was right – it had come from the town tip.

Les had grumbled about having his bath. He always did, but she had chatted away to him, and got him in eventually. She washed him all over, so far as that was possible. Cleaning in between his legs wasn't very easy, especially as she always took care that no feelings of indignity should wash over him with the bath-water. It was impossible to clean his bottom while he was sitting down, of course, but what she usually did was help him stand up, grasping the handrails, and then she'd give his bum a quick soaping and a rinse before throwing a towel over his shoulders and guiding him out of the bath. It's what she was starting to do this time, when the trouble started.

She emptied the water, then made sure that the rubber mat was securely stuck to the bottom by its little suckers. She reminded Les for the hundredth time which handrail he should hold on to, and steadied him while he heaved himself up. He nearly managed it. But his sense of balance deserted him when he was halfway there, causing him to sit down suddenly and heavily. His considerable weight came down on one side of the chair, which shifted fractionally sideways. Hardly at all, really, but just enough to destroy whatever vestige of balance Les retained. He keeled over in one direction, the chair in the other. Now he was sitting down in the bottom of the bath, unhurt, but really, really cross.

Ruth didn't know how much heavier Les was than herself. It couldn't have been twice as much. But perhaps not far off it. What she did know was that heaving and pulling weren't going to work. The other thing she knew was that there was no point in calling Social Services for help. Their salaried caregivers wouldn't even try to hoist Les to his feet. All they'd do was ring for an ambulance. Or even a fire engine. Ruth had been through all this before. It was one of the reasons why she'd put in for a bath lift.

So what she did instead was get all the towels out of the airing cupboard and stack them on the floor beside the bath. She removed the plastic chair, and put a folded towel alongside Les's left buttock. Chatting cheerfully to him, she got him to roll his weight on to his right side while she manoeuvred the towel under the raised left buttock. Now she folded another towel, but this time so that it was thicker than the one Les was now half-sitting on. She persuaded him to roll his weight over to the left, and slid the new towel under his right buttock. After that she paused to rub him down to dry and warm him. And she never stopped talking about what it was they were trying to achieve, interspersed with little stories about people Les remembered.

This story is taking a long time to tell, I know. But not half as long as the time it took Ruth to get Les out of the bath. She kept rolling him from side to side, gradually increasing the height of the seat she was building out of the towels. Eventually she had him raised high enough to be able to grasp the lowest of the handrails, and after a bit more time to think and summon up a burst of energy he'd pulled himself upright. And then she helped him out.

Les was safe; Ruth had avoided straining her back; and the fire engines were still inside the fire station being polished. The whole performance had taken four hours. Household duties, ha! And that was just what she'd done in the morning.

There *are* professional carers, but they're different

There are websites for carers like us, and some of them feature message boards and chat rooms in which we can sound off about our problems and frustrations. I've noticed that care officers employed by Social Services and other organisations come in for a severe bashing on these sites. A lot of carers (our sort of carers) resent the fact that people who care for a living seem to have so much going for them, while we have so little.

People in the caring profession (that's the other sort of carer) get a regular salary cheque, a pension, recognition, paid holidays, and days off. Many of them belong to unions who stand up for their interests. They benefit from training, and from rules and regulations which won't allow them to do certain things. And because their 'clients' are just that, clients rather than piglets, carers like these enjoy the luxury of not being so emotionally and painfully involved. In short, they live a structured, pampered, life, and it seems we HATE them for it.

We shouldn't, though. They don't get paid such a vast amount. More than us, it goes without saying, but they're none of them what you might call 'fat cats'. And almost all of them have their hearts in the right place. After all, why did they take up this career in the first place? Not to get rich, not for an easy life. I suspect that most of them felt a genuine desire to help. And they do help. Not a lot, but that isn't their fault. They do what they can. Which is more than can be said for just about everybody else.

Anyway, this book isn't for them. It's for us. There are plenty of books and training manuals and videos and courses for *them*. The point of this book is to emphasise to you that, just because you're not the other type of carer, it doesn't mean you're not just as professional. In many ways you have to be more professional than they are. You certainly have to be more resourceful because you don't have the back-up that they have.

So I say again: you're not a member of what the public or the politicians think of as the 'caring profession'. But you're a professional, for all that.

Friends refuse to think of you as a professional carer

They may sympathise with you, praise you behind your back, occasionally even (not often) offer to help. But the weird thing is that they hardly ever recognise that what you're doing amounts to a job. *They've* got jobs, but to them their jobs are real ones. Yours isn't, as far as they're concerned.

Sometimes they even seem to want to seduce you away from your caring job. They say: 'Can you get away to come and have a meal?' Or 'I've seen the perfect job for you, advertised in the *Courier*. You really ought to apply for it."

The problem is that they're your friends. You like them, and in most matters you're of the same opinion as them. So when it becomes apparent that they think you're not really working or doing anything worthwhile, it's easy for you to start to come round to their way of thinking.

Well, DON'T.

What, doing your own shopping?

Bruce was pushing a trolley round the supermarket. He was filling it methodically, going as fast as he could, because Lisa, his wife, was waiting in her wheelchair just beyond the checkout area and she wouldn't wait there patiently for long. Suddenly, who should saunter round the corner of an aisle, with his hands in his pockets, but an old friend, Dirk. Libby, Dirk's wife, was nearby, busily picking things off shelves.

Dirk looked at Bruce, amused. 'Doing your own shopping, are you?'

Now, Dirk was more than an acquaintance. He was a friend. He was even an old friend, in that he had known Bruce and Lisa for years and years. He knew all about Lisa's increasing disability. He was aware that Bruce had given up his job to care for her. But somehow he didn't seem to have taken any of this on board.

Did he really think that Lisa whizzed round the supermarket, efficiently stocking up on things they were going to need for the coming week? That she piled her wheelchair in the back of the car along with the shopping, drove Bruce home, and cooked supper? Did he really think that Bruce normally came along just for the ride?

The fact is that Dirk didn't think at all. If Bruce had been head-hunted from his old job to take up an even better-paid post somewhere else, Dirk would have understood that, all right. But giving up a job to care full-time for your wife? No, that couldn't be a job. So all Dirk saw was his old friend ignominiously doing his own shopping. And he was amused.

Lady of leisure

Mary-Joyce had been rapidly climbing the ladder in her career, but had had to step off it in order to look after her mother, who was suffering from Alzheimer's. It meant that MJ's income had disappeared, her lifestyle had crumbled, and her hopes and ambitions had been shattered. She, too, bumped into a long-standing friend one day.

'How are you enjoying life as a lady of leisure?' asked the friend who to this day is totally unaware that she was lucky to escape without being punched in the face, knocked to the ground, and trampled on.

In fact, you're more than professional

For them, it's just a job

I'm reluctant to seem critical of those care-workers who do it for a living. Maybe I shouldn't use that derogatory word 'just'. Okay, then, for them it's a job. Whereas for you it's your life.

Care-workers get to have two lives. One is their job. The other life kicks in when they go home, and consists of all the things they do in the evenings, on their days off, and on holiday.

If professionalism were ever judged by the number of hours put into a job, we'd unquestionably come out tops. Not only do we work far longer hours, but we have fewer, if any, breaks.

Part timers

The outside world sees us (if it sees us at all) as kind of part-time carers because we don't 'go to work'. We're looking after our piglet 'for the time being'. Eventually we'll stop, and get a proper job again.

In fact, it's the other way round. We're the ones who are working full-on, full-time. It's everybody else who only works some of the time, and has the rest of their time to themselves.

Qualifications

We don't have any qualifications on paper. They do, so anyone would think they were the professionals. Yes, but you're the one with the real hands-on experience. When your piglet needs some serious help, which is more important – a bit of paper? Or what you do for them?

Pay

This may be the nub of the problem. They get paid, you don't. Therefore they must be worth it, you can't be. Pay is the semantic defining difference between amateurs and professionals. So they are professional, and you're not.

It's possible that the likes of us will go on being seen as well-meaning amateurs ('She's a saint, bless her') for as long as we go on being unpaid.

But – see below.

How to acquire a professional mindset

Time to yourself

I'm sitting at my laptop knocking out these words, partly to produce a book that I hope may be of some use to you. But there's another side to it as well: I'm making time for myself.

My piglet thinks I'm working, so she doesn't mind my hiding myself away for an hour or two each day. I've discovered that this bit of time I have to myself is crucial to the way I do my caring job.

When I can't get it, I become crabby. When I *do* get it, I'm a much better carer. In fact, I'm much more professional.

Professionals don't work 24 hours a day, and neither should we.

Say: 'I'm a carer'

When people ask what you do, tell them you're a carer. Pretend you expect them to appreciate all the implications. If they don't, feel sorry for them. Behave in exactly the same way as a surgeon would. Expect an equivalent acknowledgement and level of recognition.

If there's no box in the questionnaire, draw one.

Training

I've been trying to think of other jobs or trades for which training is unavailable. Not doctors, lawyers, teachers, ambulance drivers, fire-fighters, journalists, graphic designers, plumbers, first-aiders, carpenters, electricians, nurses, accountants, computer programmers, pilots, oh shut up.

There's plenty of training, or information at any rate, available for people involved with specific disabilities. But it's all centred on the piglets. Quite rightly, most people will say. Yes, but the sort of stuff we're talking about in this book, which is common to all carers, is never taught, never explained. Or if it is, it never was to me.

Hang on a mo.

No, I can't find any. I suddenly thought that this all seems so crazy I must be wrong. So I checked on the internet and in the library. I made a few calls and asked around. I actually found quite a lot of information under the heading: 'training for carers'. But on closer inspection it all turned out to be either training for people who care for a living, or ways of training people like us to do other jobs. For example, to learn book-keeping at home in between looking after our piglets.

There seems to be a general assumption that there's nothing to tell; or that we're too stupid to learn; or that we're too unimportant to matter. Or maybe it's more sinister than that, and for the likes of us training is withheld in the same way that education was withheld from women in the old days, or from blacks in pre-Mandela South Africa: to keep us in our place.

In a way, it's worked. Professionals get trained, we reason, and we don't, so we obviously aren't professional, which means we don't count for much.

Now look. This is all the most utter and appalling b******s. (Note to editor: Why did you do that, dammit?) We ARE professional, and we DO get trained. We get trained by necessity, and by time. After a year or two of caring, we will not only have put in more hours than the other kind of carer, but we'll have more expertise. Our training exists, all right. It's just that it's not organised or formal.

Attitude to pay

I remember longing for my first job. Or, more accurately, my first pay cheque. After years of being a student, and therefore not a grown-up, I was desperate to earn money. In my mind, earning a wage was a mark of adulthood. When somebody paid me real and regular money, I would have made it.

It finally happened. I slit open that first-ever little brown envelope, and was as proud as an Olympic gold medallist. Everything was different. Now I could hold my own views, and make my own decisions. I had become a person in my own right. And what made it all real and clear was the money. It didn't matter how much or little it was. What mattered was that it was money, and somebody was paying it to me because I was worth it.

We carers are worth a lot of money, but nobody's ever going to pay it to us. If we're lucky and determined, we may get a pittance. Some of us don't get even that because we don't claim it, or because it's too difficult to fill in all the forms and takes too much time, or because we don't want to compromise our position as loving carers. In my case I didn't claim it to begin with because I didn't know I could. Nobody told me.

But then I did claim. I spent months wading through the morass of Officialdom, and finally received my first carer's pay cheque (Invalid Care Allowance, it was called then). The amount was minuscule, but the effect on my morale was huge. I was still my piglet's husband; that hadn't changed. But suddenly I was a professional carer as well. And immediately I found I could bear the hard parts of caring with equanimity. Now I was a pro.

There's a lot more about money in Chapter 13. You'll need to look in there to check the other ways we carers are affected by it, not just in our wallets but in our heads.

CHAPTER 7

Officialdom and Chaos Theory

Ignore it

What this book means by Officialdom

What it's for

Money
Information
Services to help us look after our piglets
Services to help us look after ourselves

Then why does it drive us nuts?

What it isn't

It isn't hostile
It isn't Big Brother
It's not a system

So what's the problem?

It's big and we're small
It functions in a different time-scale
It has to be accountable

Result is a muddle

Carers get let down
The general public loses out as well
Cock-up or conspiracy?

Chaos Theory

Random results from normal equations
Order out of chaos
Chaos is good

How to reduce randomness, and increase order

Work out what you want from Officialdom
Money
Information
Become a formologist
Become an assessment ace
The customer is always right
Find the person
Keep at it

Cheerful thought

Sombre thought

PS

Officialdom and Chaos Theory

It's not a hundred per cent inevitable that you'll find yourself floundering about in the chaotic world of Officialdom. Just ninety-nine per cent.

In fact, by the time you've reached this chapter, you'll probably have run up against 'the system' already. And you'll be all too familiar with its infuriating, frustrating, and occasionally (though not often enough) hilarious, vagaries.

You may even have opened the book at this section in the hope of finding some bright ideas on dealing with it.

It's equally possible that you're only here in a spirit of mild curiosity, having more or less decided not to bother with it at all. After all, carers aren't exactly obliged to place themselves and their piglets in the hands of the powers-that-be. You're well aware that to do so involves horrible hassle. And you strongly suspect, or are even convinced, that the pain is more than the gain.

Is there an alternative to getting involved with Officialdom?

Yes, there is.

Ignore it

Hmmmm. Trouble is, ignoring Officialdom in the belief that it will then leave you alone is like expecting to win the Lottery. It *could* happen. It's just that it probably won't.

In fact, pretending it isn't there might even make it harder to handle when eventually you have to.

Even so, some carers do try to side-step it. Are you, or have you been, one of them? In that case, one or other of the following scenarios may fit your case:

- You have quite a lot of money. Because of this, you haven't really felt the need to ask for outside help. Even if you were mildly tempted, perhaps you decided it wasn't worth the bother. So you used your own financial resources to modify your home and buy whatever specialist equipment your piglet needed. You probably pay professional care-givers to come in every day. You may even hire a live-in nursing team. Loss of income hasn't bothered you in the way it bothers other carers who have to give up their jobs – you're not dependent on working for a living. Or you *are* dependent on it, but by getting in hired help you can go to work and carry on earning

- You're one of those lovely people who choose not to think of themselves as carers at all – even though you are (see the previous chapter). According to your self-image you're an ordinary person quietly getting on with doing what has to be done. So it hasn't occurred to you to seek help from the State. On the rare occasions when you haven't been able to do something unaided you've asked a friend or neighbour or a relation to lend a hand. And so far they've always come up trumps. You may or may not possess an enormous amount of money, but you regard that as being of secondary importance. So you haven't bothered to claim any financial benefits, or even to find out what you or your piglet are entitled to. Well, so far so good. But it doesn't follow that the authorities won't become aware of you and your piglet in the course of time. Or that you'll be able to go on being self-sufficient for ever

- You're a specially vulnerable carer – a teenager, say, or even a child. Or perhaps you have a disability yourself. Do you harbour a sneaking suspicion that by rights you oughtn't to be a carer at all? But you want to be allowed to go on looking after your piglet? You're convinced you're the only one who can care for them properly? Are you a little bit scared of the authorities? Do you even see them as the enemy? You're worried that, if they find out about you, they'll try to take over and perhaps break up the family? You're not so much ignoring Officialdom as hiding from it.

Well, it's not my job to encourage you to turn yourself in to the authorities when you don't need or want to. But what if you're already lost in the middle of a paperwork jungle? Hacking desperately at the overhanging red tape? Frantically fending off the official forms?

The thing about Officialdom is that, though it's foisted on some, others seek it out because they need the things it offers. You're probably in that situation yourself. Maybe it's suddenly become rather important to install a stair lift, or a ramp for the wheelchair. Or what if there isn't enough money coming in and your caring role is preventing you going out and earning more? Perhaps you've reached the point when you've got to have some time to yourself or explode, but your friends, who *are* all working, haven't got time to step in and relieve you. What if you're aware that you don't know enough about how to care, and urgently need advice from people who do?

Yep. You're one of the ninety-nine per cent. Read on.

What this book means by Officialdom

I'm talking about the people in suits and white coats. The ones who sit behind desks, stare at you over the tops of their glasses, ask intrusive, embarrassing, questions and seem doubtful about your replies.

I'm talking about those others who turn up at your home armed with bags stuffed full of paperwork. And more than anything else I'm thinking of those damn forms, those multi-page questionnaires along with the accompanying multi-page explanations, which start out so clearly on page one but turn into gobbledegook by page three.

All government officials (national, regional and local) are automatically included. So are people employed by organisations that are funded by government. Or answerable to government. And so are any members of the medical profession who still cling to the old 'doctor knows best' way of thinking, whoever pays their fees.

Am I beginning to sound like someone who hates the authorities because he's frightened of them? Well, I don't and I'm not. But I *am* a carer, and I know just how hugely Officialdom can loom in our lives.

It's not exactly a necessary evil. That's because it's not evil. But it is, without any question at all, a necessary pain in the neck.

Need a reminder about why it might be necessary?

What it's for

Well, that rather depends on which side of the fence you are. The point of Officialdom as far as the government's concerned is to keep us carers caring. They don't want to take over the responsibility if they can possibly help it. So they watch us to see how we're getting on, and give us a helping hand where necessary. Which requires a bit of organisation, seeing as how there are quite a lot of us, and we all have different circumstances and requirements, and we're scattered all over the place. Officialdom is the machinery they use to tackle the job.

From the carers' side of the fence, Officialdom is there to give us stuff we need. We know it either is available or ought to be available. It's true that getting at it can be incredibly hard. Or even impossible. But it's there all right.

What have they got that we need?

Money

Disability is likely to have a drastic effect on your finances. Your piglet may not be able to earn anything, and even if *you* are it almost certainly won't be anything like as much as you would if you weren't a carer. For full-time carers, your earning power may be zero. So you'll need income to replace the flow of money which has dried up.

But it's worse than that. Because of the disability, you may well need all kinds of gadgets, help and other support which are expensive and which you wouldn't otherwise have needed.

You're in a financial black hole. Your inability to earn is compounded by the necessity to spend more. Officialdom will never plug the hole, but it'll help.

You're still going to be poor, though. To find out how to cope with this, you'll have to pop across to Chapter 13. But don't go there yet.

Information

The needs of carers are so diverse, multifarious, complex, and fluctuating that government has had to create the enormous sub-world of Officialdom to provide for them. The officials who live in this world and administer it have more than likely received some training (though it's sometimes hard to be sure).

But we haven't. So one of the resources that Officialdom has, and that we need, is knowledge. How to exist, how to care, what buttons to push and levers to pull in this new life we and our piglets find ourselves in.

Services to help us look after our piglets

Imagine for a minute that the State was looking after your piglet, and you were off doing something else. Stuff like wheelchairs, stair lifts, whatever your piglet needs, would be produced just like that. There'd be a team of people to do what you're doing at the moment on your own. The jobs which you find so onerous, whether they're directly associated with caring (like bathing and feeding) or indirectly (like cleaning up the mess) would be shared out among an army of professional carers.

Well, all that equipment and all those people exist. And even though you're not somewhere else doing your own thing, but here being a carer all on your own, Officialdom can put it at your disposal. If you know how to get at it.

Services to help us look after ourselves

Officialdom is concerned about *your* welfare just as much as your piglet's. It's not so concerned that it's about to say: 'Okay, you've done a great job and we recognise that you've had a hard time, so we're going to send you on a six-month sabbatical to Hawaii.'

But the last thing it wants you to do is burn out. So it'll do its best to take your piglet off your hands from time to time, or send someone in to keep an eye on them while you go to the pub. In theory, at least. Again, the trick is to know how to make this happen without actually burning out first.

Then why does it drive us nuts?

Considering how crucial Officialdom can be for most of us carers, you'd think we'd be really grateful for what it can do for us. You'd expect carers to go about saying things like:

'Thank goodness for Officialdom.' And 'Where would we be without it?'

But not many of us do that. What we tend to do instead is go: 'Aaaaaaaaaaaaaargh.' Quite loudly.

Aaoaaaaaaaaaargh!

Why? Because Officialdom is only really helpful in theory. In practice, it's illogical, time-consuming, obscure, usually demeaning, often unproductive, and always unpredictable.

But one thing about it is totally certain. This is enshrined in the Selfish Pig's Law of Ambient Tripwires (SPLAT) which says that the greater your need for help, the greater the number of bureaucratic obstacles that are placed in your path, and the more likely you are to trip up over them.

No wonder a brush with Officialdom can cause bile to flood through a carer's body and . . .

. . . scald and viper through her until her ears fall off like figs, her toes grow big and black as balloons, and steam comes screaming out of her navel.

Dylan Thomas, Under Milk Wood

But the trick is to bear in mind what Officialdom isn't.

. . . and I can say 'no' in 26 languages!

MISSION STATEMENT

What it isn't

Oddly enough, Officialdom isn't really any of the things people suspect. We sometimes get to thinking of it in negative terms because of the SPLAT principle. But before retreating to a corner in grumpy silence, we ought at least to consider the case for the defence.

It isn't hostile

Officialdom is not the enemy. It's actually the opposite. It's the State's way of saying: 'May I give you a hand?' It says this in incomprehensible officialese, but that's what it means.

How do I know this? Well, think about it. The State can't afford to take over the responsibility of caring for all the piglets in the country. So it wants *you* to care for yours. To make certain you do, it's prepared to help. Of course, it's not going to come up with so much aid that it would be effectively taking over the caring role. Or not in most cases. It wants to help just enough to keep you in the job.

There may be instances, particularly in the case of young carers, when the State will form the opinion that it'll have to take over. That the carer can't, in all justice, be saddled with the responsibility. When it does come to this conclusion, it'll be thinking both of the carer and the piglet. But it'll be a reluctant conclusion. It would much rather not have to take over. So it'll be open to argument, and keen to find a way for you to carry on caring.

No, Officialdom may be heavy-handed, and it may be occasionally clumsy in its use of language, but it's definitely on your side.

It isn't Big Brother

Social Services come in for devastating criticism when they fall down on the job, however reasonable their excuse. So they don't want to fall down on yours. That's what would happen, or would be *judged* to have happened, if it turned out that you were neglecting, abusing, or in some way not caring properly for your piglet. So once they're aware of your case they're bound to keep an eye on you.

But this doesn't make them Big Brother, watching your every move, earwigging on your every conversation and even tapping into your every thought.

'The telescreen received and transmitted simultaneously. Any sound that Winston made, above the level of a very low whisper, would be picked up by it; moreover, so long as he remained within the field of vision which the metal plaque commanded, he could be seen as well as heard. There was of course no way of knowing whether you were being watched at any given moment. How often, or on what system, the Thought Police plugged in on any indi-vidual wire was guesswork. It was even conceivable that they watched everybody all the time. But at any rate they could plug in your wire whenever they wanted to. You had to live – did live, from habit that became instinct – in the assumption that every sound you made was overheard, and except in darkness, every moment scrutinised.'

From 1984, by George Orwell

Listen, how many people work for your nearest Social Services department? Doesn't matter, I promise you it's not that many. How many hours a week do they put in? Yeah, well there's no need to be cynical. And how efficient are they? Like I said . . .

So do you really think they could spy on you like George Orwell's Big Brother, even if they wanted to?

Naturally, they'll watch you if they suspect that either you or your piglet, or both of you, are in some danger. If they're satisfied that this isn't an issue, they'll be fully occupied attending to those cases where there *is* a danger. They're on your back? They're round at your place day in day out? Then maybe they have a point. Maybe you're a bit too much of a selfish pig, after all.

But the biggest likelihood is that they won't be paying you enough attention.

It's not a system

Who said Officialdom was part of an organised system? It's no such thing. What it *is* is a collection of departments, and a range of services.

Whenever you feel that the system is breaking down, or you're getting lost in it, you're probably making the mistake of expecting it to behave in a way it can't. It isn't a system, so it's never going to be systematic.

True, there are laws and guidelines which are supposed to govern and unify the departments and services. But human beings interpret these, and not always in the same way. Plus, don't forget, you and your piglet are individuals, too. In fact, you're unique. So it isn't surprising that you don't fit perfectly into any system, particularly one that isn't.

Even if the system is one (which it isn't), it's so huge that it would be surprising if its component parts invariably worked in harmony.

So what's the problem?

Seeing as how Officialdom can offer so much, and is on our side, what's the problem?

It's big and we're small

It's complex, faceless, unable to make allowances for human individuality or leaps of logic, slow to change course, and incapable of empathising. It comprises a large number of component parts (social services, health, transport, work and pensions, you name it) which are supposed to fit snugly together, but don't always. And when they don't, you can fall between the cracks.

It functions in a different time-scale

When you need help you need it today. Right now, even. But that won't happen. In fact, you'll probably still be waiting in a couple of months' time. You'd be forgiven for concluding that the machinery has broken down. It hasn't, though. It's just that it's on machine time, which is different from human time.

For example:

- Officialdom has agreed that someone will come round to attend to your particular problem next week – only they don't appear. The explanation you're given is that they're off sick, and what's more there's no word about when they're expected back at work. Obviously, since they're sick, they can't be fired or shunted to one side. And since they're still on the department's books they've got to be paid. There's no budget to bring in another helper, so the work which that person is supposed to do is just not going to get done, is it? It stands to reason. They're sorry about it, but there's nothing they can do

- Your case has exposed some ludicrous anomaly in the way the machinery is supposed to work. For it to be fixed, the law has to be changed. Which it will be – in ten years' time.

It has to be accountable

Officialdom is paid for by government, which means it's paid for with money taken from the general public. Which in turn means that Officialdom is, has to be, extremely keen on being able to prove that they're not spending the money irresponsibly or crookedly.

This is accountability, and as a taxpayer I'm all for it. But like many excellent principles, it has a downside. Which in this case is that Officialdom is as much influenced by possible comeback as by what it can do for you and what you need from it. More, in fact, since nobody ever thanks them for getting something right, and everybody's quick to criticise when they make a mistake.

Hence all the paperwork. And the interviews in which there always seem to be more of them than there are of us. They're covering their backs.

... just make sure my back's covered...

Hence the principle that we don't need their help unless we establish beyond reasonable doubt that we do, which is the exact opposite of justice.

Hence the feeling that they can't be too careful about what kind of help they give. We might complain, or tell the media about their negligence, or if not about their negligence then the way they interfered.

Hence their habit of simply responding to our cries for help rather than initiating contact. Partly this is because they're too busy with all that paperwork. But mainly it's because they're conscious of being accountable.

Result is a muddle

Almost nobody gets what they want out of Officialdom. It may be worthy and necessary, and act the way it does for all the right reasons

but

Carers get let down

It happens all the time. Take the case of Clare and Alun, an educated, hard-working, and deserving couple.

It took more than seven months of battling before Claire Stuffins was able to claim disability benefits on behalf of her husband Alun.

He used to work as an oil analyst with BP Oil but suffered a stroke at the age of 34. Mrs Stuffins, 33, who was also employed by BP Oil but as a transport business adviser, stopped work in April 1999 to care for him.

Despite the fact that an initial application for disability benefits was rejected, Mrs Stuffins, of Hemel Hempstead, Herts, persevered until the claim was met.

She said: 'I had been given a pack for Disability Living Allowance when Alun became entitled to Incapacity Benefit, but had binned it, thinking that it didn't apply to him.

'I only applied 13 months after the stroke, after Alun had been medically retired. However, the forms were so complicated it was nigh on impossible to apply brain injury to the questions asked. So the application was rejected.'

Undeterred, she approached the Citizens Advice Bureau for help, but was told not to come back until the claim had been refused twice.

Only then, she was told, could someone help challenge the decision.

She said: 'It was only after listening to a talk at our local Headway [the brain injury association] group by somebody from Hertfordshire County Council's Money Advice Unit that I challenged the decision. She explained how brain injury impairments could be expressed in the claim forms.

'A doctor eventually came to see us, although the questions he asked weren't really relevant, and he would only speak to Alun and ask questions of him, and at that point, Alun had severely impaired insight into his problems.

'The doctor spoke to me only at the end and then had to scrap all his previous notes when I was finally allowed to explain Alun's disabilities. The award of the Disability Living Allowance benefit didn't come until seven and a half months after the claim, and although it was retrospective it had been a hell of a time.'

This was not the only obstacle Mrs Stuffins had to surmount. She then had to apply for Invalid Care Allowance when she gave up work full-time to care for Alun.

She said: 'When I was due to give up work, I phoned the local Benefits Agency to ask for guidance about what to claim. I was so confused in the end I wrote to them. They wrote back advising me to claim the Invalid Care Allowance and advised that my National Insurance Contributions would be fully credited.'

Mrs Stuffins currently receives Invalid Care Allowance worth £41.75 a week. She said: 'We also get a slight discount on our community charge. It reduces by one band because of Alun's disabilities. However, I was encouraged by a carer at the Princess Royal Trust carers' centre to apply, and the discount was backdated to the date of Alun's stroke. Nobody had explained our eligibility previously.'

> A spokesman for the trust said: 'Carers are often completely fazed by the benefits system. A large number are not claiming Invalid Care Allowance and many are on the wrong level of Disability Living Allowance. These carers had been struggling financially.'
>
> *from the* Daily Telegraph

Okay, Clare and Alun got there in the end. But they were business executives, and handy with the paperwork. What about those carers and piglets who are less able to fight for their rights? There are hundreds of thousands of them. Maybe even millions.

In fact, almost everyone who calls on Officialdom for help is faced by conflicting information, delays, confusion, and frustration. So what happens?

> Research suggests more than a billion pounds' worth of benefits go unclaimed each year.
>
> A survey by insurance firm Prudential blamed confusion and complexity in the benefits system, covering Council Tax Benefit, Housing Benefit and income support. Of those questioned, 23% had never heard of the benefits, while another 43% did not realise they were eligible.
>
> *from the* Daily Telegraph

The general public loses out as well

Not only is Officialdom failing to make the benefits available to those of us who need them, but they're handing out the money to other people who don't.

> Every year, it is estimated that benefit cheats cost £2 billion in stolen benefits.
>
> *The Department for Work and Pensions*

Brilliant, isn't it? For every pound that Officialdom fails to pass over to people like us, there are two which it gives to the cheats and conmen.

In fact, it's even worse than that, because Officialdom has to pour even more money into new schemes and departments with names like Targeting Fraud, and into prosecuting the crooks.

And that's just the situation regarding financial benefits. How many of us fail to get other kinds of benefits that we need, are owed, and which are supposedly on offer, like:

- Information
- Special equipment
- Help in the home
- Respite care?

Cock-up or conspiracy?

Here are the theories.

Cock-up: the reason that those who need it don't get it, and those who have no right to it steal it, is that Officialdom cocks it up. This could be because the officials are just plain incompetent, or that they're being strangled by their own red tape.

Conspiracy: the government deliberately makes Officialdom impossible for ordinary people to penetrate so that it doesn't have to shell out so much money.

Or there's one other possibility: it's neither cock-up nor conspiracy. It's what is technically known to science as chaos.

Chaos Theory

Meteorologist Edward Lorenz was working on a weather-prediction computer program in 1961. He kept feeding in the same parameters, but again and again getting different results. In the end he concluded that the workings of the earth's atmosphere were so complex, and affected by so many tiny influences, that anything could happen and it was impossible to predict what would.

> The flapping of a single butterfly's wing today produces a tiny change in the state of the atmosphere. Over a period of time, what the atmosphere actually does diverges from what it would have done. So, in a month's time, a tornado that would have devastated the Indonesian coast doesn't happen. Or maybe one that wasn't going to happen, does.
>
> *Ian Stewart,* Does God Play Dice? The Mathematics of Chaos

This is 'the butterfly effect', and it was the beginning of Chaos Theory, which went on to become a serious avenue of scientific research.

Between then and now, Chaos Theory has been applied to population growth, the outcome of tossing a coin, cotton price fluctuations, musical composition, and the beating of a human heart. But as far as I know the scientists haven't yet applied it to the claiming of benefits, or any other aspect of Officialdom.

And indeed, why would they? According to the theory, chaos produces:

- Random results from normal equations

- Order from apparent chaos.

Which is exactly what happens in the world of Officialdom, and you don't have to be a research scientist to recognise this.

What you have to be is a carer.

Random results from normal equations

Try getting together with any group of carers, and swap notes on experiences with Officialdom. You'll see straight away that carers with broadly similar needs and backgrounds are getting totally different responses from the authorities. The only obvious pattern is that there isn't an obvious pattern.

The whole thing seems crazy and, worse than that, unkind. Why should *she* get that grant when *I* can't?

Aha, but this is not craziness. It's chaos, which is, in its own way, predictable, and a lot more hopeful.

Order out of chaos

Talk a bit more to the victims, no, sorry, I meant carers, and you'll very likely find one or two who persisted in their battle for justice, and in the end got the support they were looking for.

For them, order eventually resulted from apparent chaos.

Sometimes this can take the shape of something you weren't even looking for and didn't know existed.

Chaos is good

Chaos is miles better than either conspiracy or cock-up. If the State was conspiring against you, you'd never win.

And if it's true that it's completely inept and disorganised, you haven't got much chance of getting what you need either.

Under Chaos Theory, all you've got to do is keep trying. The results will be random, and sooner or later one will be the one you want. Furthermore, the longer you keep it up the greater the chance that order will emerge out of chaos.

Trouble is, you need it now – not at some theoretical point in the future.

How to reduce randomness, and increase order

This is where you have to stop thinking like a scientist, and start acting like a carer.

What scientists do, after they've set up an experiment, is to observe the results. They don't try to influence the outcome, if they can help it. But that's exactly what we have to do.

As soon as we come into contact with Officialdom, we need to be aware that we're in for a spot of chaos. We're almost certainly going to feel confused, angry, frustrated, and despairing. But the trick is to pay no attention to any of those feelings. Instead, just plug away at 'the system' in as unchaotic a way as possible, till some good comes out of it.

Work out what you want from Officialdom

Surprisingly, hardly any of us do this. When you become a carer for the first time, you probably don't even stop to think that you are a carer. You're more focused on your piglet than on yourself. And in any case, it's all new to you. How do you know what you need? Nobody tells you.

The other thing nobody tells you is what help is *available*. Which makes it hard to figure out what help you need. Sometimes it's only when you hear what benefit or assistance somebody else gets that you realise it's exactly what you need too.

So you have to concentrate. Investigate other carers and other piglets to find out what support they're getting. Think about your own situation, and list the parts you're finding hard. Be aware that no relief is going to come unless you ask for it, and it's no use just shouting HELP. You have to apply specifically for each bit of help, which means knowing exactly what help you want.

Money

Money is available (or not, as the case may be) from the State in both hard cash and in the form of substitutes for money, like travel passes, tax relief, and concessions.

To get your hands on most of it, you need to be poor. But not all benefits are means-tested, so even if you're filthy rich some of it will come your way. Which is fair enough: you've paid your tax dues, and now you're saving the State money by caring for your piglet.

But don't expect to be able to second-guess the logic behind what the State says you're entitled to and what you're not.

In Britain at the time this book was being written (don't worry about checking it out; it's probably changed by now), the Occupational Therapy section of Social Services could supply and fit, free of charge, small items of equipment like handrails in the home of anyone who needed them. Slightly bigger and more expensive items, like bath lifts, could be supplied on permanent loan, also free of charge. But modifications to the home, such as the installation of a shower or stairlift or wheelchair ramp, were classified as 'major works', and means-tested. In order to qualify for a grant, the piglet needed to have hardly any savings at all.

> Eileen and Johnny, when they retired, sold the house they had brought the children up in, moved to a much smaller one, and invested the difference. They used the interest to supplement their pensions. When Johnny had a stroke, Eileen put in for some modifications to the home, but was refused a grant on the grounds that they were too rich.
>
> Nick and Charleen, when they retired, hung on to their big house. Their only pension was the State one, which they were hard-pressed to live on. Charleen had a stroke, and Nick put in for a grant towards having a lift installed. He was awarded not only the grant, but also extra funds to supplement their income.

Are you seeing a moral in this story? That, say, the more responsible your attitude to your own money, the less seriously will you be taken by the State? Or that the more disabled the piglet, and in consequence the more onerous the job of the carer, the less likely are you to receive any help?

Nah. It isn't that. It's just chaos, that's all. And if there's a moral, it's that you should keep trying. Need money? Can't get it from Occupational Therapy? Then look elsewhere in the system. It'll almost certainly come from somewhere if you really need it.

Information

You'd think there'd be an official somewhere who would look at your case and tell you exactly and definitively how the State could help. But there isn't.

There are plenty of sources of information, some of them part of Officialdom and some of them independent. And they all tell you different stories.

The most useful sources are almost certainly going to be other carers and piglets, and particularly carer support groups. Inevitably they're going to have more direct experience of what help is available than Officialdom, which doesn't specialise in carers.

What you have to do is glean ideas and possibilities from wherever you can, and then go to the relevant authority to apply. They may say: 'No, sorry, you're not eligible.' Or they may equally well reply, in a surprised tone of voice: 'Yes, that's a good idea.'

> • Less than half (42%) of respondents have been given sufficient help/support or information about lifting, handling and moving.

- Only 42% of carers responding have been given sufficient help/support or information on giving injections or the use of catheters/dialysis.

- On help with key caring tasks, 30% reported that they have not been given what they perceive to be sufficient help or information.

- It is a matter of some concern that almost a third (32%) of carers found the sources of help and advice available to them to be either fairly or very difficult to use. Of those who found these sources to be either very or fairly difficult to use, over half (53%) said that this was due to lack of information on the help available.

- Significantly, 26% identified transport or travelling difficulties and 17% identified their own lack of confidence as barriers to using sources of advice and help.

- The proportion of those who found the sources very or fairly difficult to use was higher among younger carers (35% for those aged under 45) than older carers (28% of those aged 65 or more). Those with most difficulty were caring for people who were aged 16 to 29 years.

- Other groups who found significantly more difficulty were those caring for more than one person; those caring for people with a physical illness or learning disability and those spending a longer time caring.

- It may be a cause of concern that 11% of respondents have identified a publication of some sort, rather than a professional or a local agency, as their major source of information about the diagnosis and future development of the person they are caring for. While such sources can clearly be useful additional sources it seems worrying that they are being cited by so many carers as their main sources of information about the health needs of the person they are caring for.

- Those who have most difficulty with sources of advice and help are also those who get most of their information from newspapers or leaflets (rather than from contact with professionals).

From Carers Speak Out Project
a survey undertaken by The Princess Royal Trust for Carers in the UK

See? You're not the only one who can't find out what you need to know, either about or from Officialdom. If you're the studious type, or a compulsive picker-up of leaflets, that doesn't mean you're going to get all the info you need. It actually works the other way; you'll get a lot less than carers who are good at networking and asking questions of all and sundry. And how about this? Lack of confidence is a barrier to acquiring information. To get that one sorted, see the section below headed 'The customer is always right'.

Become a formologist

Okay, we've established that Chaos Theory is a valid and respectable branch of science. Well, the study of official forms, or formology, ought to be another one.

It's impossible to communicate at all with Officialdom unless you can speak the language of forms. Which is not easy.

Here's what happened to me:

I finished filling out a particularly long-winded form, and spent some time amassing the documentary evidence that had to accompany it (doctor's certificate, piglet's photograph, copy of some benefit previously awarded, etc). There was a checklist at the end of the form, and I carefully ticked each item as I appended the document.

I stuffed everything in a large envelope and took it along to the relevant government office, where it was opened in front of me by an important and experienced person. He read through the completed form, checking that I had filled out each box in block capitals, and then he turned to the documentary evidence, meticulously inspecting each piece.

Aha. Triumph. 'You haven't attached the birth certificate.'

I replied patiently: 'If you look at the checklist, you'll see that I've attached every item listed on it.'

He smiled smugly. 'It's not on the checklist.'

'Then how was I supposed to know you were going to ask for it?'

'You're supposed to read the other form, the one entitled "Notes on Completing the Form". It makes it clear in there that you have to produce a birth certificate.'

Now it was my turn to be smug. 'I have the Notes right here.'

He ran through them quickly, then turned back to the beginning and went through them again more slowly. No success. Back he went to the beginning and started again, this time laying a ruler under each line as he read it. Triumph once more, mixed with relief: 'Here it is.' He swivelled the form round and showed it to me.

I threw my arms out. 'If the birth certificate is essential, then why on earth isn't it on the checklist? What's the point of having a damn checklist if it isn't comprehensive?'

'May I ask you to keep your voice down?'

'Look,' I said. 'I'm a person who messes about with words every day. Words are my business. If *I* can't understand what I'm supposed to do, who the hell can?'

'Do you want to complain?'

'I AM complaining.'

He stared at me, astonished at my ignorance. 'No, no, no, it's no use complaining to me. You need to fill out this complaints form and send it to the address on the back page – with the necessary documentary evidence, of course.'

But what if words are *not* your business, and no matter how many times you read and reread the form, you still can't understand what it's all about Don't guess. It's too important for that. Mess it up and you could miss out on some much-needed money or support. Do you have a friend who's better at this kind of thing than you are? Then get them in to help.

Can't think of anyone? Then get some official help. That sounds like a stupid idea, since it's Officialdom which is causing the problem in the first place. But the Citizens Advice Bureau is a sort of halfway house between Officialdom and you. The people who work there are volunteers, but they've all been trained in formology. They should be able to help you not only sort out what the form's all about, but even get it filled out for you.

Even when you understand forms, and know what bits and pieces you're supposed to attach to them, filling them out can be a demeaning business. It's the questions they ask. Can the piglet get dressed/go to the toilet/eat without help. 'Of course I can,' roars the piglet, even though it's not true.

The problem is that *you* need the help which you're applying for in the form, and the piglets need their independence and self-respect. How to achieve the one without compromising the other?

There's more on this in Chapter 16. But here, we're studying formology – the science of completing forms in such a way that they achieve the objective. And the first rule is to resist the temptation to lie. It's not going to work. Pander to your piglet and write down on the form that they're able-bodied, and you won't get the help you're looking for. But go too far the other way and say they can't do a single thing for themselves when in fact they can, and you'll only be found out.

What you have to do is tell it the way it is, even if your piglet doesn't want you to do this. Which is why another temptation interposes itself at this point. Go behind the piglet's back. Don't tell them what you're doing. If necessary forge their signature. But this is another bad idea. You're concerned about their self-respect? Then how does deceiving them help that? In any case, everything you put down in the forms is going to be assessed at an interview later on.

It may be a good idea to bring in some trusted friend to help when you're completing the forms. Someone who's not quite so close to the piglet as you are can often defuse what would otherwise be an explosive situation.

Even then, it can be hard to know exactly how to answer some questions. How far can the piglet walk on their own, for example. Well, obviously it depends how they're feeling. Some days, they can stagger all the way to the Post Office; others, they're hard put to get to the bathroom. So you compromise and invent a distance – 50 metres, say. But in six months' time, when you're still negotiating for this particular benefit, can you remember what you said? And has your piglet's long-distance walking ability increased or decreased? You may need to know. So make a photocopy of each form before sending it off, and hang on to it.

A better idea still is to ask around to see if anybody knows what answers Officialdom is looking for. It may be that there's a crucial figure for how far the piglet can walk; 49 metres, and they qualify for a benefit, 51 metres and they don't. Ask before you fill the form in.

And don't undersell. Officialdom expects you to give your answers based on the 'worst case'. So if the piglet can walk half a mile on good days but only stagger 25 metres on bad days, put 25. It's what you're supposed to do.

Become an assessment ace

Getting help from Officialdom isn't just a question of sending in some forms. You'll be assessed, face-to-face, as well. Which sounds like a good idea, except that in some ways assessments are even more difficult than forms.

At least with a form you have time to consider what you're going to say, and even to cross out your answer and have another go. But when an assessing doctor asks your piglet how well they can walk, whereupon the piglet leaps out of the chair and strides about the room like a champion sprinter limbering up, all you can do is mutter sheepishly: 'They're not usually like this.'

Part of the reason for the assessments is so that Officialdom can see for itself how disabled your piglet is. But you can also ask to be assessed yourself so it can gauge how hard a time you're having looking after them.

The people conducting the assessments usually say whether they want you and your piglet in the room together or apart. But you may be allowed to choose. Either way it's a hard one.

When it's the piglet who's being assessed, what do you do if they lie through their teeth? They probably will, because

- they're jealous of their independence and self-respect

- they may not appreciate everything you do for them or the grief it causes you

- sometimes the questions are phrased incompetently ('Can you get dressed all by yourself?' 'Yes, thank you.').

So you may want to be on hand at piglet assessments, if only to inject the occasional raised eyebrow.

On the other hand, it might be better for *you* to be assessed on your own. Otherwise the temptation is to say: 'Yes, I'm getting on fine, thank you very much,' when what you really want to do is wail: 'I think I'm going mad,' or 'I'm completely exhausted, and I can't go on any more.'

No doubt the crooks who steal billions from Officialdom are expert at assessments. That's because they're good at lying. But we SPs can be too self-effacing. We have a habit of playing problems down instead of up. And as a result we end up with less support than we deserve.

There are all kinds of reasons why assessments are so hard to get right. They can be acutely embarrassing. They can put you on the defensive. And you may not even be clear what the assessors are looking for.

So what's the trick? It's to steel yourself beforehand to tell it the way it is. And during the assessment, don't sit back if the wrong message seems to be coming across. You tell 'em.

The customer is always right

When you ask Officialdom for help, you're not a scrounger. What you are is a customer. The services that Officialdom provides have been put there for you. So you needn't think you're asking for a favour.

Daunted because they're the experts and you're a beginner? Because they're professional and you're amateur? Because they have all the power and you don't have any?

Rubbish. You're doing the State a favour. Just keep thinking how much it would cost them if you fell down on the job.

Not getting the information or the services or the money you need to allow you to carry on caring? Then it's the State who's falling down on the job.

It's a weird thing, but what you get out of Officialdom doesn't always depend on what you and your piglet need. It can be determined by your relationship with it.

- You can be a young carer, or one on a seriously low income, and you'd benefit hugely from help. But if you're scared of them you may not get any

- You might happen to be a middle-aged carer in full control of your life and finances. You're confident, articulate and pushy. You stand a good chance of getting quite a lot.

It's all a question of your attitude. So, if Officialdom is being a bit negative or playing hard-to-get, don't hold back, and don't give up. You're more important than you think. Never mind about upsetting them. Carers have traditionally hung about in the background being self-effacing. That's why we're in the mess we're now in. Go for it. It's yours. It belongs to you.

We're not talking charity here. If we were primitive people, we'd live in a village, and the other villagers would gather round and help. Well, we *do* live in a village – a big one. And the villagers have appointed officials to organise the helping.

The only problem is, we have to fill in forms to get them to do anything.

Find the person

Officialdom isn't all forms and numbers and gobbledegook. The people that toil inside the corridors of power are the same as us. Admittedly very few of them have been carers, so they probably won't understand your point of view in the same way that other carers do.

But they're still people, and it's easier to build a relationship with a person than with a system. So whenever you talk to one, on the telephone or in person, get their name and make sure they've got yours. Next time you have to go back to that department, head for that person first.

Be a person yourself, not a number. If you have to make a nuisance of yourself to get something done, be a nuisance to a person and not just the system.

Keep at it

> 'You get all these statements of intent to help, have these meetings, fill in dozens of multi-page forms, and then nothing happens. Except more talk, more forms, and endless waiting.'
>
> *Bernard, a disillusioned carer, who gave up on Officialdom*

Remember your Chaos Theory and never give up till order has emerged from the muddle.

Cheerful thought

It gets easier

- once you're in the system, and Officialdom recognises who you are

- when you've found your way around and know the ropes

- once some help has been made available to you, so that you feel stronger and have more time to tackle the next step

- after your first 'hit' with the system, and your confidence has been given a boost.

Sombre thought

Officials are professional, so you have to be professional too. In fact, you need to be better at the game than they are.

How?

- Whenever you have dealings with Officialdom, keep a note in a diary of what was said or done.

- Check out what you're entitled to, and stay up to date.

- Keep copies of any forms you've filled out.

- Keep files of correspondence.

- Take the business of Officialdom seriously.

Remember Officialdom is now as much part of your job as it is for the officials themselves. It's as intrinsic as your other caring skills.

You'll meet other carers who complain about Officialdom. That makes about as much sense as a sailor complaining about the sea.

PS

If you've been thumbing through the pages of this section looking for detailed advice on what benefits to claim, where to get help with the stair lift, how to organise respite care, you'll be disappointed and irritated. Well, I'm sorry. I haven't supplied any of this stuff because:

- they'll have changed the rules, names, places and amounts by the time the printers have got the pages bound and the shops have got the book on the shelves, and

- everything's different not only in each country, but also in each part of each country, and depending on who you talk to in each department.

But there'll be a support group near you that will be able to give you good and up-to-date advice. Get it.

CHAPTER 8

Your body

Warning: caring can be bad for your health

It's harder for us than for care-workers

Training
Equipment
Going it alone

What gives?

Backs are at the forefront

Minding your back

Tools
The home
Not being an idiot
Keeping fit
    Specialist muscles
    Anti-stress
    Slow slow quick quick slow

Technique
    Positioning prior to standing from
        chair/toilet/commode/bed etc
    Rolling in bed
    A falling or fallen person
    Techniques
    Assisting the fallen person up from the floor

Take care, now. Look after yourself

Your body

How are you feeling today? Fine? That's great. As it happens, so am I. Which means that we're both in the minority.

Surveys show that between 60% and 75% of carers (depending on the survey) suffer health problems as a result of their caring. And the British government, in their National Strategy for Carers document, admit '51% of carers had suffered a physical injury such as a strained back since they began to care'.

So if you're feeling well, you're either lucky, or it's temporary, or you're doing something right.

Mind you, those health problems that most of us suffer from, they're not all physical ones. There's anxiety (80% of the carers who reported bad health experienced this), and depression (almost half had to put up with that).

So morale and mental health are big issues. But that's all you're going to hear about them in this section. On the other hand, there's plenty about that side of things in Chapters 10, 11 and 12, so if this is what most concerns you, you'd better whiz over there now.

Here, I'm thinking about our bodies in general, and our backs in particular. That's because 40% of the carers in the surveys had back pain at one time or another – some of them all the time – and they believed it was as a direct result of their caring role.

Warning: caring can be bad for your health

The likelihood of becoming a carer increases with age. And as we age we tend to experience more health problems. So it isn't surprising that, statistically, caring is unhealthy.

> Question: Why am I like a statistic?
> Answer: I've been broken down by age and sex.
>
> Christmas cracker joke.

As usual, statistics don't know what they're talking about. The real reason that our bodies start to crack under the strain is that caring can be hard, physical work. And that most of us are forced to do it on our own, without help. What's more, since we don't get any training, we almost invariably go about it the wrong way.

Another reason is that it can be exhausting emotionally. Oops, I just said I wouldn't refer to this till later. Sorry, but I can't stay away completely because they're linked. Stress and anxiety can stiffen you. Not stiffen your moral fibre, enabling you to brace up and carry on. No, stiffen your body, literally, which can quickly lead to muscle strain. And make a bad back worse.

Talking of muscles, it turns out that your muscles actually weaken when you're clinically depressed. Did you know that? I didn't, but now that I do it explains why being in a bad mental state can cause you to be in a bad physical state. In other words, caring can get you down literally as well as figuratively.

Add in the need to lug a heavy piglet around, and work at an awkward angle or in a posture that's unsound from an engineering point of view, and some body is going to complain. Guess who that body belongs to:

you.

It's harder for us than for care-workers

I'll tell you one thing: it's got nothing to do with ability. It IS harder for us unpaid carers than for paid care-workers to look after piglets without risking our health, and it is NOT because we're less capable than they are.

It's because they're equipped for the job, and we're not. They're armed with

- training (whereas we are given no information)
- specialist equipment (which we can only get if we know what to ask for, which we don't since we haven't been given any information)
- assistants (we have to carry out our caring alone and unaided).

Training

'Training in moving and handling is a vital aspect of implementing safe systems of work for staff.'

Excerpt from Safer Handling of People in the Community, *a handbook intended for paid managers of paid care-workers.*

Doesn't that irritate you? So training in moving and handling is vital, eh? Then why the hell doesn't anyone train us?

The handbook goes on: 'Employers have a general duty to provide suitable and sufficient information, instruction, training and supervision to safeguard the health, safety and welfare of their staff while at work. There is a requirement for training to be provided before staff are exposed to a hazard, or if the level of risk changes. Staff, therefore, require training on induction, if new equipment or work practices are introduced, and on a regular basis.'

In researching this book (well, once I'd started writing it, it seemed only fair to find out a bit about what went on in other homes, and with other types of carer) I attended seminars, interviewed professionals, and read books. I constantly came across advice about the necessity of training in order to avoid injury to the carer.

> 'Lifting or supporting people with disabilities is a practice which requires training if injuries are to be avoided.'
>
> *from* Children who Care

I actually attended a training session – or what I thought was going to be a training session. It was organised by a carers' charity (bless their hearts), and they'd got the professionals in to tell us what we ought to know about moving and handling piglets. But a lot of the advice in it turned out to be for piglets: how to walk with a stick, how to get out of a chair, that sort of thing. At question time I asked about some of the more specific problems I wanted answers to: how to move a piglet when they were in bed, how to help them get up once they've fallen on the floor, how to sit them straight on the toilet if they tended to crash down on it suddenly and askew. But the lecturer, a physiotherapist, said these problems were individual ones to me and could only be answered after an assessment had been carried out.

Naturally I applied for an assessment there and then, but nothing happened. After two weeks I contacted the physiotherapist and reminded her. She assured me that I had not been forgotten and that somebody would come to see us. They never did, and nothing more was ever heard.*

---

* Correction: I did hear, after six months. I received a letter assuring me that I had not been forgotten.

Of course, if I had been a professional care-worker, it would have been the other way round. I would not have been allowed to put myself at risk handling patients without being shown how to do it. My employers wouldn't have permitted it; nor would my union. Everybody on that side of the fence knows what would happen if a care-worker damaged their back on the job as a result of inadequate training. The care-worker would sue the employer, the union would call all the other workers out, questions would be asked in high places, articles would be aired in the media.

We, on the other hand, are expected somehow just to know how to heave our piglets about without doing ourselves a mischief. Or, if we don't know, then to learn on the job. If we put our backs out, are we going to sue? Who?

Get the union on our side? What union?

Equipment

Professionals have access to far more in the way of equipment than we do. They go in for hoists, special beds, frictionless sheets, and who knows what else. A lot of this stuff is expensive, and some of it needs to be installed. Even if we discover that it exists and is appropriate for our circumstances, we might not be able to afford to buy it without assistance, and that would mean the usual forms. There'd be a lot of resistance on the part of Officialdom. Even if we jumped successfully through all the hoops there'd be delays.

There is an alternative, of course.

- Find out what's appropriate and available

- Go out and buy it

- Pay someone to put it in.

And then again, there's the other option, which is what most of us plump for. Go on as we are, till eventually we injure ourselves.

Going it alone

Professionals tend to work in pairs, whereas we usually go it alone in caring matters.

It's true there are plenty of couples who share the caring. For example, parents of a disabled child. Or a couple who accommodate an elderly relative in their home. But even then, one member of the duo will often be out at work or off doing the shopping or looking after the other members of the family, and at those times there is only one active carer on duty.

The sheer logistics of ordinary life dictate that an unpaid carer is likely to be heaving and shoving on their own in a situation where professionals would be doing it in pairs.

What gives?

When the mule is overloaded, there's a good chance that it'll collapse sooner or later. Which bit gives way, exactly, is hard to predict. Symptoms could seem to have more to do with the mind than the body: anxiety, perpetual tiredness, a feeling of hopelessness.

Or they could be clearly physical: joint strains and back pain.

As it happens, they're probably all interlinked. Attention to the mental problems may well have a beneficial effect on the physical ones.

Even so, there's one bit that's in the front line of danger. And that's your back.

Backs are at the forefront

We've all been taught that our backs were designed for walking on all fours. But don't try caring for your piglet on all fours because it isn't going to work. I just tried, to see.

My piglet's bed was at the wrong height, and so was she. As for getting her in and out of the car, there was no way.

No, you have to stand up, and you have to lean over to heave and lift. You have to bend your neck, and distort your spine. You have to do all the things that you know are going to put a strain on your back. It goes with the job.

> 'Adults are too heavy to be physically lifted by two people, and bodily lifting is a high-risk activity.'
>
> The Lancet

TWO people, note. As for us, who are coping on our own, well, high-risk isn't in it. You *know* you're going to hurt yourself sooner or later.

Take Eileen, who is 83 and small. She cares for her husband, who's a big man. When he has a fall, there's no way she can get him up and into his chair. She has to call the ambulance. So what she tries to do is prevent him falling in the first place. Sometimes – well, all right, often – this means she needs to use her small reserves of physical strength (she has a lot more mental strength) to prop him up, redirect his barely controlled movements, channel his lurches. Guess what? Eileen suffers from a bad back.

Dan is 35, and fit. His disabled daughter is small for her age, and thin with it. Even so, lifting her out of the car caused him to bend over forwards and sideways at the same time, while taking her weight. Afterwards he had to be helped to the surgery.

Jules is a teenager. Her mum can do a lot for herself. It's just that she sometimes doesn't. So Jules always (well, not always, because she's a teenager and goes in for the usual bolshy patches, but certainly often), does things for her. And because she's young she sometimes attempts things which, if she was older and wiser, she wouldn't. What Jules doesn't know, and to be fair her mum doesn't think about either, is that her future health and development are being endangered by these activities.

In all these cases, it's the back that's first to go. And before it goes, the thing you're doing that's going to make it go seems unavoidable. For example:

- Lugging the wheelchair into and out of a car

- Leaning over to do up a seat belt

- Helping the piglet at bath time

- Helping them on or off the toilet

- Helping them get comfortable in bed, or to get out of bed, or back in

- Preventing falls, or helping a piglet get back up after a fall.

Minding your back

When politicians protect their own backs, it's metaphorical. In our case though, it needs to be real, and physical.

But the first action to take is a mental one. It's to realise that risking your back in the first place is probably a bit stupid. We do it because we're being conscientious, which sounds like the best of reasons, but isn't.

When a professional care-worker refuses to heave a stuck patient out of the bath, they aren't being lazy or selfish. They're being professional. They know they won't be a whole lot of use to anybody if they're in a wheelchair themselves.

Your next action should be to find out what steps you can take to go easy on your back while at the same time getting the job done.

Tools

Where I live there's a department at one of the big hospitals* which stocks just about every gadget imaginable, and some you never imagined, for helping disabled people. It's like the underground laboratory presided over by Q in a James Bond movie.

A guided tour of this amazing place opens your eyes to all kinds of possibilities, some affordable and some less so. I don't know whether there's something similar where you live, but it's worth asking. Just because we haven't been trained to do our job doesn't mean we can't take the law into our own hands and find out what we should be doing, and how.

The home

This is so obvious I wouldn't even mention it if it weren't for the fact that I didn't think about it till somebody pointed it out to me. It's this: you can do a lot to protect your back simply by preventing some of the situations which put a strain on it. For example, if your piglet has fallen once or twice on their way to watch television, could it be that a corner of a rug trips them up?

---

* Aid and Equipment, at the Royal South Hants Hospital, Southampton, UK.

In which case, removing the rug could be all you need to do to prevent a recurrence.

I apologise for that. It's so annoying when somebody tells you what you already knew. I may take it out before the book goes to print. On the other hand, maybe I won't because there's a chance that you're like me – too busy concentrating on the piglet to look about and see what traps there are for the unwary.

Not being an idiot

If your back hurts, it's tempting to ignore it while you look after your piglet.

Don't. Get help.

Keeping fit

In my experience the world is divided into those who believe in keeping fit and do something about it, and those who don't and don't. Carers, probably are no different. But we should be.

The reason is that caring can be a weird mixture of long periods of sluggishness interspersed with bouts of violent, unnatural, high-risk activity. Because of your piglet's disability, you don't in the nature of things spring about at high speed. What you do is keep pace with them for much of the time. You're a hare plodding along with your tortoise. (I don't know how the piglet suddenly transmogrified into a tortoise, but it did.) Next moment you're straining and heaving, muscles creaking, vertebrae groaning, joints cracking.

A lot of what you do makes you unfit, and some of what you have to do calls for super-fitness. This is peculiar to the caring role, as far as I can see. It's something we ought to take into account.

Then again, there's the effect of time: you think you're fit; you used to be fit; then suddenly you discover you're not as fit as you thought. It's not just that old age is creeping up on you; it's hours and weeks and months of heaving and bending, in postures you were never designed for, whether on all fours or otherwise. And they're taking their toll.

Despite these sudden bursts of extreme energy and physical contortions, some carers become enormously fat. I don't really know why this is; probably the combined result of stress and eating more than you want in order to keep your piglet company.

So keeping fit is really quite important for us. Not that you need to go to the gym every day, or train to take part in the next marathon. But it is helpful to do *something*.

I've had to stop going to state-of-the-art gyms ever since my experience in one when our boat was in Malaysia. It was so hot there that taking any exercise in the open air was out of the question.

But some of the hotels boasted air-conditioned gym facilities which a transient yachtie was permitted to use. The one I visited was in Penang.

It contained dozens of hi-tech appliances, all equipped with electronic control panels.

I tried going for a run on the running-on-the-spot machine, but failed to set the controls to make it operate at the kind of pace I wanted. So I turned to a gadget where you lay on your back pushing weights up and down. I could have managed the weights if I'd been able to understand the electronics.

Finally I sat down at one of the rowing machines, which I thought I really did know something about. But it too required a lot of electronic programming before you could use it. While I was fiddling with the controls, I spotted out of the corner of my eye someone else to my left doing exactly the same thing. I didn't look across directly because

I was concentrating on the LCD screen. Eventually I was all set, and noticed that the character on my left was ready to begin rowing as well.

We both picked up our oars and pulled at the same time. It was like a race, except that we were rowing at the pace set by our electronic controls. As it happened, we both seemed to be rowing at exactly the same speed. After five minutes, I turned my head to grin at him. Only then did I discover that I was staring at a wall-to-wall mirror.

Specialist muscles

You use different muscles for moving piglets than you probably would do otherwise, so it's worth doing a few exercises that get them ready for the strenuous, sudden and occasional use that you'll put them to. I'm not about to recommend a regime, though I use the Royal Canadian Air Force 5BX plan from time to time. I have a regular routine with regard to physical fitness exercises. It starts with a realisation that I feel Sunday afternoonish on days other than Sundays. I dig out the 5BX and check through it, discover with relief that I'm now so old I don't even have to do proper press-ups, calculate which exercises I am going to do, and do them. For about a month. After that I'm so bored I can't face them any more. But I'm quite fit by then, so I don't really need to. So I stop.

I also walk for miles, sometimes on my own, at other times pushing my piglet in the wheelchair. This is an excellent answer because it gets her out in the fresh air, which is good for her, and pushing her uphill is seriously hard work, which is good for me.

It also helps to get rid of any build-up of stress.

Anti-stress

There's lots about stress and ways of relieving it a couple of chapters further on (Chapter 11). One option is to run away from the cause of the stress. You can either do this literally, by sprinting round the block, preferably yelling your head off as you go. Or in some comparable way, such as by jumping on your bike and pedalling for all you're worth.

If the exercise is strenuous, it's good for the soul as well as the body. But it's no use only taking exercise when you're stressed out. It needs to be reasonably regular, so that you not only get fit but stay that way.

Slow slow quick quick slow

Most carers are fitter and faster than most piglets – obviously. So most carers operate at a pace which is slower than their natural one – equally obviously. What this can do is make you unfit, and unready for those bursts of energy that are called for from time to time. Plus, it can drive you nuts.

Exercises, boring though they are (and they are), can be, I was almost going to say the ideal, but in fact the only, antidote.

There's one other benefit in taking exercise which I, feeling a bit disloyal, pass on. It's that your piglet cannot join in. So you have to do them on you own. Or if not on your own, then in company with someone other than your piglet. So the exercises take you away from the business of caring, if only for half-an-hour. It's a form of respite care.

Technique

Doing the weird physical work that caring calls for, and not damaging your back in the process, is all about technique. Everyone knows the trick of keeping your back straight and using your legs when you lift something heavy. What we don't know is how the hell to do this while bending over a bed, or a bath. Or helping a piglet out of a car.

As a matter of fact, I don't know, either. I've discovered that it's hardly ever necessary to bend over to clean the bath if you always use a bubble mixture (not oily, or the piglet can shoot from one end of the bath to the other and right over the end on to the floor like a world bob sleigh champion). Or if you're too mean to buy bubble mixture, then squirt a small amount of washing-up liquid in the water before pulling the plug out.

I've also learned not even to think about supporting my piglet or to try and lift her while bending, unless I can take my weight on my arm.

Oh yes, and something else. I used to help her out of a chair by standing beside her and heaving on one of her arms. Now what I do is stand in front of her chair, just out of her reach. If she stretches out for my hands, she has to move her bodyweight forward, and by the time I grasp her hands her weight is in the right place, right over her feet, and there's hardly any effort involved in pulling her upright. (I've also learned that this method is incorrect, so I'd better not advocate it here.) Well, they should have trained me, and then I'd know better.

To quote again from the *Safer Handling of People in the Community* manual:

- 'The techniques described here should not be used without formal moving and handling training.'

- 'All manual handling tasks have an inherent risk and no amount of manual handling training or provision of equipment will eliminate all risk.'

- 'If in doubt, don't do it.'

I *think* what this is about is protecting the authors' backs against being sued by care-workers who get it all wrong. Anyway, there isn't any training for the likes of us, so I can hardly insist that you get yourself trained before following their advice. All I do now is pass on the advice, AND the warning. What follows is taken from the manual.

Positioning prior to standing from chair/toilet/ commode/bed etc

- Ask the person to shuffle or rock on his bottom to the front of the chair
- Check the person's feet are flat on the floor, hip distance apart; not tucked under the chair. It may be helpful to have him position one foot slightly forward of the other
- Ask the person to lean forward so he has a 'nose over toes' position
- Gentle rocking of a person forwards and backwards sometimes helps build momentum for the move
- Ask the person to push up on the arms of the chair into a standing position. As he stands, ask him to look up and ahead, not at the floor.

- standing directly in front of the person
- underarm drag
- shoulder lift
- using linen sheets to lift or drag
- pivot transfer/bear hug/standing transfer.

Rolling in bed

Low friction rollers (sliding devices) are placed temporarily under the person and should extend from the person's shoulders beyond his buttocks. They are especially useful for turning a person when a number of turns are involved (eg bed baths requiring multiple turns). The rollers are removed when the turns are completed. They can be used by one or two carers depending on the weight of the person and the individual carer's capabilities.

A falling or fallen person

There are several techniques in current practice and each one recognises that trying to stop a falling person is very unsafe and likely to lead to injury to the carer and possibly to the person himself. It is impossible to set out parameters dealing with all situations and the ones listed below are set in a practical environment and do not deal with life-threatening situations. The following is intended as a guide only and is by no means exhaustive. The techniques described should only be used after specific training and completing a moving and handling assessment for the person.

Techniques

Falling person out of the carer's reach: It is unrealistic to physically assist the person. There is not enough time to reach him and too great a distance to reach and stretch. If there is no immediate danger of the person striking a fixed or immovable object, allow him to fall.

Falling Person, carer within close proximity but not physically touching or assisting at the time of the fall: The carer may be able to do one of the following: think ahead and where possible remove dangerous objects within the environment prior to the person walking in the area; redirect the fall by pushing or pulling the person away from dangerous or immovable objects.

Falling person, carer is in physical contact or delivering care at the time of the fall: There is no one safe way of dealing with the falling person even if the carer is in close physical contact at the time. The following guidelines may be helpful:

- The carer may have more control if she positions herself behind the falling person rather than in front

- The carer has both hands open while taking a step backwards but keeping close to the person

- The carer is likely to have more control holding the person's torso rather than his arms

- The carer bends her knees and maintains a stable base to help protect her back while allowing the person to slide to the floor

- The carer supports the person's head where possible

- The carer allow the person to fall rather than supporting them in an upright or slumped position

- Do not take all of the person's weight

- When the person is sitting on the floor and leaning against the carer, the carer may then step back and kneel down while protecting the person's head and maintaining her normal back position.

Assisting the fallen person up from the floor

The uninjured conscious fallen person:

- Stay calm and remain with the person, don't let him hurry to get up

- Place a pillow under the person's head and wait until he feels ready to try to get up

- Encourage the person to bend up both knees (one at a time) and roll onto his side, and then push up into a side sitting position

- When ready, ask him to roll onto all fours

- Bring a low stable chair or stool to the person's side

- Encourage the person to place his near hand on the seat and bring his near leg through so that he is able to push up onto the near foot

- Ask the person to push down on his raised knee with his other hand

- Encourage the person to push down on the seat and through his foot while swinging his hips round to sit onto the seat.

A carer should never manually lift a fallen person up from the floor except in a life-threatening emergency, and then only after thorough assessment.

UNSAFE TECHNIQUES

- Arm and leg lug
- Underarm drag lift
- Shoulder lift

There you are, that's what the book says. It's full of useful tips, so if you can't find an expert to come to your home and show you what to do, getting hold of a copy of the book would be the next best thing. Its advice is clearer than the excerpts I've included above because it's accompanied by illustrations.

As an untrained carer who has made every mistake in the book and who makes them still, all I can say is that training is clearly important, both for us and the wretched piglets entrusted to our care. It's just a pity that at the time of writing it's virtually unobtainable unless you're a paid care-worker. Not that we need much training. Professional care-workers have to be taught about a wide variety of conditions and piglet abilities, whereas all you need to understand is how to handle your own piglet, not mine as well.

What you can do, though, is ask for an occupational therapist to come and show you what to do. It'll be training of a kind.

Take care, now. Look after yourself

This is what people say to one another when they go their separate ways. But it's only a figure of speech. However, I'm saying it to you right now, and I mean it.

You're almost certainly neglecting your own health. It's what carers do. We ignore our own ailments, and are so busy with our caring that we forget to take preventative health measures for ourselves. Exercise, diet, regular medical examinations – you thought they were for successful business executives.

Well, they're not. They're for you and your body, whether or not you're a selfish pig.

CHAPTER 9

Sex

Can, but can't bear to?

Do, but no longer enjoy it?

Can't, and miss it?

Do without
Celibacy
Solo sex

Go for it
Someone else you love
Someone you know
Someone you don't know at all
Is lack of sex bad for you?

Want a solution?

Happy thought

Sex

Just because you're a carer, it doesn't automatically follow that you're going to have problems relating to sex. But it may. You won't have to complete a multiple-choice questionnaire to discover whether or not it's an issue in your case. You'll know, all right.

If your sex life hasn't been adversely affected by your caring, or just plain isn't a problem for you, skip this chapter. You've got enough real concerns without having to worry about this one as well.

Still here? Okay, I'm going to assume it's because you have a genuine sexual problem. It might still be better for you to omit this section, though. An awful lot of taboos hang around the subject of sex, some of them rendered impermeable by religion and culture. What I'm trying to do in this book is to face up fair and square to all the big matters that affect carers, without getting bogged down in the marshland of political or religious correctness, or cultural preconceptions. It's an approach which is bound to cause a certain amount of indignation, if not outrage.

I'm not about to apologise. Well, maybe I am, because the last thing I want to do is upset you. But I'm still determined to bring the subject out into the open for all the rest of us who feel suffocated by undiscussable frustrations and fears.

I think I'll put a page break here. If you turn over and carry on reading, let's all be clear that it's because you want to be included in the discussion. So don't bother writing in and complaining if you hate what you read after this.

CHAPTER 9

So. Your sex life has gone downhill as a result of your piglet's disability, or as a result of your role as a carer. What's to be done?

Your piglet is probably your spouse or partner.* Not necessarily, though. For most of us, our sense of identity is closely bound up with our sexuality. So if your caring role has somehow modified your belief in who you are, your sex life could also be affected. For example, let's say you're a man and that you're looking after an aged parent full-time. You could come to believe that you've been changed radically, from being a masculine bread-winner into a kind of housewife. This inadvertent sex-change (not real, of course, but perceived) could affect your sex drive or performance.

What if you're a woman, and caring for a neighbour in addition to your own family? What if you're holding down a job as well? You could easily be feeling stressed out by all this. Even if you're not at burnout stage, the heavy pressure loading might have an adverse effect on your libido. Which in turn could influence your marriage, or your relationship with your partner, for the worse.

What is more likely is that your piglet is your usual, or former, sexual partner, and that now

- although you *can* have sex, you no longer want it, so don't

- you *do* still have sex because your partner wants it, but you don't enjoy it any more

- your caring has deprived you of sex altogether, and you miss it.

Can, but can't bear to?

What's happened is that your piglet has been changed by their disability. To be fair, you both have. But your piglet is no longer the person you used to fancy. You may still love them.

---

* Incidentally, I'm not being gender specific here. Your partner might be the same sex as you. It doesn't make any difference.

Very probably you do. But perhaps in a different way. And perhaps not in that way.

It could be that making love to this person, who's no longer the same as the one you used to have that wonderful sex with, is horrible to you. You just can't bear it. It might be a relatively small thing, like their sense of touch.

Good sex requires sensitivity on both sides and, if one partner has lost that, it probably won't be much fun for the other one. Or it might be something much more physical and much more basic than that. Some piglets retain what the books call 'a healthy sexual appetite' even though they've lost some control of other bodily functions. The thought of your piglet losing control of their bladder or even their bowels while you're in the act of making love might not even bear thinking about.

But now life suddenly gets incredibly complicated. They want it, but you can't bear to give it to them. And yet they're your piglet. They're the person you used to have sex with, and they're the person you now 'give love and endless therapy to'. You probably feel terrible about withholding this most intimate and important of all therapies. They're your spouse, aren't they? So are you denying them something you ought to be freely giving? They're the person you care for, aren't they? Does caring have to include sex?

What are you looking at me like that for? You think I've got an answer to all this? Nope. Sorry. I've got plenty of sympathy, but that's not a help. All I can really do is remind you that the most important person out of you and your piglet is you.* If you try to do something you really can't bear to do, you'll be the first person to suffer but not the only person. Sooner or later your piglet will, too. If you stop being able to do your caring job, what then? So lighten up. You can't bear to have sex? Okay, you can't bear to have sex. Don't worry about it.

Do, but no longer enjoy it?

One of the defence mechanisms which piglets often deploy is denial. They deny to themselves that there's anything wrong with them. It seems to me that this can be a good thing if it helps them carry on with life. But it can be hard for you if they want to continue having sex in order to reinforce their image of themselves as a well person. *You're* not in denial. Nor can you let yourself be, if you're to do your caring job with your eyes wide open. So having sex in these circumstances can be the very opposite of an open, intimate act. It's the equivalent of a white lie: an act of dishonesty committed out of altruistic, even loving, motives. But it's still a lie. And it might be a painful one for you – mentally, physically, or both.

This is the kind of thing which contributes to the pressures of caring. (Turn to Chapter 11 to bone up on this, if you haven't been there already.) Once you let the pressure reach too high a level, even if you don't quite get to the burnout stage, the level

---

* Do I really mean this? It sounds pretty heartless, I know. And when the chips are down, of course I don't really one hundred per cent absolutely-set-in-concrete mean it. But then again, I've said much the same thing in other parts of the book, so I must have sort of meant it. If you're upset or incredulous, turn to the note at the very back of the book. Maybe that will put matters straight.

of your sex hormones can be lowered. It's a negative double whammy: you don't want to have sex with your piglet but you go ahead anyway, you hate it, it makes you miserable, and next thing your hormones go into retreat which makes the prospect of sex even less appealing.

Can it really be right for you to go ahead with sex on this basis? I don't think so. It may be time, instead, for you to catch up on your studies on how to become more of an SP.

Can't, and miss it?

This is much more likely to be the scenario that faces you. Your piglet is ill and can't have sex; you're not ill, but you can't have it either. They don't miss it because they're ill; you bloody well do. You can either go out and get it, or learn to live without it. But which?

Luckily for you, you may in fact have no choice. I say luckily, because choices are always complicated, and when there isn't one, at least you benefit from the simplicity.

Why no choice? Well, getting respite care in the form of a day off is hard enough to achieve; respite sex from Social Services isn't even on the menu. How about friends, then? The trouble is, they don't ever seem to consider that you might be starving to death from lack of sex. A friend of mine had a successful prostate cancer operation. He came round to tell me in gleeful, wicked detail about the firmness of his erections and what he was able to do with them. He wasn't gloating. He was merely joyful on his own account and eager for me to share his happiness. Did it occur to him that sex was no longer a possibility for me, for quite a different reason? That I could bear it provided I didn't have to hear about other people's romps? Did it hell.

And as for female friends, I'm waiting for the phone call that goes like this: 'Molly and I are coming round this evening; Molly will look after your piglet while you and I pop into the spare room for an hour or so and rip each other's clothes off.' It hasn't happened yet.

Do without

I've explained in that last section why you may have to learn to live without sex for practical reasons. You may also be forced into this course of inaction by your sense of morality, or religion. You may be married to your piglet, and find yourself unprepared to break those vows. Whatever the background, you're now on your own as far as sex is concerned. What does this mean?

Celibacy

You can choose real celibacy. You know, in which you don't even think about it, let alone do anything about it. Or if you do think about it, you immediately banish the thought – whoosh, gone.

This may be easier said than done, depending on your past habits, your temperament, and your age. If you're not by nature a saint, there's a danger that you'll end up feeling deprived, resentful and unfulfilled. And there's also that dreaded thought which haunts so many of us carers: 'By the time I get my life back, it'll be too late. Why have I got to be old before my time?'

Solo sex

As it's not essential to have a partner on hand in order to experience some sort of sex, at least you'll be able to achieve a measure of physical relief, however unsatisfactory. This is good and bad news. The good news is that it takes hardly any time at all and doesn't require you to be out of the house and away from your piglet; you won't have to make complicated arrangements about meeting someone else, or finding a piglet-sitter while you're away having a sexual adventure; and there's no conflict of loyalty.

The bad news is that masturbation produces no emotional release, and may even increase emotional tension.

Even so, going it alone may be a better option than total celibacy. Needless to say, you won't want to talk about it to other people, or even your piglet, the way we're discussing it here. But you don't have to feel bad about it either. You're not doing it because you're a sad pervert. You're doing it because you're a good carer.

But before plumping for the No Sex option, you may at least want to check out the alternatives.

Go for it

Okay, you can't have sex with your piglet, but doing without sex isn't right for you either. Nor is solo sex. What you need is a partner.

Someone else you love

There might be somebody right there, ready and waiting. You love them. It doesn't stop you caring for your piglet. But this other person exists. They want to have sex with you, and you want to have sex with them. My God, this is a complicated one. There's almost no way I can tackle it without being facile. Let's try, anyway.

- What you've been doing as a carer is handing out love to your piglet. They appreciate it, some of the time at least. But on the whole it's been a one-way street. Now, though, you've got the opportunity to be on the receiving end of love. Not just to dish it out, but get it back in full measure. This is something your whole being has cried out for. It's something that's satisfying not just physically, but at some deep primal level. This is real respite care. It's something that can stand between you and burnout. Something that can keep you human.

- It's also something that can come between you and your piglet. Giving care to your piglet can be hard enough when you love them. It could become harder still if you love someone else as well. It could change everything. Thoughts

151

of treachery and guilt could easily come stealing up. At best, this new love could make your caring role harder; at worst it could make it impossible.

Someone you know

What if you have the opportunity (and take it) of having sex with a good friend. I'm thinking about someone you've always fancied, but never loved. This could be the answer you were looking for. You get the physical and emotional release of real sex, as opposed to the pseudo-release of masturbation. But love doesn't come poking its nose in where it doesn't belong. You and your piglet go on as before. In fact, better than before because instead of being repressed, frustrated and bitter you're now able to bask in the glow of a rewarding sex life as well.

Or is that pie in the sky? Experience shows that nothing ever stays the same, so one thing you can be absolutely certain about is that this relationship will change. It might start out as an uncomplicated but rewarding one. But how will it progress? Is life about to get horribly messy for all three of you?

Well, yes, it almost certainly is, let's face it. Can you cope with that? What'll it do to your pressure levels?

Someone you don't know at all

Looking at this thing logically, we have to consider sex with someone totally outside the circle of friends and family. Someone with whom there's no history of friendship, let alone temptation to love. For example:

- With a prostitute. I know, I know, the health risks are so lethally high that the option, if it is one, almost certainly doesn't deserve a place in this book. Even if that appalling danger could be overcome, the financial cost would probably rule it out, given that most carers scarcely have enough money to buy the groceries. And yet, and yet. A prostitute doesn't have to be some wretched creature picked up on the street. It could be someone very like the good friend from the previous section. And what would be on offer, and in theory achievable, would be much the same: real, rewarding, sex without entanglement. It may be that paid-for sexual respite care comes under the same heading as legalisation of drugs – something that has arguable, theoretical benefits, but which is politically and practically unlikely to be acceptable to the majority

- You're not the only one who'd like more sex than you're getting (which I assume to be the case, since you're still reading this part of the book). All those people who visit singles bars and go on special holidays for like-minded individuals are on the lookout for it too. Again in theory, there's nothing to stop you finding one of them and forming a temporary liaison for mutual sex. In a way, this is a worse option than the one above because you'd need to invest a lot more time (more than you have, probably), it'll cost just as much and be just as risky.

Is lack of sex bad for you?

President Jack Kennedy notoriously shocked and embarrassed Prime Minister Harold Macmillan by informing him that he always developed a headache if he didn't have a woman at least once a day. SP or not, he'd have made a terrible carer.

As for the rest of us, who have neither presidential pull nor a crowd of secret service bodyguards to smooth our path, sex is likely to become a thing of the past. It'll go the way of popping down to the pub, doing things on the spur of the moment, and whizzing about the place. You'll certainly miss it, and there'll be times when you yearn for it.

But is it bad for you to do without? Well, all the things that you used to do, can't now do, and long to do, contribute to the build-up of pressure, so nudge you one step nearer to burnout.

But plenty of other people, carers and non-carers, do without, and they don't die of it.

It might help to remember two things:

- It can change. In either direction. If you're not getting it now and want it, you may get it later. If you *are* getting it now and don't want it, you may come back to wanting it in time

- Friedrich Nietzsche: 'What doesn't kill you makes you stronger.'

Want a solution?

I'm sorry, but you won't find a solution here. Enforced absence from the pleasures of sex is only one of the many problems of being a carer. Some of the others are isolation, burnout, back pain, money. Hardly any of them are addressed openly, but sex is embedded in the deepest silence of the lot. So: if you want it and find a way of getting it, fair enough. No criticism from where I stand, or from where any other carer stands, I suspect.

If you want it and don't get it, well, haven't you been here before? It didn't kill you then, and it won't now. Might give you a headache, though.

Happy thought

Think of all the complications, heartache and expense you'll be saved.

THE KISS

CHAPTER 10

Your mind

What makes you think you've gone off your trolley?

Change
    Change of relationship
    Change of circumstances
    Change of identity
    Change of future
Conflict
Being out of control
Shame
Isolation
    Friends
    Officialdom
    Even you won't listen
Trapped!
Loss
Guilt
Piglet-think

What to do to hang on to your sanity

Time
    Journeys
    Doing things with other people
    Watch your piglet's clock
    Allow sinking-in time

Take control again
    Act like a pro
    Tell everyone you're a carer
    Don't be too ambitious
Do your own thing
Get some respite
Talk, talk, talk
Cool it before you burn out

What not to do

Push them down the stairs
Jump off the roof
Keep it to yourself
Do everything yourself
Pretend

By the way

Your mind

Didn't make you smile this time? Then how about a different one, specifically for carers:

Caring has driven me nuts – and it isn't helping at all.

And now for some news that's good or bad depending on your point of view:

More than 50% of carers suffer mental health problems as a result of their caring.

If you think you're going nuts, that item may be quite good news. It means you're not alone.

Alternatively, it might be rather depressing news. Before, you only *felt* as if you were going off your trolley. Now you think it's probably true.

It can be the little things which drive you crazy. A carer I know says her piglet goes to sleep in the afternoon and wakes up thinking it's tomorrow morning. If she goes along with this, it means she has to produce a second breakfast, and the rest of the day's schedule is thrown out of kilter. It disconcerts both of them. So what the carer has taken to doing is to write on a piece of paper: 'Today is STILL Wednesday,' and leave it where the piglet can see it when she wakes up.

It doesn't do any good. The piglet opens her eyes, reads the

CHAPTER 10

paper, chucks it to one side and says dismissively: 'That was the paper for yesterday.'

Englishman goes into newsagent's in remote Irish village.

'Do you have a newspaper?'

'Yes, Sir, certainly, Sir. Would you like yesterday's or today's?'

'Oh well, I think I'll have today's.'

'In that case, you'll have to come back tomorrow.'

Silly joke.

Well, it has a certain logic.

So does that famous sketch from *The Goon Show*:

Bluebottle: What's the time Eccles?

Eccles: Just a minute. I've got it written down on a piece of paper. A nice man wrote it down for me. If anyone asks me the time, I show them.

Bluebottle: Let me see the paper. It is writted here that it is 8 o'clock. Here, what happens if they ask you and it's not 8 o'clock?

Eccles: Then I don't show them the piece of paper!

Bluebottle: But how do you know if it's 8 o'clock?

Eccles: I've got it written down on this piece of paper!

Excerpt from The Goon Show, *BBC; written by Spike Milligan*

What makes you think you've gone off your trolley?

It's when you stop seeing the funny side of things, and give in, despite yourself, to – well you know – rages, terrible depressions, sudden irrational feelings of resentment. And it's when you start entertaining thoughts of doing things you know are wrong, unthinkable, and crazy.

Fair enough. You probably have gone a bit mad. After all, according to the Oxford English Dictionary, insanity is to be 'in a state of mind that precludes normal perception and behaviour, and ordinary social intercourse'.

Yeah, you're nuts all right. And what's caused it is this disability, this caring. The fact is, you wouldn't be normal if the impossible position you're in didn't have this effect on you.

Exam question: 'For carers, madness is normal.' Discuss.

By the way, feeling you're going mad is part of burnout. There's a whole lot about that in the next chapter. The section you're reading at the moment is about what it is that drives you crazy. And then, in a minute, it's about what, if anything, you can do about it.

Change

This is one of the big things (that pushes you towards the edge). And the hardest to put your finger on.

Human beings are amazingly adaptable. We can get used to more or less anything if we have to. But only if the change is welcome. Or, if it's not all that welcome, when we at least know we've brought it on our-selves. But this caring role has been foisted on us by fate. And it's not a small, insignificant change. It has radically changed every-thing we were used to.

The change may have been sudden – for example, if your piglet suffered a stroke. In that case, everything changes dramatically in an instant, and there's no time to adapt.

Or the disability may be one that builds up gradually. In which case you might suppose you'd get used to it gradually and be able to cope with the change more easily. Sorry, no. When things happen that slowly, you often don't see the changes until suddenly you're aware that the situation is different. Which is much the same as a sudden change.

In either case, there you are, in trouble.

Your caring situation may even be one where there is no discernible change – to the outside world, at any rate. If your child was born with a severe disability, for example. But the fact is, there's always change. The piglet gets older and, as they grow, so do the problems of caring for them. And you're getting older, too, watching your life slide away and away.

The kind of changes which can drive us nuts are:

Change of relationship

When a parent or a spouse suddenly turns into a piglet, it's hard to know who you're dealing with. They're no longer who they used to be. Or, even more complicatedly, sometimes they are and sometimes they aren't. This is incredibly disorienting.

Change of circumstances

One moment you were a circus trapeze artist – or whatever it was that you used to be – and now you're a carer. Or maybe you're still a circus trapeze artist AND a carer. Either way, it won't be just your job that's changed. It'll be your life.

160

Change of identity

When you were a circus trapeze artist, you knew exactly who you were. And so did everyone else. Now you're not at all sure. And neither is anyone else.

So when you suddenly lose it, and go mad, is it really so surprising? You've lost yourself.

Change of future

You might have been one of those people who take life by the scruff of its neck and force it to head the way you want it to. Or were you more easy-going than that, and pretty well content to go with the flow, reserving your decisions for tactical matters such as where to take your holiday this year?

Whatever your personality type, the future is totally out of your hands now. It has taken over.

Conflict

It's the conflicting demands of caring which can seem to tear you into little pieces.

- You focus a hundred per cent of your attention on your piglet, and next thing everybody else is suffering from neglect. Your family. Your partner. Your friends. Your children, even, if you've got any and they're still at home

- OK, so you try to look after everybody's needs – piglet, family etc – only to find you're neglecting yourself

- Your caring is preventing you from earning money. At the same time it's costing you money you wouldn't otherwise have had to spend. If you *do* go on working to make the money you so desperately need in order to care for your piglet, you can't do your caring job as well as you think you ought to. The dilemma gets you down. And depression is a form of mental illness*

- The more severe the illness of your piglet, the more absorbing, time-consuming and demanding the care they require. The better you do the job, the more you prolong it. And the more you prolong it, the harder it gets. Modern medicine and new technology exacerbates this conflict. In the old days piglets either got better or they died. Nowadays caring, like a diamond, is for ever. This is an aspect which nobody talks about. You probably don't. But you think about it. And it's this that drives you mad.

Being out of control

You feel as if you've lost control of your life. Yet with all this responsibility that you have for your piglet, you need to be more in control than ever.

You can go round and round in circles trying to figure this one out.

- The more dependent on you they are, the more control you exercise over them, and the greater the contrast with the lack of control you have over how long it's going to go on, and what's going to happen next

- You may feel you can't go on, but you know you have to. And sometimes you may even believe that you shouldn't, but can't see what the alternative is

---

* Working parents of non-disabled children face this conflict as well. But for them it's a little bit more out in the open, whereas your conflict is concealed behind closed doors.

- If you literally can't cope, either physically or mentally, and get help, then you've become a dependant too. You've lost even more control

- To live and carry on caring you need more money. Yet there's no way you can raise it. Your finances are hopelessly out of control.

Shame

Carers really ought to be proud of themselves. But we're not. We're more often ashamed of the mess we're making of things (well, perhaps not literally; it's the piglet who does that). But we suspect we should have found a better way of handling this situation, and feel a bit ashamed that we haven't been able to.

Society, if that's the right word for all of them out there, doesn't help. They treat us as if we're out of work, or are incapable of doing anything better, or are losers because we don't have as much money as them. And it's easy to forget how important we really are.

A sense of failure, when it's combined with the vital job of keeping someone alive, is enough to drive anyone bonkers.

Isolation

You're alone with your piglet, and cut off from the rest of humanity. Or so it seems. You get no feedback, so it's like playing squash on a court without walls. No matter how hard or accurately you hit the ball, it never bounces back.

When there's no feedback, there's no surefire way of telling what's real and what's imaginary. You can begin to lose touch with reality. This really is madness.

How can you take a logical view when it's impossible to test the logic? It's hard to do. Maybe even impossible. It's one of the effects of isolation. There's more on this, back in Chapter 4.

Maybe the trick is to remember you're not isolated literally. You're surrounded by, for example:

Friends
Friends are so well-meaning. Where would we be without them? Yet they don't half drive you mad, the things they say.

'Your piglet is wonderful'	Part of you is proud and pleased. The other bit wants to shout: 'What about me?'
'I don't suppose your piglet really understands'	When they really do. In fact, your piglet probably understands more than the friend seems to. But how can you talk to a friend who can't see what's happening?
'Your piglet understands exactly what's going on'	This is what they say when your piglet has a cognitive or mental impairment. It makes normal satisfying conversation impossible with the piglet, so you turn to your friends for it. But then they don't understand either. They think they do. In fact, they seem to think they know more than you do. Aaaaaaaargh!
'Of course, what's happening to your piglet is only what's going to happen to all of us in the end'	It's supposed to be a comfort that just when you stop being a carer (if you ever do), you'll be so old or in such a bad way that you'll need caring for yourself? You're supposed not to mind that the best years of your life are being taken from you? You're supposed to look at your piglet and feel astonishing pleasure that you'll be going the same way yourself in a year or two?

I feel a bit guilty, writing this bit. My friends, the ones who aren't carers, have mostly tried so hard to help. Sometimes they've even succeeded. And to them, of course, I'm eternally grateful. But some of the others, well, there have been occasions when their efforts have not only NOT helped, but actually made things worse. It hasn't been their fault. How could they understand? After all, they never see what's really going on. It's all happening behind closed doors. They're outside, and you're inside. Isolated. Cut off. On your own. Going bananas.

Officialdom

Officialdom is there to help. They're supposed to be the ones who de-isolate you.

- But do they listen? Mmmmm. Perhaps, a bit, in their own way

- Even if they listen, do they hear what you say? Well, sometimes you wonder

- Even if they hear, do they believe you? They often act as though they don't

- And even if they believe you, do they understand what it's like for you? Do they, hell.

Alternatively, do they wrap their heads in paperwork so they can't see you bashing your head against a brick wall?

Yep.

Even you won't listen

Going mad is not what you might call a socially acceptable phenomenon. Or so you suspect. So you cover it up.

'How are you doing?'

'Fine.' When you're not.

This might be a conversation between you and someone else. Or it might be between you and yourself.

You're not up front. Out in the open. Instead you're in hiding. You're isolated.

Trapped!

You really are in solitary confinement, because you can't get out. You're trapped in there, who knows for how long?

Loss

You've lost the person you knew. Or in the case of a child who was born with the disability, you've lost the child you once thought you were going to have.

Guilt

Your piglet can't help being disabled. *Of course* they can't. You know that. Sometimes, when you feel you're going really mad, you tell this to yourself over and over. But you still can't bear it.

You can try to shut out this feeling. In which case you further isolate yourself, and drive yourself even more crazy. Or you can own up, and feel overwhelmed by guilt.

'What am I doing, hating them for cramping my style? I must be totally evil.'

There's another thing that happens which brings on this wave of guilt. You knock yourself out doing something that your piglet will really, really appreciate. Only they don't. And you mind like hell that they don't. You don't want to mind. The piglet has a pretty bloody good excuse for not noticing the effort you made. But you still mind. You vow never to do anything as good for them again. Phrases like 'stew in their own juice' spring to mind. Quickly followed by that relentless guilt. So you DO do it again. You make another stupendous effort. And once again . . .

Piglet-think

Your piglet's mind may well be every bit as sharp as yours. Or even sharper. But if there's any kind of mental impairment or modification, so that they go in for bizarre and illogical thought processes and remarks, it's going to have an effect on your mind.

> Dogs look like their masters.
>
> *Old saying, which I'm sure is true*
> *(or is it the other way round?)*

It's my belief that carers start to take on some of the characteristics of their piglets, given enough time.

Such-and-such a disability leads to dementia, according to the books. Yes, but dementia in whom? The piglet or you? They don't tell you that.

What to do to hang on to your sanity

> 'There's nothing either good or bad but thinking makes it so.'
>
> Hamlet, *by Shakespeare*

Aha, now we come to the nub of the matter. It's thinking that makes things seem unbearable. It's thinking that drives you nuts.

So, logically, if you've thought yourself into this state, you can think yourself out of it.

Or put it another way. When you find you're beginning to go bananas, your instinctive response is to try to change whatever

167

it is that's driving you bananas. But you can't, because it's not capable of change. So you get worse.

But you might well be able to change something. Namely, yourself. And you *can* do that. At least, you can change the way you look at the situation, which comes to the same thing. For example:

Time

Well, you can't change the nature of time, obviously. Or even comprehend it, unless you're the Lucasian Professor of Mathematics at Cambridge University. But you can take the frustration out of it.

Piglet time is different from conventional human time. It's often slower (it takes so long to move anywhere, do anything). It can be more rigid (meals have to appear at the very moment that the clock strikes).

If one of you is operating on piglet time and the other on real-world time, it can drive you mad. Answer: both of you should operate on piglet time. For example:

Journeys

Let's say you need to go to the hospital and in real-world time the trip should take about an hour. Well, forget that. The question is how long will it take in piglet time? There's the long process of getting ready to go out and getting yourselves to whatever transport you'll be using. Then the equivalent procedure at the other end. The whole thing might easily take twice as long. So allow two hours for the journey. And don't even bother comparing this with the time it would take if you didn't have a piglet. If you didn't have a piglet you wouldn't be making the trip in the first place.

Doing things with other people

I mean, other people who aren't piglets and carers. Real-world people. What if a movie comes to town that you want to see? A bunch of friends are going, and ask you to join them.

Don't.

They'll want to go to the evening performance, which would mean keeping your piglet up late. This would have appalling consequences the following day.

They would set off late for the cinema, rush there, dive in just before the start of the main programme, and afterwards want to go and eat pizza somewhere where there'd be a queue.

So here's what you do instead. Go to an afternoon performance all by yourselves, leaving in good time even if there's a danger of arriving early. When you get to the cinema there'll be no need to hurry to pick up the tickets and find your way to your seats. The house lights will still be up, and as it's the afternoon performance there won't be hundreds of pairs of legs ready to trip you up. When you come out, you'll easily be able to get home in time for the usual routine of going to bed.

Watch your piglet's clock

A lot of piglets get tired faster than they used to, and faster than you. So use the time when they're most alert (could be the mornings, but you'll know) to have sensible conversations.

Allow sinking-in time

This was a bit of advice given to me by our support group, and it made a fantastic difference. The suggestion was to think ahead and give plenty of warning about things that were going to happen. For example, my piglet likes to accompany me to the town tip when an accumulation of bottles and old newspapers is ready to be chucked out. Now, instead of saying: 'Come on, let's go to the tip' and immediately helping her out of her chair, I announce: 'We need to go to the tip tomorrow.' Then, first thing next morning, I remind her. And now she gets twice as much pleasure from these little excursions as a result of the anticipation, and half as much stress because she doesn't feel suddenly pressured.

Because it's more fun, and easier, for my piglet, so it is for me.

Take control again

One of the things that drove you berserk was the feeling that events had taken over your life so that you were no longer in control. Okay, you can't change the fact of the disability. But you *can* do things to put you back in the driving seat:

Act like a pro

That's right, a professional. How can you be a victim, in the hands of fate, when you're running your caring job like a professional?

Take a pride in doing well all those things that have been getting you down. Things that didn't seem worth doing, but which you find yourself doing all the time, are part of the job and therefore they *are* worth doing. Once you realise that, and take pride in doing them well, suddenly they stop being maddening and become satisfying.

Maybe this isn't anything to do with professionalism. Perhaps there's a better name for it, though I can't think what it is. One of the jobs which used to drive me up the wall was getting my piglet dressed in the morning. I'm a slob and usually wear whatever clothes I find lying on the floor in the morning. My piglet, on the other hand, takes a creative interest in what she wears. So I can't just dress her in any old thing. She always has a very clear idea of what she wants to wear. It's just that she can't express it very well.

'I want the blouse that Jane gave me the Christmas before last, and the skirt that matches it,' she instructs me. And I have absolutely no idea which the blouse is. Even if I had, I wouldn't know what skirt matches it. So I hunt around in her drawers and the wardrobe, suggesting this and that.

'No-o-o-o-o-o,' she yells, exasperated. And in the end, in the past, I would have left the room to indulge in a five-minute break of bashing my head against a brick wall for light relief. But another carer, who had been there, done that and got the tee-shirt, reminded me that stress occurs when there's a marked difference between what you want to do and what you have to do. What I had to do was find the clothes my piglet wanted, whereas what I wanted to do was finish the dressing so I could get on with writing this book. So what I did was take a pride in learning which garment was given to my piglet by whom, which one she had bought, where, and when, and what went with what.

After a while, when she'd demand the stretch trousers and the matching top, I'd know what she meant and where I'd put them. I'd hold them up for her inspection. 'Yes, that's right,' she'd tell me. Satisfaction all round, instead of encroaching mania.

Tell everyone you're a carer
'And what do you do?' asks the person you've just met for the first time.

'Nothing, now. I can't go out to work.'	Wrong.
'I stay at home and look after my piglet.'	Better, but still wrong.
'I'm a full-time carer.'	That's it. Now you've got it.

You're not a nobody. You're not out of work. You do have a value. You are important. You definitely *are* in control.

Don't be too ambitious
Oh dear. That sounds like a counsel of despair. But it isn't. This is all about doing the things which you and your piglet can now do, and doing them in a satisfying way. What happens when you're new to caring is that you try to do the things you *used* to do, and either fail or do them badly. Frustration is one of the things that drives you bonkers.

Focus on what can be done, not on what can't.

171

This is no excuse for not attempting new stuff. Or giving up and doing nothing at all. All it means is that triumphs, success and pleasure in achievement are now achieved differently. They're still achievable, though. By both of you.

If you find that doing things is driving you barmy, it's probable that you're still trying to do the wrong things. Rethink your ambitions, and stay in control.

Do your own thing

We're back to the selfishness of the pig. The more I write this book, and the more I think about it, the more I realise how over-unselfish most of us are. Is that a word? It is now.

What we do is put so much time, thought and effort into our caring that we give up some of the activities that we love.

Can't play in that band any more? Go for long, hard walks? Sail? Fly? Go to the races? Listen to music? Whatever it was you used to enjoy so much?

Nonsense.

Put it back on your timetable. Be a bit more selfish.

Think about it. Why was it a good thing to do in pre-caring days? Because, however illogically, it did you good. Well, not doing it isn't doing you any good. Or, by extension, doing your piglet any good.

So make whatever arrangements are necessary to make it possible for you to do it again. Regularly.

Get some respite

You have to take a break, you really do. The fact that it may seem almost impossible mustn't stop you. There's a lot more on this terrible topic in Chapter 15, and you ought to head over there soon if you haven't been there already. Because it IS possible. When you know how.

Check this out with any other carers you can find who thought they were going nuts and then had a break. Did it sort the problem for them?

Well, then. It'll work for you too. So don't try all those 'It's too difficult, too expensive, my piglet wouldn't like it' excuses on me. There are ways, and it could be vital for both of you.

Talk, talk, talk

Talk your way out of solitary confinement. Talk to whoever will listen. Friends, social workers, relations, the people next door, the man who comes to read the meter.

They don't really want to hear? Doesn't matter. Being a bore to outsiders is better than going mad as a result of isolation.

Got a computer? Try talking on the chatrooms of carers' websites. Or any chatrooms, come to that.

Got a telephone? Talk down it till it melts.

You might drive everybody else mad this way, but you could save your own sanity. And as I keep telling you (are you sure you're listening?), you need to be MORE SELFISH.

Cool it before you burn out

If you feel you're going mad and do nothing about it, the consequence is that you burn out. And the consequence of *that* is quite likely to be something really unhelpful for all concerned.

There's a long chapter on burnout coming up next. Maybe that'll give you a few ideas.

What not to do

The trouble with going bonkers is that half the ideas you come up with for making you feel better are crazy. Not crazily good. Bad crazy. Not good at all. For example:

Push them down the stairs

This is an idea that strikes lots of carers as being a sensible solution at one time or another. The probability, though, is that it might well drive you right over the edge – as well as your piglet.

Jump off the roof

Ditto above.

Keep it to yourself

Feeling as if you're going mad is one of the things most people don't want to talk about. Apparently it's shameful or embarrassing or something.

So they keep it to themselves until the men in white coats come and wrap them gently (or not) in a strait-jacket, and take them away in a van without any windows.

Do NOT keep it to yourself.

Do everything yourself

'I somehow feel as if I ought to be able to manage.'

Yeah, yeah, yeah. This is what we all feel. And then we can't manage. And then we feel guilty that we can't. It's all rubbish.

Pay no attention to this inner voice. It doesn't know what it's talking about.

Your inner voice belongs to someone who feels inadequate. But this is only because that someone hasn't been trained, isn't paid, isn't accorded any respect by them out there.

Suppose you *were* being paid, and that you were an employee in a big company. What would you do if your job made you feel this way? Go on strike, probably. What you wouldn't do is go on working all those hours under those conditions for that money. And you absolutely certainly wouldn't do it on your own without support, without relief.

So DON'T.

That way madness lies.

Pretend

I think it must be something to do with the reluctance of all of us to be total outsiders. What we like to do is to fit in. Be normal.

But everybody else is rushing about, going to work, going on holiday, spending money, living frenetically. And you're not. So what do you do?

Pretend. That you're just like everyone else. Which is a lie. Oh, all right then: deception. And what a tangled web we weave when first we practise to deceive.

The other mad thing we do is pretend there's nothing wrong with the piglet. Or at least, not as much wrong as there really is. We're encouraged in this deception by all of them out there.

'Aren't they doing well?' they say, encouragingly. And 'You'd hardly know, would you?'

Etc etc. All well intended, no doubt. I suppose *they* want you to be included in their circle, as well. Or at least, to feel as if you were.

But it works the other way round. Because the whole thing's a lie, you can lose your grasp of what's really real, if you're not careful.

No, pretending certainly isn't an antidote to madness. It might be a contributing factor.

By the way

Just one more thought on the 'You don't have to be nuts to work here, but it helps' notice. Just change it to:

> You don't have to be nuts to work here.

Because you don't.

CHAPTER 11

Burnout

How it happens

Pressure from beneath
Downward pressure
Sideways squeeze

Recognising the symptoms

Doing something about it

Lower the upward pressure
Lift the downward pressure
Push out the sideways pressure

What *not* to do about it

Suicide
Murder
Bearing the burden on your own

The importance of being selfish

What the books say you should do

Deep breathing
Imagine a hostile animal
Imagine a peaceful place

Physical movement
Punchbag therapy
Respite

What the books say you should not do

Booze
Valium
Violence

Cheerful note

Burnout

This is another word I haven't looked up. It may not feature in the Oxford English Dictionary. Whether it does or not, burnout is a phenomenon that's real enough to just about every single one of us carers. I'm not talking about the mental shenanigans of the previous chapter. They can give rise to a sudden explosion or outburst. But they don't constitute burnout.

Burnout is a longer-term effect. It comes from a build-up of frustration and doubt. And it's nurtured by isolation. If you

- feel overwhelmed by a sense of defeat
- tell yourself you can't go on
- suddenly find yourself engulfed by paroxysms of racking sobs
- have no energy for anything
- blame 'things' for having got on top of you recently
- decide you might as well give up

that's burnout.

And guess what? It's a consequence of the job you do. It's an occupational hazard. One day people will click their tongues in disapproval at the way carers' health used to be put regularly and needlessly at risk. Carers' burnout will be categorised alongside pneumoconiosis and emphysema for miners and asbestosis for building workers. There'll be demonstrations in the streets and items on the news about it. Burnout for carers will be established and recognised and respectable.

There are stirrings already – but not enough. The solutions that have been put forward by government agencies don't work. And there's no compensation.

The thing to remember is that if your lungs get clogged up by asbestos dust, it doesn't mean you're a failure or a hopeless case. And it doesn't mean that, either, when you suffer from burnout.

The good news about burnout is that you can do something about it.

How it happens

Burnout is a product of prolonged stress. The reason it's not fully recognised is because stress is more associated with a frantic working environment, or with crushing responsibilities, than with caring – which can look to an outsider like a gentle, slow-paced, even pleasant occupation. At least, I *think* that's why government agencies don't do much about it. On the other hand, maybe it's because

- it would overstretch the system and be too expensive

- carers don't have enough power to force the issue.

Anyway, that's all a subject for another time. Right now our job is to look at stress, see what it is, and understand why we carers are so subject to it. At this point I have to repeat that I'm no psychologist. All I can tell you is what I think is going on here. If you're not sure that I'm making any sense, or if you want to get it straight from the horse's mouth, check out one of the textbooks on the subject. I've listed some of them at the back of the book.

Meantime, this is the way it seems to me.

Stress is three-dimensional. It's like a box, which has height and width and depth. With stress, though, the dimensions are different. There's the force that buoys you up from underneath; the load which weighs on you from above; and the squeeze effect of time. For us carers, the killer is the time dimension. But let's look at the other two first.

Pressure from beneath

Nobody, whether they're a carer or not, exists in a pressure-free world. There's always some of it about, and for most people there's quite a lot. The strange thing is, we like it that way. When there isn't quite enough we get bored and try to do something about it. We go in search of stimulation or entertainment. This doesn't feel like pressure, but that's what it is. It's pressure from underneath. We all need this upward force for buoyancy. If you're lucky, your work provides upward pressure. Or maybe not if you've got a horribly repetitive and boring job. If that's the case, you'll depend on after-hours entertainment and socialising, and on looking forward to your next holiday, for your buoyancy. But most jobs produce a certain amount of challenge and stimulation. That's why retirement has such a bad name. ('Got to have a job to keep the old brain active.')

The trouble is, though, that the moment there's some springy, pleasant buoyancy underneath you, that's when you usually start to feel some downward pressure.

Downward pressure

Let's say you've got a new project: to put a shelf up in the kitchen. Okay, that's only moderately exciting. But if it isn't something you do every day, it'll stretch you a bit (yeah, yeah, but I meant mentally, as you know very well). You'll have to work out what the finished job is going to look like, what materials you should use, where you're going to get them, and whether you have the right tools. All the while, you're thinking about the effect the new shelf is going to have on your life.

Then, as soon as you start to put the materials and tools together, the downward pressure begins. Can you get the shelf precisely level? Will it be strong enough? Will it look as good as you'd hoped? Or maybe the shop has just sold out of what you need, or as soon as you start work you discover that you haven't got the right parts, or you *have* got the right ones but not enough of them.

This downward pressure is more or less inevitable. It's almost as if you can't have the pleasure of upward pressure without the limiting effect of the downward pressure. Or perhaps if there isn't enough of a pressure difference then you don't really feel any satisfaction. In order to feel fulfilled, you need the opposing forces. Or something like that. Who knows? Anyway, here's what happens next: when you start drilling into the wall, the bit won't go in properly, but chews out a kind of bomb crater.

Now you're suddenly in a different situation. The downward pressure has become uncomfortable. When you're scuba-diving and feel such a build-up of pressure that your ear drums begin to ache, the trick is to stop descending, or even go up a bit. You pinch your nose and try to blow. With any luck that'll equalise the pressure in your ears so that you can't feel it any more. Then you can carry on descending. But life is a lot simpler for scuba-divers than it is for you trying to put this shelf up. How are you going to relieve the pressure when you've just drilled a bloody great crater in the kitchen wall? It's good if somebody comes into the room at this point and starts talking to you, because that gives you the opportunity to swear at them and explain it was all their fault. Failing that, you can always hurl the drill on the floor and stamp on it.

What's going on here is that you're caught between the upward buoyancy that came from planning the project, and the downward pressure of actually trying to do the work. If you overcome the difficulties you may feel a mild degree of triumph, which you wouldn't have felt if there hadn't been any downward pressure. If on the other hand you make a complete cobblers of the job and end up wishing you'd never started it, you're still unlikely to feel too much stress. A bit, but not a mega amount. The job wasn't important enough to merit that. Whatever discomfort you feel, you'll get over it. It's highly unlikely, anyway, that you'll suffer from burnout, as a result. For that, you need the third dimension to come into play: time.

Sideways squeeze

Okay, you're putting up this shelf, and everything's going reasonably well. But halfway through the job you discover that it's got to be finished by tonight. You thought you'd got tomorrow morning, but now you remember you promised to do something else tomorrow. The pressure increases because the time frame has narrowed. You're being squeezed.

Or what if your next-door neighbour sees what you're doing, and asks if you can possibly stick some shelves up for her? And so does the old fellow at the other end of the street. You agree because you think you ought to, but now the job has converted into a much longer one – too long to be enjoyable. It's been turned into a chore by the amount of time you're going to have to give to it.

This is what time does to carers. It squeezes the other two dimensions of pressure.

Did you do any babysitting when you were a teenager? Did the horrible brats ever behave badly, make a mess, refuse to go to bed, etc? And did you cope with that all right?

If you did, it was probably because you knew you'd only have to put up with it for the one evening – and in any case, you were getting paid. But what if it wasn't for the one evening only; if it was all day and every day; and if you weren't getting paid? Different story?

I know that's how it is for parents. And they don't get stressed out, or not usually. This may be because we're genetically programmed to look after kids. Or perhaps parents are somehow kept sane by the knowledge that the kids are growing up, and that there's a time limit. It's a longer one than the babysitter's, but a time limit all the same.

Most carers, though, can't comfort themselves with the thought that their troubles will soon be over. Most caring goes on for an awful long time. And whereas parents can watch their kids growing up and developing into people who hardly require any care, piglets are different. Some of them are going to deteriorate gradually, requiring more and more care as time goes on. Others are going to remain stable, indefinitely, while you, the carer, grow old. Whatever the condition of your piglet, it's the relentless, day-in-day-out never-endingness of being a carer which can eventually get to you. It's the dimension of time.

Time can squeeze the upward and downward pressure, exaggerating and increasing it to the point where it crushes you. If it wasn't for time, you'd be able to do the job and do it well. You started out doing it well. You went on doing it well for ages. But now it's got to you. And you feel you can't do it any more.

Or maybe it's some other aspect of time. Maybe it's the way your piglet has to do everything very slowly, so that time for you, too, has been slowed down to the point where sometimes you can't bear it. Or perhaps they have a habit of doing something over and over again (asking the same question, or making the same mistake) till you feel you're going to burst.

It's time. Squeezing the already considerable pressure of being a carer. It's time, that never seems to stop. And you think it never will. Or not till it's too late.

That's burnout.

Recognising the symptoms

Do you know when you're starting to burn out? What are the things that start to happen to you when you are burning out? Some of the general symptoms of burn out are that you no longer feel any pleasure. Things become burdensome. There's no pleasure in your actions or the usual things that used to give you pleasure. Things start to bother you more. You become more irritable. Things that don't usually bother you suddenly begin to do so. You just can't stand that the toothpaste cap wasn't put back on. You can't stand that the cup is turned this way rather than the way it should or there's a smudge of lipstick on the rim. You find yourself not returning phone calls from your friends or from Aunty Bessie, who you usually like to talk to. You find yourself putting things off more frequently, not answering letters, not taking care of errands and so on. You know you are burning out when you start to withdraw socially and when you're not sleeping well at night and you find yourself drinking alcohol more than usual. These are the general things that people who are overtaxed tend to report when they are just reaching the point of 'losing it'.

The key to successful caregiving is not allowing yourself to reach the breaking point. This means in advance recognising that you are near to the burn out point, near to, but not yet at the edge. When you reach that early point you still have an opportunity to turn things around, to obtain the help or respite you need to refuel you emotionally and physically. Caregivers of HD patients tell me about the personal signals that clue them that they are reaching the edge.

It might be a sudden migraine or an increased tendency to forget simple details ('I never forget to put salt into the soup, but this time I did. I knew I was in trouble.')

'The forgotten person in Huntington's disease'
by Dr Seymour Kessler

I read this in an HDA newsletter at a time when my piglet and I were still sailing round the world. It was becoming clear that Cathie wouldn't be able to go on much longer. Neither of us had really come to terms with this, and we were not happy about it. But I thought I was in control of the situation.

Singapore was the 30th country we had visited in our boat, so I could deal with Customs formalities blindfold by then. Yet we sailed out of Singapore without our passports. It turned out that I'd left them on the counter in the Immigration office. Anyone who's travelled in other countries, whether backpacking or on business or in luxury tourist mode, knows that you don't let your passport out of your sight if you can help it. Yet I'd just strolled away from ours, winched the anchor up and sailed out. As soon as I discovered what I'd done, it was like the man said: I knew I was in trouble.

But how exactly are you supposed to 'obtain the help or respite you need to refuel you emotionally and physically'? Yeah. Good question. The trouble is, you don't seem to have the power to think any more, let alone the energy to do anything. What you'd like is for someone to come along and relieve you of the load, or for something miraculous to happen. But you know that no-one will come, and nothing will happen. And that just makes you feel more dejected, more helpless, and more doomed.

So perhaps there isn't anything you can do? Well, actually, there is.

Doing something about it

This is going to sound like another piece of fatuous self-help advice, I know. All I can say is, if you're suffering from burnout or sense that you're dangerously close, try it. Try easing the pressure in one of these ways. If you don't, but just carry on sitting there in stultifying misery, things are not going to get any better. And remember the saying:

> God helps those who help themselves, and the government helps the rest.

Well, it's not true. Whether or not God can help you I have no idea, but I'm quite certain the government won't. If you're burnt out, or near to it, you have to pull back by yourself – and you can. What you have to do is relieve that crushing pressure. You can do that by pushing down, or pushing up, or pushing sideways.

Lower the upward pressure

This is easy for the person who's feeling stressed out when erecting a shelf. All they have to do is give up. Either decide not to have a shelf there after all, or get someone in to do it for them. The bottom will fall out of their pressure box, and their heartbeat will return to normal. Admittedly, they'll feel a bit low as a result. A bit inadequate, perhaps. But at least they'll no longer have to hurl electric drills through plate-glass windows.

The upward pressure for carers, too, comes from the job itself. Only it's not quite so easy to walk away from it. What you *can* do, though, is make a big effort to do the job less conscientiously. Don't be such a good carer. Work to rule. Do only what's necessary. Lower your standards.

Sacrilege? Well, I wouldn't be telling you to do this if you really were an SP. I wouldn't really want to make life unpleasant for your piglet. I certainly wouldn't want to endanger them. But I don't think you'll let that happen.

Anyway, try it. Try being a bit more of an SP, and see if you feel better. If it works, you'll do the job even better.

187

Lift the downward pressure

Again, this is easier if you're putting up a shelf than if you're caring for a piglet. Digging craters in the wall? Try a new drill bit of the correct type. Use a more powerful drill. Drill in a different place. Worried about getting it level? Ask somebody to lend a hand and hold the spirit level while you make pencil marks on the wall.

But how do you apply the same technique to your caring? First, try to identify the part of caring that's applying the downward pressure. Some parts are bound to be worse than others. It might be something that anyone can understand, like helping your piglet go to the toilet and cleaning up afterwards. Or it might be something that you think other people will regard as a very small matter but which nevertheless is driving you nuts. Whatever it is, try getting someone in to help with this particular problem – or to show you how to make it easier to cope with.

The immediate problem here is that you suspect, or know, that your piglet won't be happy about this. Well, tough.* They'll just have to lump it. You're in trouble here, and for the good of both of you the pressure has got to be eased. And if this is what it takes, then this is what has got to happen.

Push out the sideways pressure

The sideways squeeze comes from time, remember? And this is the dimension which is the most likely to produce burnout in carers. Caring is a process that goes on and on and on, relentlessly. Things would be different if you could work 9–5 and have

---

* Do I really mean this? Perhaps not 100%. When all's said and done, they're the one who can't do things for themselves, so you're bound to put them first. The trick is to try not to, quite so much, from time to time. It's useful to remember that you BOTH suffer from the disability. They're the ones who have it, clinically speaking; but you share it with them. And sharing is exactly what needs to be done. One moment their needs are paramount, and the next yours are.

Saturdays and Sundays off. Or if you knew you had another six weeks on duty and could then have a three-week break.

There's nothing you can do about the duration of your caring. But there are two things you can do to push back the pressure.

- Set yourself a time limit. Tell yourself you'll perform your caring role for the next six months, then stop. Now the thing is contained. You can bear anything if the end is in sight. What will happen when the six months is up? Doesn't matter. Just tell yourself that something will happen and then you'll be out of it

- Force regular breaks from your caring. I say 'force' because this is a really hard thing to do. The day centres are full, friends are too busy. Up to now you've caved in and just got on with the job. No longer. Shout, kick, insist, do whatever you have to do. But take time off, and take it off regularly. Make it happen. The very act of reorganising time will help to ease the squeeze.

What *not* to do about it

The first thing that burnout cases generally do is: nothing. They're beyond taking any action at all. Well, sometimes this can work. After all, one of the dimensions of burnout is time, and time is fickle. It can ease off by itself, so that burnout drops down to ordinary stress.

If this is all you can manage (ie, nothing), that's fine. So long as you *do* do something the moment you feel you can. If you continue to take no action even then, time will start to squeeze you again soon, just when you're not ready for it, just when you're unable to bear it.

Weirdly, the three things that occur to most of us at burnout time are the very three things that don't work. They are:

Suicide

This can seem like a really sensible option. Being a carer is killing you anyway, you reason. If you bring things to their natural conclusion, everything will work out for the best. You walk out of life, somebody else takes over the caring role, your piglet gets better care, and you no longer have the angst and the aggro. Everybody wins.

Wrong.

Burnout is temporary. Suicide is permanent.

There's lots of other stuff here, which you can consider when the burnout phase has receded. How it hurts everybody around you so much that they never really recover. How you'd have to be the most selfish of all selfish pigs to inflict that on them. How you'd miss the good things which are lying in wait.

I'm deliberately not bringing religion or the law into this. When you're contemplating suicide, these things probably won't seem to count for much.

Don't care whether suicide is the answer or not? Believe you can't go on, whatever the rights and wrongs?

You can.

Murder

The other day I read a questionnaire on a website about carers' health, and found that one of the questions was:

> Have you ever wanted to harm the person you care for?

Till then I used to think it was just me who secretly harboured thoughts of murder. I had no idea that other people ever felt the same way.

190

The more I thought about it, the more I realised that if this question had found its way into a mass-circulation questionnaire, then the issue must be a common one. It's just that nobody talks about it. Even the compiler of the questionnaire couldn't quite bring himself to talk about it openly. 'Harming the person you care for' clearly meant murdering your piglet.

If you're one of the thousands if not millions who've thought about it, the first thing to do is to understand that it's a common reaction, and that you're not actually evil. Next, turn to Chapter 12 (no, not to find out how, you fool).

For now, though, since we're on the subject, let's just say that murder might seem like a good idea at the time, but isn't. It doesn't solve the problem.

And like suicide, it's permanent. Whereas burnout is temporary.

Bearing the burden on your own

It's almost inevitable that you'll be isolated in your caring. Have you been to Chapter 4 yet? There's a lot about loneliness and isolation in there.

It's also inevitable that isolation will increase your stress, and hasten your ultimate burnout. That's what isolation does to people.

So the other thing you mustn't do – apart from committing suicide or murder – is go on being isolated. It's not a luxury to share the burden with other people. It's an absolute necessity. If you haven't been to Chapter 17 yet, go there NOW. Go on.

The importance of being selfish

I said at the beginning of this book that you weren't as selfish as you thought. I may even have said that you weren't selfish at all. Well, you should be. And now's the time to start.

The thing is, it's not as easy as it sounds. In fact, for a carer, it's a surprisingly hard thing to do. You actually have to steel yourself.

Why is being more selfish a good idea? Well, what you've got to do is push out the parts of the box which are causing the excess pressure. And the top and bottom parts are directly concerned with the job you're doing. The more conscientious you are at caring, the harder the job, and the more pressure. The more pressure, and the longer it goes on, the sooner you burn out.

Don't forget there are two people in this scenario: you and your piglet.

One is getting some pretty good care; the other is burning out. What would happen if the emphasis of care shifted a bit from the piglet to you? Is the piglet going to suffer? Not a lot. Are you going to get a new lease of life? Yes you are. And who benefits from that? Both of you.

Here's the kind of thing you can do:

- Say no sometimes. You don't always have to do what your piglet wants immediately they ask. Sometimes you do. Just not every single time. Springing into action becomes a habit. Break it occasionally. And don't feel guilty when you do

- Lower your standards once in a while, and see if the world falls apart. It hasn't? Did anyone even notice? Well then, do it more often

- Insist on getting help from time to time. I don't mean ask for help. Insist on it. From the care authorities, from your friends. Before, when you've asked, did you apologise? Beg, even? Next time, tell them what you need and when you need it.

Don't worry that being a selfish pig will become such a habit that you'll stop being a proper carer. It'll work the other way, I promise you. You'll become a better carer.

What the books say you should do

According to the books, when you were a caveman confronted by a stressful situation – a charging mammoth, say – your instincts told you either to run away or stand and fight. The books say that this 'fight or flight' response is what takes over when we get stressed out today.

What they say is that, when you suddenly find yourself in a situation with your piglet that makes you want to rush out of the house (flight) or push them down the stairs (fight), you can employ some cunning modern techniques to minimise your ancient response.

For example:

Deep breathing

The mammoth has appeared at the entrance to your cave. Your breathing rate automatically increases and becomes more shallow in readiness for whichever response you choose: fight or flight. But the mammoth isn't real. It was there one and a half million years ago, but it isn't there now. You can drag your body back into the 21st century by calming your breathing. Take a series of slow deep breaths.

Yeah, right. Your piglet does that thing that they do which always drives you totally round the bend. Your hands are inches from their throat, your teeth are bared, a horrible snarl is emerging from your throat. All you have to do is say 'Yes, dear,' then go and stand in the corner, breathing deeply. Next thing, they say it again, and never mind taking shallow breaths, you find yourself uttering a long blood-curdling howl.

Imagine a hostile animal

A great big woolly mammoth, say. Now you can see that you're responding to something ridiculous, something that doesn't really exist.

Yeah, right. Now there are three of you in this situation: your piglet, you, and a bloody great imaginary wild animal that's on the point of trampling you to death.

Imagine a peaceful place

The theory is that when you're somewhere stressful, somewhere where you don't want to be, simply imagine yourself to somewhere peaceful and idyllic, and the stress will go away.

Yeah, right. You're stuck in this room being tortured by the demands of your piglet who doesn't realise what they're doing to you; so you imagine you're somewhere else, and for a moment there you almost believe it. Then you open your eyes and suddenly things are even worse than they were before.

Physical movement

Your body needs to run away. So stride about, waving your arms. Or if you can leave the house, jump on your bike and ride round the block.	Yeah. And get reported to Social Services for neglecting your piglet. (I was once, for doing just this.)

Punchbag therapy

Your body needs to fight, so take it out on a punchbag you've borrowed from the local gym.	Yeah, but what you want to do is kill something, and no matter how hard you hit that punchbag, it won't die. Better to slam a door or two. Then at least the plaster will fall down and a huge crack will appear which you'll have to spend the next day filling.

Respite

Get away from it all for a few hours, a day, or a week.	Yeah, right. Assuming you can achieve that (in which case you're cleverer than I thought) you'll just have time to rediscover your pre-caring self, before you'll be jerked back into the present, hoping it won't be even more difficult as a result.

No, but seriously, they're worth a try. You might get good at some of them if you practise a bit. The trouble is, all of them are short-term remedies whereas burnout is a long-term thing and out of reach of tricks like these. But if just one of them succeeds in relieving the pressure for some time, it will have staved off burnout.

What the books say you should not do

Booze

You mustn't take to the bottle. You can't be a drunk and a carer at the same time.

No, but what you can do is pour yourself a glass of wine which you can drink all by yourself while practising how to be more of an SP.

Valium

You mustn't take drugs.

No, you mustn't depend on any drug. But when deep breathing has failed, a Valium might be just what's needed to save your piglet from grievous bodily harm.

Violence

You mustn't lash out at your piglet. Nor must you abuse them psychologically.

No, you mustn't. Not even when they're abusing you, which they very well might. In this, the books are right.

Cheerful note

You get better at managing pressure. You do. You become more familiar with its causes. And by practising different ways of alleviating it, you learn the tricks that work for you.

Plus, don't forget, nothing in this world is static, and both you and your piglet are going to change, which in itself will alter the loading.

That's not a lot of encouragement in the short term. Which is where this book comes in. If it helps you to appreciate that all carers are subject to burnout, that it's common and dangerous, that the support agencies are aware of it, have done studies on it, and are working at ways of minimising it, you may begin to realise that you're not burning out in isolation. You're in good company.

CHAPTER 12

Pushing them down the stairs

No joke

But no harm done – yet

Murder in the dark

A professional job

Why on earth?

Power
Punishment
Fight *and* flight
   Chinese water torture
   Psychological abuse
It's madness
Easy target
Exhaustion

You could be the victim, too

The whip hand

Guilty as charged?

Stop it, stop it, stop it

Stop caring temporarily
Stop caring altogether
Stop whatever it is that starts the madness
Get help?

Pushing them down the stairs

Our friend Bill introduced me to his new girlfriend. She turned out to be a part-time nurse in a care home, so I immediately started to pick her brains. She was cheerful, open, voluble and, it seemed to me, compassionate. You could see straight off that she was a good carer.

'Don't they just drive you mad?' she asked happily. 'The only reason I haven't pushed them down the stairs is because I'd be found out.'

And that's what started me thinking about this chapter.

No joke

Like so many really important bits of information, it was imparted in the guise of a joke and accompanied by a little laugh to emphasise that it shouldn't be taken literally. And in time-honoured fashion I laughed back.

It wouldn't have been in the spirit of the conversation to have pressed her on the subject. I rather wish I had. I'd like to have asked:

- How close to the truth had that throwaway remark actually been
- Whether she had ever done such a thing
- Or something like it
- Or almost done it
- Whether any of her colleagues had
- How she reconciled murderous thoughts with her caring philosophy
- How they affected her relationship with her patients
- Whether the patients knew or sensed how close they and she had come to the brink
- How they responded to her afterwards.

I should have asked all these questions. The trouble was that I didn't dare. Because I knew exactly how she felt. And although it was clear she had been joking, in my case it wasn't a joke at all. I actually had come dangerously close to pushing my piglet down the stairs.

But no harm done – yet

Then, later on, I received a questionnaire about the effects of caring on the mental health of carers. One of the questions was whether I had ever wanted to harm my piglet. And I started to put two and two together.

I realised that perhaps, after all, this was a common phenomenon. It wasn't only me who came close to murder. Perhaps all carers did.*

Murder in the dark

I decided it was a pity I wasn't a writer of detective stories, because the murder of a piglet could make an ideal murder plot.

---

* Coming close to murder is of course different from committing it. Every now and then a case of actual piglet murder comes to light.

Wendolyn Markcrow cared for her Down's Syndrome son, Patrick, for 36 years. As he grew older he developed autistic traits and became violent. During one of these bouts he blinded himself in one eye.

Wendolyn enlisted the help of her doctor, and for years they pleaded with the local authorities for help with Patrick's care. Finally, when she was 67 years old and exhausted, she sedated Patrick, put a plastic bag over his head and held it there till he stopped breathing. Then she took a kitchen knife and tried, but failed, to kill herself.

Her family said they didn't know how close to the edge she was.

The judge, in sentencing her, said: 'You will be punished as long as you live by the knowledge of what you have done.'

Her lawyers throughout the trial maintained that she had committed the act at a time of 'diminished responsibility'.

And millions of carers, reading the story in their newspapers, wondered where the diminished responsibility lay.

A physically frail, mentally confused person is found at the foot of the stairs, dead. The carer had 'popped out' for five minutes at the time of the 'accident'. It looked as though the piglet had tried to operate the stairlift, or been going to the bathroom past the head of the stairs, on their own, and fallen.

The primary suspect is the carer, who was the last person to see the piglet alive. But the police can't find any real motive, and there's no history of domestic violence. They interview the family, friends and neighbours who all attest that the carer not only seemed genuinely fond of the piglet but had looked after the piglet tenderly for years. 'A wonderful person. A saint,' they told the police.

The denouement of the story is that the detective, who once looked after an aged parent and is therefore full of insight, understands that the culprit was indeed the carer, but that the carer hadn't, technically speaking, pushed the piglet down the stairs. What really happened was that the piglet had been driving the carer mad all day, and that when the piglet happened to be poised at the head of the stairs, the desperate carer lunged past in a bid to escape the sound of the piglet's voice. In hastily brushing past, the carer inadvertently knocked the piglet off balance, and down the stairs they went.

The carer hadn't meant that to happen – or had they? Maybe they had, subconsciously? Was it flight, or was it fight? The story ends on a note of uncertainty.

A professional job

And then I got to thinking about known instances of patient abuse in special hospitals and care homes, where there is no recognisable motive, but a nurse has either neglected or tortured an inmate. It seems it can happen anywhere; you don't have to be an unpaid carer to come close to the edge. It can be a professional job as well.

One of the differences between paid care-workers and us (apart from the matter of pay) is that their caring happens in public. Or if not exactly in public, then in the company of other workers and other patients. In cases of abuse, there's a good chance that somebody will blow the whistle, and the mistreatment will be exposed. Eventually.

But our caring goes on behind closed doors. Friends and neighbours talk about us behind our backs and say that we're saints, but they don't often come and have a look for themselves to see whether we really are or not. If they did, and if they happened to see us in some of our less tolerant moments, might they not blow the whistle on us? Report us to the authorities for piglet abuse? Say that we were a threat to the piglet's safety?

All right, they probably wouldn't go that far. But they might very well stop thinking of us as saints.

Why on earth?

Anyone who has cared for somebody else long-term can understand (or thinks they can) the temptation to lash out, verbally if not physically. Just as everybody knows it's something you mustn't do, everybody also knows there are times when you're stretched beyond the limit of patience. But is it as simple as that? Do people like my friend's cheerful nurse/girlfriend have a finite supply of patience and goodwill in the way that a bath can only contain so much water? And when that limit is exceeded the bath overflows all over the floor, or the nurse girlfriend lifts her hands to push a patient down the stairs?

The chances are, it's more complicated than that. After all, there are millions of us carers, so it's highly likely there are at least hundreds of possible reasons why any one of us should lose our cool.

Like what, for instance?

Power

We see that happening, in politics of course, in business, and in the corridors of Officialdom. But we probably don't relate it to our own situation. Nevertheless, we *do* have power over our piglets. By definition they are dependent on us. Could it be true that we are being corrupted – not absolutely, but relatively?

Patients in mental hospitals are the ultimate in powerlessness; they can exercise control over neither their minds nor bodies. The nurses/warders may not have much power outside the walls of the institution, but their relative power inside them is immense. The power differential may in fact be so great that the tendency to corruption is close to being irresistible.

At home, our piglets probably have more independence, so that the power differential will be less. But it'll still exist. Is there a sliding scale of corruption? Does a tiny bit of power corrupt a tiny bit? What's the power:corruption ratio?

Luckily, I don't know what I'm talking about here. I simply put forward the hypothesis that you may be tempted to abuse your piglet, on the rare occasions when you are, by the simple fact that you have power over them, and the fact of having this power, even though you never wanted it in the first place, is not doing you much good.

Punishment

Whatever the illness or disability that's affecting your piglet and making them dependent, it's also affecting you. Let's say, for the sake of argument, that they suffer from MS. Your life has been changed as a direct result of this, so it could be said that you *both* suffer from MS.

But they're the ones who contracted it. Clinically speaking, it's their disability, not yours. Somehow they managed to inflict it on you. You hate what it's doing to both of you. Maybe deep inside you hate the piglet for involving you in their problem.

The whole thing is their fault, and there are times when you want to punish them for it.

Fight *and* flight

In moments of extreme stress (in other words, when you're going bananas), your atavistic and instinctive responses are pretty well limited to two options: fight or flee. The problem is, there's never any time to choose. Even if there is, it doesn't do you much good when flight is out of the question. Suppose, for example, your piglet is standing in a doorway, immobile, apparently welded to the floor, and the telephone is ringing on the other side. You know it's the call you've been waiting for and that you really, really want to take. Not being able to get to it is driving you frantic. In an explosion of stress you dive straight between the piglet and the doorpost, and between fight and flight. Your sudden outburst of energy takes you simultaneously away from the piglet and towards the telephone. But it also knocks the piglet over in the process.

You may say, breathlessly, to the person on the other end of the telephone that you can't talk because your piglet has just fallen over, and they believe you. The piglet may think it's true as well. But *you* know, if you allow yourself to know, what really happened. All right, you didn't push them down the stairs. But it was a close thing.

You can't relate to any of these scenarios? Well maybe you're a saint after all. Or are you? After all it's not necessary to knock a piglet over to abuse them. There are other, subtler ways of getting your revenge.

Chinese water torture

Well, not literally. But if you feel so inclined you can apply physical abuse by, for example, being rough while helping the piglet to get dressed. Or when brushing their hair. If they look as if they're about to knock over a cup of tea, you could prevent the accident by lightly tapping their hand. You're not slapping them, how could anybody think that?

Alternatively you can always apply torture by failing to perform some little task that you normally do for them, or that they need having done for them. Not giving them a wash when they want it and are looking forward to it can be a fairly satisfactory kind of punishment if you're feeling the need to be a bit vicious. Not that you'll want to repeat this several days on the trot or it might punish you more than them.

A popular method of abuse in care homes, reputedly at least, is 'inappropriate use of medication' – in other words, sedation. This one has two things going for it: it reduces the patient to a semi-vegetative state (that'll teach them), and it makes the care-worker's job nice and cushy.

Psychological abuse

Mafia thugs know exactly how to beat somebody up in such a way that they leave no visible bruising or cuts. Carers can achieve the same objective with psychological unkindness. All you have to do is constantly remind the piglet that they're in your power. The list of torments is as long as the menu in a bad restaurant.

- Just say: 'You know you can't get out of that chair on your own' when they're having a go in a bid for independence

- Make an indignant fuss over any unpleasant mess, and clean it up with exaggerated disgust

- Roll your eyes heavenward and utter a long-suffering sigh when they say or do something wrong, particularly when it irks them that they can't do it properly

205

- Tell them: 'If this sort of thing goes on I'm going to have you put away'

- Fail to remind them that their favourite television programme is about to start

- Point out that they've missed it once it's finished

- Leave them on their own, particularly at times when they're frightened or sad.

It's madness

Don't worry, I know very well that calculated abuse of that kind isn't your scene. You have to be a lot more heartless than a simple Selfish Pig to indulge in deliberate cruelty. On the other hand, I'm prepared to bet there have been moments when you came close to a single act of major abuse. And I suspect I know the reason: you were being driven mad.

It's complete nonsense to think that 'sticks and stones may break my bones but words can never hurt me'. It's words which are behind our worst impulses. Your piglet could chuck the china at you without having any more damaging effect than making you laugh. But the things they say – ah, they're very different.

It can be some bizarre and illogical remark that makes you feel as if you're going as mad as they are. It can be a habit of speech on their part; maybe they repeat things over and over again, or speak indistinctly so that it's a real effort to listen to them. And since they seldom say anything worth hearing, you get to the point when you just want to stop the noise

It can be a criticism, even. Just when you've bent so far over backwards to help them that you consider you're due for a special award for bravery, they complain that you treat them really badly and never do anything for them.

Words that hurt can make you want to respond in kind. Only, sometimes words are inadequate for a reply. You may not be able to summon the precise words which can deliver the maximum impact. Or it could be that you can't reason with your piglet because of their mental confusion. Just as likely, you cannot discuss a subject because of some taboo or other. When this happens, when words won't work, this is when you feel the compelling need to do something physical and cruel.

We've all seen this phenomenon in children. One moment they're playing happily; next thing war has broken out and atrocities are being committed. It's not just that children are wild animals. It's that they're inarticulate. When words fail them, they hit out.

Easy target

Nobody says that adjusting to being a carer is easy. It isn't. In fact, it can be so frustrating and infuriating that it can make you want to take it out on somebody. But who?

> Any person suffering from a chronic disease can become an easy target for abuse. This can be a result of the mental and physical changes that he or she has undergone, the caregiver's inability to adapt fast enough, or the fact that the patient with the disease is an easily identified victim.
>
> *Advice leaflet for care-givers*

Do you sometimes feel that you and your piglet are alone in the world? This is the notorious carers' isolation syndrome. One of its effects is that, when you need a victim so that you can get your own back on the injustice of your situation, there's only one possible person: your piglet. There they are, and here you are, and nobody can see you.

Exhaustion

Long-distance lorry drivers are required by law to limit the time they spend behind the wheel. Whenever they bend the law, which from time to time they do, they often bend something else as well. Fatigue affects the way we function, and is known to be dangerous.

Carers, unlike lorry drivers, are not prohibited by law from spending too long on the job. In fact, we're encouraged to do just that. In the UK, piglets only qualify for the maximum amount of Disability Living Allowance* if their carers have to get up and tend to them several times a night, several nights a week. It's a kind of reward from the government: keep your carer on the go night and day, and we'll give you extra money.

The inevitable result is that something gets bent, and what you have to hope is that it isn't your piglet.

You could be the victim, too

> The abuse can be either way. A caregiver can abuse the patient and the patient can abuse the caregiver and the rest of the family.
>
> *Advice leaflet for caregivers*

Piglets with dementia may develop abusive or aggressive behaviour. Others can undergo disruptive mood changes. Even the very young and the very old can pose a threat which invites retaliation.

But I suspect the most usual form of carer abuse by piglets

---

* Disability Living Allowance rates are decided by the piglet's care and mobility requirements. The care component has three levels, of which the highest is only awarded when the carer has to render assistance throughout the 24-hour period.

stems from something much more ordinary: they're frightened. Frightened of losing control, of being alone, of death. Seized by fear the piglet, unable to do anything to make the nightmare go away, may lash out (verbally or physically) at the carer. These are important and understandable concerns, so that you'd think any one of us would be able to handle them, and respond with kindness and reassurance. Yes, but that isn't how it seems at the time.

Them:	You:
'I want you to clip my nails.'	'Your nails don't need clipping; I did them yesterday.'
'No you didn't. Feel this one.'	'It's fine, I promise you. If I cut it any shorter I'd make you bleed.'
'That's probably what you'd like to do.'	'That's nonsense. You know I wouldn't want to do anything of the sort.'
'Well, you only ever do things for me when you absolutely have to. You hate doing things for me.'	(Diplomatic silence)
'You're supposed to take care of me. That's what the government pays you to do.'	'As a matter of fact, they don't. They give me a wretched stingy allowance to compensate me for not being able to earn decent money in some other kind of job.'
'See? You resent having to look after me. You hate me.'	'Of course I don't hate you.'
'You do, and I hate you back.'	Aaaaaaaaaaaargh!

The whip hand

This kind of interchange can develop into a war. The good thing about it is that they're unlikely to be able to push you down the stairs. The bad thing is that you could push them.

There are marriages like that. Or households in which, say, two elderly sisters live together, seeming to feed off their mutual antagonism. Maybe you and your piglet were a case in point, before the disability? No, all right, you weren't. But such things have been known.

There's an instance of a couple who were on the verge of splitting up when one of them had a stroke. Afterwards, the one that was left undamaged felt obliged to stay on, looking after the other one. But the stroke didn't make an unsatisfactory relationship more satisfying. The impartial observer, whoever that might be, could possibly have concluded that it made the relationship even harder to bear, for both of them.

Anyway, we're not here to discuss them, or anyone else. What we're doing here is looking at you and your situation. And the point is, if you get into a war with your piglet, where will it end? It is a horrible fact that domestic violence, once it has established a pattern, rarely stops. In fact, it tends to get worse.

I know, I know, you and your piglet swearing at each other hardly fall into the category of domestic violence. But refusing to say goodnight could lead on to something else. Manhandling them into their clothes, for example. And then to combing their hair so violently that it hurts them. After that you might feel it necessary to threaten to have them put away. You might even give them a smack. Or a whack. And finally, what – push them down the stairs?

Is your relationship different from what it once was? If it seems to have deteriorated (I don't say it has, mind) is it because the piglet/carer thing has got in the way? This may not be the way it is for you at all. But it is for some. And for them, there's always the risk that they'll allow the process to continue to the point where they find themselves ruining each other's lives.

It isn't your piglet who got you into this mess. It's the disability. But what happens next is in your hands. They're dependent on you, for the future of the relationship as well as everything else. And you're the carer. You've got the whip hand. Almost literally.

Guilty as charged?

Carers are guilty.

That's to say, we often *feel* guilty. We're certain somebody else would manage the caring role better. We're convinced we make mistakes that are terrible, and that another carer would never have made.

My friend Mary looked after her husband, a big, determined man. She told me: 'Once I gave him a slap. He slapped me right back, but I still felt truly awful about it. Not because he slapped me. It served me right. No, it was because I was supposed to be looking after him and yet I slapped him. Slapped him! How could I have done that?'

Yes, but her piglet was her husband. Their relationship wasn't that of nurse and patient. It was much closer than that. And people in close relationships almost always row. In fact, the closer you huddle people together, the more likely they are to row, the more often they'll do it, and the more bitter the rows will be.

Come on, Mary, what did you expect – that the arguments would disappear just because your husband suffered a stroke?

What if he hadn't been her piglet when she slapped him? Would she still have been overcome by guilt (bearing in mind that he not only seriously provoked her but gave as good as he got)?

Carers are ridiculous. We think we ought to be perfect, and are surprised and disillusioned when it turns out that we're not.

Stop it, stop it, stop it

Domestic violence has to be stopped in its tracks. I'm not sure that it matters whether it's a parent abusing a child, a man beating up his partner, or a carer exerting psychological cruelty over their piglet. And by stopping I don't mean pushing them down the stairs. I mean changing the normal pattern of events in which violence increases with use.

You'll never be perfect. At least, it's unlikely. So there are going to be moments when you say or do something you later regret. But the trick is not to let it become a habit.

How?

Stop caring temporarily

The moment you find yourself at the top of the stairs, hands raised and ready to push, is the moment to realise that you're burning out. You've been at it for too long. You're no longer yourself. It doesn't matter whether the urge to push is a sudden aberration or the last link in what you think is an entirely logical chain, the fact remains that you're not rational. You're not yourself.

What you need is a break. What you may *want is* a permanent break, but what you have to have is a break of some kind. There's a whole section on this later (Chapter 15) because respite care, though easy to talk about, can be almost impossible to achieve.

But you must. Not only that, but you must achieve it on a regular basis. It's no use thinking that by taking a quick break you'll cure the problem for good and all. You might. It's highly likely that you'll come back restored. It's also highly likely that the whole relentless process will begin again and that at some point in the future you'll find yourself once more poised at the top of the stairs.

Stop caring altogether

My friend Tricia's husband developed MS while their three children were still very young. For a time life became very fraught for all five of them. Then, one day, when they were sitting round the kitchen table, she leaned forward and tapped him on the forehead with the spoon she was using to eat her boiled egg. Not long afterwards she divorced him, left home, took the children with her and brought them up on her own.

She said: 'It was a hard thing to do. Abandoning your husband just when he needs you looks a bit heartless to the outside world. It doesn't feel like the right thing to do, either, especially if you're someone who actually believes in the sanctity of the marriage vows. But when I tapped him with that spoon, I could see that it was going to happen again. And I wasn't convinced I would always be able to restrict myself to a spoon. The only safe solution I could think of was to remove myself and the children from that situation.'

For most carers, there may be no visible option other than to carry on caring. And yet, for most carers, there is. Even when other family members are too far away, or too committed, or nonexistent; even when care homes are full, or too expensive; even when Officialdom claims it can't help, there *has* to be a better option than caring till you push.

Walking away may look irresponsible. It may seem to be the act of a truly selfish pig. But there's just a chance that it could be the most caring thing you could do.

Stop whatever it is that starts the madness

Not your piglet's madness. Yours. What is it that triggers these wild emotions? Perhaps it's something that can be changed. Or, failing that, perhaps there's something in you that minds terribly, and maybe *that* can be changed.

Let's say, for example, that there's a carer out there somewhere who feels so frustrated about not being able to get on with their real life that they've started to consider pushing their piglet down the stairs. This carer can justify it easily. It would be the kindest thing for the piglet, and for the rest of the family. It would actually lessen everybody's suffering in the long run. Plus, it would release the carer to get on with a productive, worthwhile life.

Okay, now let's imagine that this carer comes round to seeing the caring role in a different light. What if they came to believe that it was an important thing to be doing? What if their old job, the one they had been longing to get back to, suddenly seemed trivial by comparison? What if they were publicly praised for the work they were doing, and given a high-profile award (all right, I've gone too far, but you get the idea)? If this change of perspective, this epiphany, came about, the danger to the piglet would evaporate. The stairs would return to being something to ascend or descend at a stately pace.

I don't really know whether a change of attitude as big as this can be engineered. I do know that it sometimes comes about. It happened to me. Luckily, in the nick of time.

Get help?

This is what the books say. Or, to be fair, what they advise is that you should *seek* help. Seeking it and getting it are two different things. One's fairly difficult, but the other is about as likely as making a fortune out of a pyramid selling scheme.

Nevertheless, it's worth trying, if only because seeking help is an admission – to yourself – that you need it.

CHAPTER 13

New money

You've been reclassified

Spangle

Actual hardship

Relative hardship

The consumers
The competitors

How to deprogram yourself

Island living
A different way of keeping score

Earning extra

The money
Identity
Self-esteem
Friends
Respite

What to do

At home
Away from home

But will anyone employ you?

Money for your piglet

It's in your head not your pocket

New money

Old money is what you used to earn. It was an inseparable part of your lifestyle, and of who you were.

But now you're a carer and everything has changed. Freedom has gone up the spout, all your priorities have been radically reshuffled, time has taken on a new meaning, AND you're quite likely to be broke.

There's nothing new about having less money than you'd like. Everybody has less money than they'd like. Before you became a carer, would you have refused an increase, or a bonus? Handed back a tax rebate? Said: 'No thanks, I don't need it,' to a windfall profit? Immediately passed on to someone else a bequest from an unexpected uncle?

I don't think so.

But there *is* something new about your finances now. And it's not just that you're strapped for cash.

You've been reclassified

What's happened is that you've been dropped into a lower socioeconomic bracket. Even if you were teetering on a very low rung of the ladder before you became a carer, at least you could cling to the knowledge that you stood a good chance of climbing higher. Now you can't. Because you're a carer you have hardly any opportunity of making money. In fact it's quite likely, especially if you're a full-time carer, that your earning potential is zero.

Being broke is uncomfortable for practical reasons. But being officially a low earner, publicly dependent on benefits, recognisably poor – that can be worse than uncomfortable. It can be humiliating.

It doesn't have to be, though. As always, there's an alternative. What you need to do is look at money from a new angle. Once you see it from the perspective of a carer, instead of from the viewpoint of where you used to stand, surprising things happen.

Spangle

From the Selfish Pig's angle (SPANGLE), money has a completely different value. In fact, it's new money.

And the great thing about this new money is, you don't need so much of it.

Hold on, hold on. Don't go away just yet. You've turned to this chapter because you HATE being poor. You're outraged that the money you get isn't enough for the weekly shop, and even when it hits your bank account it's so paltry that you're restricted to the cheapest of everything.

You feel belittled that you can't afford the tiniest treat, ever. You think you've been sidelined by the State, and that you're worth better treatment than this, and the absolutely *last* thing you need to read about here is unrealistic, sentimental claptrap about how to think yourself out of poverty when, dammit, the fact of the matter is that you haven't got enough money to live on, and it's NOT RIGHT.

Yeah. I know all this. And like you, I can't do anything about it. About the money, that is. I can't get you more of it. I can't tell you how to fiddle the system so that you do. Or give you an address you've never heard of till now, where a nice person will hand the stuff over to you just for the asking.

But I still might be able to help you cope. Stick with me for a page or two more.

Actual hardship

It's true that being a cash-free zone can induce real hardship. If you

- are literally starving
- can't keep warm and dry
- are ill and can't get treatment

then this is actual, undeniable hardship. What's more, it can kill you. And there are plenty of people, far too many, in that situation.

But are you one of them? That's to say, two of them, because your piglet's more or less bound to be in the same financial position as you. Well, are you?

What's more likely is that you're *on* the poverty line, rather than below it. You can live. It's just that you can't live well. Yes, life is hard. The question is, is it seriously hard, impossibly hard, totally unbearably hard?

Or is it *relatively* hard?

Relative hardship

I'm in danger of losing you again, aren't I? You don't give a damn about the theoretical difference between actual and relative hardship, whatever that may be. All you know is that you haven't got enough money, and because you're a carer you can't do anything about it.

Ah, but you can. And that's because the kind of poverty you're almost certainly experiencing (relative poverty) can be eased by other methods beside the obvious one of throwing large amounts of cash at it.

What you have to do first is consider why you feel bad about being poor, even though you're not actually starving and you do have a roof over your head.

It's because of all those other people.

The consumers

They (you know who I mean: all of THEM out there) have more of everything than you do, and it's this which makes it so hard to bear being poor. You get your nose rubbed in it before you even set foot outside your front door. Switch on the telly, open a newspaper or magazine, pick up one of those catalogues that come thudding unasked through the letterbox, and there is all the stuff which THEY can get but you can't. Head down to the shop and you can't avoid them. They're all at it: buying stuff, driving about in cars, wearing new clothes, coming out of restaurants wiping their mouths.

It's a consumer society, and everyone but you is consuming away as hard as they can. And, instinctively, you want to be there with them, consuming your share.

But the thing is, they aren't really enjoying themselves. They may think they are because they've been told they ought to be. But all this frenzied consuming is giving them a hard time. Doesn't matter how much they earn, they'll never be able to have enough. There's too much pressure. You see, consumers don't have any choice. They *have* to spend money. It's how they're programmed.

Poor them.

Consumers are a vital part of the economy. Their purpose in life is to buy whatever products and services are churned out by industry. If they don't, the world stops going round. So they're programmed to play their part, whether they want to or not.

It's actually worse than that, even. If the economy is to be healthy, it has to grow every year. That means that more products and services have to be made, which means that poor old consumers have to buy more of them. So they're programmed to want more. Not just more than they have, or more than the people next door. Just more. Every year.

But not us. We're lucky. We only have one job, which is to be a carer. We're exempt from the responsibility of being consumers too. So it's not compulsory to join in the, let's face it, slightly obscene feeding frenzy.

You've experienced many instances where you've felt, as a carer, that you were on the outside of society, looking in. And you didn't like it much. Well, here's one instance where it's really rather relaxing. Phew!

The competitors

For all of them out there, there's an additional burden. Poor old consumers are not just programmed to consume. There's more urgency to it than that. They're programmed to compete against one another. Whoever consumes the most wins the competition.

Money isn't just about what they can buy with it. It's about keeping score. And they have to post the results up in public, for all to see.

You thought money was just a system of tokens? Something that was invented because bartering was so time-consuming? ('I'll give you my tent if you give me that donkey.' And then later: 'My tent is worth ten tokens, but your donkey is only worth five, so if I give you ten tokens you have to give me two donkeys.')

Not any more. Tokens are now desirable for their own sake. ('She's worth ten million tokens.') Why? Because they're points on the scoreboard, and the one who has the most is the winner of the competition. And, of course, the other way around. Whoever has the lowest score is the all-time loser.

There's nothing particularly new about this. 150 years ago fat stomachs were praiseworthy and desirable; they publicly showed that you not only had enough to eat, but more than enough. Now it's cars and houses.

But we're excused. We're not expected to compete.

Or hadn't you realised?

How to deprogram yourself

Again luckily, it's not really necessary to *do* anything at all to de-program yourself from the consumer mindset. The business of caring will do it for you. It's certainly occurred to you that among the differences between you, an unpaid carer, and somebody else with a job that's recognised are that you don't qualify for

- overtime
- a minimum wage
- uninterrupted meal breaks
- health insurance
- sick leave
- maternity leave
- employment rights
- limited working hours
- a paid holiday
- a pension
- time off.

But maybe you didn't see the upside of all this? Well now you do:

- You don't have to be a consumer
- You don't have to compete.

Because you can't.

Island living

'Are you going anywhere this year?' is the question that innocently pops up when consumers get to talking about their holidays. Of course, they're all name-dropping exotic locations, and sooner or later you start to feel you want to go where they're going. Then you long to. And because you can't afford it, you feel aggrieved.

But what if you already lived on a remote island in the South Pacific? Imagine it. There are few people, no television, no shop, no clothes, no cars. On the other hand there's breadfruit on the trees, there are bananas and mangoes, and the fish in the lagoon are moderately easy to catch.

Who's rich and who's poor now?

Oddly enough, we carers *do* live on an island. How often have you felt isolated? Well, isolation is the exact condition you're in when you're on an island. So now you can feel good about it.

You don't have to buy a large-screen digital telly just because the ads tell you to. There aren't any ads, and even if there were there aren't any televisions. Nor are there neighbours with bigger sets than yours.

Okay, so you don't live in the middle of the South Pacific. But you're a carer, which comes to much the same thing. All those aspirations which consumers are programmed to have are pointless to you. You *can't* go skiing because of your piglet. Or climbing in the Himalayas. So you're excused from having to want to.

The problem is the pressure which is applied to ordinary consumers. It needs to be huge to get them to consume enough. And even though you're officially exempt from consuming, it's hard to escape the pressure.

My piglet and I wandered about in our boat for years. We had no access to television, and when we spent any time in one place we got about by walking as we didn't possess a car.

Once back in a house again, we were bombarded by car ads. But they seemed ridiculous to me and I didn't relate to them at all.

I observed them, though, with fascination. And within a year I found myself lusting after a shiny new car.

It was the pressure.

This is one of the reasons why it's pleasant, relaxing and re-assuring to associate with other carers. They're in the same boat, if you'll excuse the expression. Like you, they're unpaid non-consumers. They're a counter-balance to all those consumers and all that pressure.

Also like you, they can't get out much. So even if they had any money, they wouldn't be in a position to spend it. Which, in turn and in time, should cut down the longing to spend.

The tiny world of a carer can, at the end of the day, be quite a comfortable place. So long as you don't let it turn into a cell.

A different way of keeping score

My friend Roy always runs a big car. He's a businessman, and according to him it helps him get the contracts.

'It's what's in the car park,' he says, flashing his cuffs and adjusting his tie.

Money as a measurement of success is meaningless in our world. Nobody's impressed by what you've got (or don't have) in the car park.

How can you correlate your caring with the money you get for doing it? You can't, and we don't.

Your points are earned by doing the job. And they don't need to be counted or measured.

Even so, leaving all that philosophical stuff to one side, you could be excused for wishing you had a bit more disposable income, if only because it would make your caring job easier. It could buy you the means to transport your piglet to the doctor.

Or acquire those aids which Occupational Therapy have promised but not delivered. Or buy you some respite care.

So let's take a quick look at the prospect of topping up your benefits and earning a bit extra.

Earning extra

Adjusting your frame of mind is the best and first way to feel less poor. But the next is to generate more money. Once you've achieved the first, a very small amount of extra cash will go a long way, so you'll be really quite rich. Well, relatively rich (sorry, that word again).

But whether you *can* generate more or not will mostly depend on your piglet and their disability. And your real job, the caring job, has to take precedence. Start a second job and allow it to assume more importance than the caring, and you could find yourself in difficulties.

Don't let's get bogged down by the problems, though. What are the compensations of doing some work on the side?

The money

Of course. That's what this is all about. But remember that anything you earn may, and probably will, affect whatever State benefits you receive. You may only be allowed to earn so much before the benefits are reduced or stopped.

The obvious course of action is to calculate what these effects will be, before starting in on the work you have in mind. Yes, well. Obvious it may be, but it won't be easy. You're dealing with Officialdom here, and you know what *that* means.

Nevertheless, it's essential to do the sums first if you don't want to find yourself saddled with all the inconvenience of doing a job but not actually making as much money out of it as you expected.

Your second job (ie, not the caring job but the other one) may be the one you held down before your piglet's disability came about and before you became a carer. In this case, hanging on to it, even on a different and perhaps part-time basis, has another upside in that you'll keep your pension rights. Millions of carers give up paid work in order to care for their piglets, and discover later that they have to endure poverty not only as carers, but right through into their own old age because they've lost out on their pension.

Identity

Being invisible, we carers tend to lose our sense of identity. We forget who we are, and become merged with our piglet. That's why, when anyone asks me what I do, or when I have to complete the 'Occupation' section of a questionaire, I say I'm a carer.

But I have to struggle a bit. After all, I'm just living with my piglet, not going out to work. So I find that the words which spring to mind are 'unemployed', or even plain 'nothing'.

Whereas, if I got a job, it would be easier and more reassuring to say 'plumber' or 'librarian' or 'executive', as the case may be.

As it happens, at the moment I *am* working – if you call writing a book working. But because I've been thinking about this business of identity and what we're for, I don't say 'I'm a writer' when someone asks me what I do. Instead I say, loudly and clearly: 'I'm a carer.' And later I may add that I do a bit of writing on the side.

Funnily enough, caring isn't the only profession that gets its knickers in a twist about identity. There's the person who carries out the maintenance on the swings in the children's playgrounds but claims he's a helicopter stunt pilot. The waiters who are really actors.

It even works the other way round. An airline pilot down the road from me, fed up with being envied, now says he's a traveller in metal tubing.

And how about all those women: 'I'm just a housewife'?

How did I get started on this? Oh yes, identity. Well, if you have trouble saying you're a carer, doing some other work as well may ease the difficulty.

Self-esteem

Because we're all products of the consumer society, it's hard to forget about the points system. We're not paid, only given hand-outs (and they're inadequate), so it's easy to believe that we're not worth anything.

One of the great things about receiving a wodge of money or a pay cheque for something you've done is that you can say to yourself 'I earned that', and feel your self-esteem soar.

But for every upside there's a downside, and in this case it's the danger that the more money you make, and the better you feel about the new job, the worse you might feel about your caring.

Friends

One of the characteristics of caring is the isolation, and though I've pointed out one advantage of this, the unmistakable minus is that it's easy to get lonely. When people come to call on you and your piglet at home (if they ever do), you're in your caring environment, and conversation may not stray too far from that theme. Whereas at work you're in another world. You can forget about caring, have a laugh, exchange all kinds of ideas, and get a new perspective on life.

This is why working from home isn't as popular as you might expect. People miss their mates.

There's still a downside, though. The ones you meet at work are locked into that consumer society. They're all competing, and they have priorities and desires that you've been weaned away from. But they're your friends and colleagues, and you find yourself wanting to see things the same way they do. You start to get sucked back into all that. Next thing, your caring duties start to seem even more confining and onerous than they did before.

Also, a lot of the social side of work takes place after hours, when people go to the pub before going home, or whatever. But not you. You have to get back to your piglet, and can't join in. Or if you do you feel guilty about it.

Even so, work outside your home and away from your piglet can be wonderful respite care for you. Just not perfect, that's all.

Respite

If you're a full-time carer, the business of looking after your piglet can dominate your every waking thought. Obviously so – you're on duty all the time.

Concentrating on some other work, even for short periods and even if it's only in the spare room or at the kitchen table, can take your mind off the caring, and be as good as a rest.

What to do

Your second job (let's get it quite straight that your caring has to be your primary occupation) will pretty well have to involve work that you know about, and have probably done before. For example, if you trained as a physiotherapist and earned your living at that before you became a carer, it'll probably be your immediate choice for a second job now.

Or if your favourite pastime is water-colour painting, you might think of painting some pictures which you could sell.

Both of these you could do from home, so let's look at that sort of job first.

At home

If you choose a job you can do from home, it'll probably be because your caring job won't let you go to work somewhere else. So it would be best to opt for something not just that you know about, but that you can drop at a moment's notice and go back to when each caring crisis has been resolved. The kind of jobs you might be able to do are:

- Computer programming
- Bookkeeping
- Clock repair
- Secretarial services
- Or even writing a book.

You might be lucky and be able to allocate a certain part of the day for this work, rather than turning to it in spare moments. Piglets can be very demanding, and this is only partly because they need constant attention. The other part is because they *get* constant attention, and come to depend on it and insist on it. I've said somewhere else that it might do no harm to practise being more of an SP than you are by nature. But it's often not that easy. Announce that you're going to have a quiet half-hour and read a book on your own, and within five minutes there's a cry for attention. But if you say you're working and mustn't be disturbed until the hands on the clock point to the six, you might get away with it. Might.

Away from home

Your away job may be the one you had before you became a carer. Maybe you've never left it. Or perhaps it's the same occupation, but now you're working for somebody else.

Whatever it is, work which takes you away from your caring environment is quite likely to be better paid than working from home. It also stands a chance of providing more accentuated and prolonged respite care.

But of course, you won't get off lightly. There'll be times when there's a conflict of interest. There'll be occasions when your time is over-stretched.

Your stress level may go up in line with your bank balance. Sometimes you won't be able to do the away job properly because you're exhausted, or have to rush back to attend to your piglet, or stay at home for days on end.

Then again, the costs of working away from home can be higher than you remember. The travelling, the clothes, maybe special equipment you need for the job. I'm not trying to depress you. It's just that when you're broke and some extra work comes into view, most people are so busy staring at the money that they don't look at the rest.

Freelance work is probably the least good idea because with freelancing you have to put so much time into getting the work, as opposed to doing it.

The work you need is the sort where you can get out, get the job done, get paid, and get back.

But will anyone employ you?

In theory, and on average, carers are highly employable. That's because the chances of your becoming a carer increase with age, which means that the more experienced you are at your job, the more likely you are to become a carer.

But that won't necessarily be the way other people see it. Ever heard of ageism? It may not matter how experienced and in theory valuable you are; if you left the company to become a carer and are trying to come back on a different basis, or if you didn't leave, but want to change the terms of your employment, you might not seem quite as valuable to your employers as you believe you should be.

Optimists maintain that businesses are beginning to realise it's costing them money when they lose people to caring, so they're starting to develop carer-friendly strategies, which not only reduce their staff loss but also present a good corporate image.

Hmmmmm. Maybe. Some employers.

Money for your piglet

Now, I know this is a book for and about you, the carer. But while we're on the subject of money, let's not forget your piglet. They're having to cope with cashlessness as well. They may not have as much as they were used to, or would like.

It's one thing for you to overcome the difficulties by either changing your attitude or earning a bit extra, or both. But it may well be that neither of these is an option for your piglet. So you can stand by for a storm.

Most of the State benefits will be awarded to the piglet rather than to you, and you may find that the piglet is reluctant to hand it over to you, even for housekeeping and groceries. It's their money, and they're damn well going to hang on to it. Fair enough, in a way. Their disability has robbed them of so much else, it's only natural they should want to hang on to what they can.

Another scenario is that you handle all the finances, and the piglet is amenable to this. But what happens if they want to buy you a present or, come to that, buy *themselves* a present? Piglets who are disabled mentally may not be able to handle money under any circumstances, but others may like to have access to a bit.

It's good for all of us to have a disposable income. Whether it's the old stuff, or the new variety.

It's in your head not your pocket

Oh no, here he goes again, philosophising.

I don't care. This could be important.

It's a fact, and a relevant one for us carers, that the way you look at money affects the amount of money you have. Millionaires think they're poor by comparison with billionaires.

If being a carer enables you to see money for what it is, then in a way you're lucky to be a carer. It has showed you a way out of the trap.

You don't have to compete, because you're doing a more valuable job than you would be if you were working in a shop, factory or office. Which is more important, being a money broker earning as much as a small country, or someone who's saving a life?

The rest of the world (THEM) are accustomed to valuing a job, and the person who does it, on the basis of how well it's paid. No wonder we're invisible. We're unpaid, so we can't be worth a second thought. Not by them, anyway. Luckily, we don't make the same mistake.

The world may claim and believe that a high-earning divorce lawyer is more important than someone caring for their granny. But only because the lawyer earns more. What if it was the other way round, and the State paid you more to look after granny than the lawyer was able to charge the unhappy couple?

I've learned not to care what the world thinks I'm worth. I *know* I'm indispensable when I can't find anyone else to do the things I do for my piglet.

CHAPTER 14

The hands on the clock

No end to it

Not your time

Hibernation

The big bang theory

The fourth dimension

Adjusting the clock

Keep time with it
It's not a waste of time
Stop the pendulum
Regulate it

Time out

The hands on the clock

Your caring experience is different from mine. And a third carer will have a different experience from yours. But one of the really big factors for the whole lot of us is time. Time is what gives caring the characteristics which make it so different from anything else, and it's time which can make it so hard to cope with.

If that sounds a bit philosophical and airy-fairy, I'll try to run through it briefly. But run through it I will, because I have an idea that getting a handle on the special relationship between time and caring makes the whole thing clearer, and somehow easier.

No end to it

Caring is long term. At least it is for most of us. For some carers, such as parents of disabled children, it can be a life's work. For others, there *will* be an end to it, but it won't be soon.

Patients with a short-term disability are to be found in hospitals, and they're not what I call piglets. Piglets are people we give love and *endless* therapy to. At least, it seems endless.

The knowledge that there's nothing you can do to speed the clock up or let it wind down can be wearying. The uncertainty about whether you can last the course can be frightening.

If we all knew that we would have to care for our piglets for no longer than six weeks, and then we could get back to normal, there'd be no need for this book.

Not your time

This enormous span of time stretching ahead is not really your time. It's your piglet's. But in some incomprehensible way your time has been subsumed into your piglet's. Your life has been taken over.

Jane wanted to wail: 'What about me? By the time he's off my hands I'll be a geriatric myself.'

This is one of the problems: while the hands of the clock are going round for your piglet, they're going round for you too.

Hibernation

Caring changes the nature of time. When a grizzly bear hibernates, its metabolism changes and its heart rate slows. It has moved into a zone where time moves at a different speed. Something similar could be happening to you. Whatever your natural pace, you have to modify it to match your piglet's – or you do if you're not to go berserk.

Let's say your piglet takes ten minutes to get through a doorway and along the passage. It's no use trying to hurry them up, either by pulling them along or uttering encouraging cries. This is the rate they can manage, so it had better be the rate you choose too. At first, this is hard. But you learn; you adjust; you slow down.

Now your daily rhythms are different, not just from your natural and previous ones, but also from everybody else's. You're out of sync. 'Humans are adaptable,' you tell yourself firmly as you try to hop from time zone to time zone. But this is stressful. Like the grizzly, you find you need to be operating at hibernation speed or hunting speed, but not switching between the two.

And since you're a useless selfish pig and you habitually put your piglet first, it's easier to opt for hibernation.

The trouble with this is that it isolates you and your piglet from the rest of the world. You're in your cave, scarcely breathing, while life outside hums and whizzes. But hibernation isn't unconsciousness. You're all too well aware of what's going on outside the cave. It's just that you can't join in any more. Even though you sometimes long to.

The big bang theory

How did it all start? Not the universe, but becoming a carer. Was there a single momentous instant in which you and your piglet made the transition from your previous life to this one? That is what it might have been like if they suffered a stroke, for instance, or crashed a motorbike.

Or did their disability creep up gradually, and encroach on your awareness insidiously?

Either way, time will have been a vital component in the process. The first instance may have been like a shocking explosion after which suddenly everything was completely different and would never be the same again. In the second instance it may have taken you years to wake up to the fact that you had become a carer. You simply didn't notice the hands on the clock going round. Then one day you looked at the clock face and understood what had happened.

The fourth dimension

Everyone lives in the same physical world. It has three conventional dimensions and a fourth: time.

But for carers time is not the fourth dimension. It's the first.

Adjusting the clock

Can you? Should you?

You can, sort of. At least, you can make certain adjustments which make it feel as if something has been achieved. And since perception of time, rather than time itself, is all we're bothered about, this works just fine.

Keep time with it

Once you alter your own rhythm so that it beats in time with your piglet's clock, all the frustration (no, that's not right; but a lot of it; the worst part of it) evaporates.

When you're new to caring, you'll be anxious to get on with your own stuff, so it's really hard to be in harmony. But after a while you feel the new rhythm, and learn to go with it.

And then it's better.

There'll be opposition, mind. The rest of the world won't be happy to see you slowly ticking along at piglet pace. They'll want to shake you out of it. They'll want you to keep their time. After a while you'll have learned not to listen.

And then it's better.

It's not a waste of time

When it takes an hour to do something that used to be accomplished in ten minutes, and if you're by nature a busy person to whom time is precious, you'll chafe at the waste. You'll chafe even more painfully if that hour is spent doing something you never had to do at all in the old days, like cutting your piglet's toenails. That really will seem like a waste of time – time which you could be devoting to some of the hundreds of things of your own that you're anxious to be getting on with.

But when, eventually, you pick up the beat of piglet time, and also when you accept that this is your job now, it starts to become clear that time isn't being wasted after all.

True, there'll be moments when you falter, and feel an ago-nised 'Aaaaaaargh!' coming on. But there's a useful trick you can pull here. Remember the last fatuous form-filling exercise you carried out for Officialdom, or the delaying tactics they employed in response, and ask yourself: 'Who's really wasting time around here, them or me?'

It isn't you, I promise.

CHAPTER 14

Stop the pendulum

This is a method of influencing time that may occur to you in moments of approaching burnout. Stop the pendulum. Stop that bloody ticking altogether.

You could achieve that by pushing your piglet down the stairs, or pushing yourself. Or both. There's more than enough about all that in Chapters 11 and 12. If you haven't been there yet, and are casting longing glances at the stairwell now, better pop over there before you do anything else. No, not the stairwell. Chapter 11 or 12.

Regulate it

Piglets are hooked on routine. To an extent, we're all attached to it, but most of us need a break from it occasionally. Piglets want fewer breaks, and derive more satisfaction from always doing the same things at the same time. At least, mine does. And yours may.

In Chapter 22 there's a bit about a carer who stuck to the

routine for some time after her piglet had died. She discovered that far from being the irritant which she had assumed it was, it had become a comfort.

You may have established a routine for your piglet's sake. Well, let it regulate your life as well. It won't mean that you're becoming old before your time. What you're doing is living comfortably in your piglet's time.

Our own time will come, and when it does we'll be better equipped to adjust to it after living in piglet time – for the time being.

Time out

Despite all these adjustments, the fact remains that piglet time isn't really your time. You'll still need a break. The next chapter is all about this.

CHAPTER 15

Give me a break

TGIF-IW

Reality or mirage?

It's the carers who say no

The piglet isn't keen
Can't afford it
Don't know how to begin
All too difficult
Martyrdom
Guilt
Tried, failed, won't go through that again

Choking the cat

Friends
Day centres
Time to yourself in another room
Catnapping

Three conventional types of respite care

Piglet goes away
Piglet stays at home
You both go away together

How would you like to pay?

How to spend it

Re-entering the atmosphere

Give me a break

The train pulls into the terminus, and you heave your big, full, awkward suitcase down on to the platform. There are no trolleys in sight, so you set off towards the barrier, carrying the case. It's heavy, but not too heavy. You can handle it. And anyway there'll probably be a trolley somewhere on the main concourse.

You lug the suitcase past the barrier, then put it down while you cast around for a trolley. There aren't any, as it turns out, but at least you've had a brief rest. The trouble is, you've got a long walk ahead of you. Oh well, it can't be helped. You pick up the suitcase again, and heft it in your hand. No, it's not too bad. You can manage it all right.

But after five minutes, there's no denying it: the suitcase *is* seriously heavy. Much heavier than you'd thought. You try switching it to the other hand. Yes, that's better.

On you trudge, alternately switching the case from hand to hand. But it's not getting any lighter. Your arms are aching badly now. So are both your shoulders. What's more your back is sending out warning signals, and your fingers are on fire. But there's still a long way to go. You set yourself a target. You'll get as far as the hamburger stall before putting the suitcase down for a rest.

You really, really try, but you don't make it. Your body was telling you that if you persisted, then some sort of damage would result. You'd pull a muscle or slip a disc. So you stop, put the case on the ground, and sit on it. You allow yourself five minutes.

But what if it's impossible, for some reason, to put the suitcase down? What if there's no alternative to go on lugging that enormous, and by now harmful, load?

Hmmmmmm. Good question. Mind you, it's only a hypothetical one, because NOBODY goes on carrying their own bag when it's become that heavy. Doesn't

245

matter what's in it, doesn't matter if they're halfway across a road at the time – down it goes, albeit for only a few seconds. But carers can't do that. They may be aching, they may be breaking, but they're stuck with carrying that load.

Is this where you are? Then you may have reached the break point. This is what it's called because

- either you take a break
- or you risk a breakdown.

TGIF-IW

You've heard of Thank God It's Friday. No, not the restaurant; what you used to say at the end of the week, in the days when you could take Saturday off. In some ways the anticipation was almost as good as the weekend itself.

Not all workers get a whole weekend off, obviously. But almost all of them take some sort of regular break which they can look forward to. All except us, that is.

Our time off is occasional, irregular, and measured in half-hours. The Thank God It's Friday feeling is not for us. The best we can do is TGIF-IW (Thank God It's Friday – I Wish).

> Owing to popular demand, tomorrow has been cancelled and today will be repeated.
>
> *Another silly office sign*

Except that it's not by popular demand in our case. No matter how much we long for a break, need a break, feel we'll crack up if we don't get a break – today is always repeated, and the break never seems to come.

Reality or mirage?

The need for carers to take a break is real enough. It's recognised and documented. What's more, a solution has been invented and given a name.

The solution:

> 'Short-term or temporary care for people with disabilities so that their families can take a break. Care can be provided in several settings, depending on the level of care needed, the urgency, personal choice and cost. It is sometimes possible to arrange in your own home.'
>
> *Official booklet issued to carers*

The name:

Respite care. I've also heard it described, irritatingly, as 'a gift of time'.*

When you first hear about respite care, you could be excused for experiencing a surge of relief such as a desert traveller might feel on sighting an oasis.

The trouble is that the respite care, like the oasis, could be a mirage. For the rider on a camel, who knows his way around the desert and may even be guided by map or GPS receiver, there's a good chance that the oasis will be real. For the carer, it probably *is* a mirage.

---

* Well, I find it irritating. Other workers get statutory holiday and paid leave, whereas we have to be grateful for a gift of time, always assuming someone will give it to us.

Or is this just depressing and unhelpful cynicism? Well, here's what happens to Carer X. She's told she needs some respite. She knows it's true. Her body and very soul are screaming for a break. She's assured by supporters and Officialdom alike that respite care is available, that she and her piglet qualify for it, and that it'll happen. But somehow or other, it never does.

She's puzzled. Is it just her? She asks around, and what she discovers is that hardly any carers get respite. Now she's even more puzzled. How can this be?

Poor old Carer X is too close to the problem, and too desperate for a break, to understand what's going on. The question she should have been asking was:

How could all carers get respite?

There isn't the infrastructure for it. Yes, it would be lovely if we could all work a five-day week and have evenings and weekends off. But there aren't enough relief carers to stand in for us, so it's clearly impossible. How about a two-week break every six months? Equally out of the question. Where would the money come from?

No, it's a lovely idea, but that's all it is.

Well, then, why don't the support groups and the officials explain this to us? Then at least we wouldn't be subjected to the gloom of disappointment and frustration.

It's because we'd stop caring or our health would give out. So what they do is give us the smell of a holiday, but not the holiday itself. And it works. We're all still here, aren't we? Caring away for all we're worth.

Oh all right, this *is* cynical. And if you're still with me, I half apologise. Only half, because there's a certain amount of truth in what I've just said, even if it isn't the whole truth.

The rest of the reason that we don't get the respite care we crave and deserve is that many of us wouldn't take it even if it was offered.

It's the carers who say no

Hang on a minute. Even though we're cracking up under the strain, even though we're desperate for some relief, and even when an opportunity to take a break arises, we deliberately choose not to take it?

Ridiculous?

Not really. Read on.

The piglet isn't keen

To be fair, if you were the piglet, would you want to be sent away? Would you want to be put in an institution, or placed in the hands of new people?

They know where they are with you. What they don't know is that you're at screaming point – even if it's them who've been screaming at you. The fact of the matter is that you *are* looking after them rather well. They're probably scared about what would happen to them if you were to stop, even temporarily.

You can explain till you're blue in the face that a change is as good as a rest, and any other comforting clichés that spring to mind. But the unknown can be daunting for anyone. For piglets, who are dependent on other people, it can be seriously frightening.

They may beg you not to leave them. Or they may do the opposite, and say: 'You ought to get away from me for a bit. You deserve it. I want you to.' But you sense that their heart's not in it. You can tell they're unhappy about it.

Either way, you decide you really can't bring yourself to subject them to it.

Can't afford it

You don't get paid to look after your piglet. But anybody who takes over from you will have to be paid – unless you're exceptionally lucky in your friends.

Moreover, if the piglet is to receive respite care in a home, there'll be accommodation charges on top. The whole thing could be so expensive that it doesn't bear thinking about.

You know there's a possibility of financial help, but that's going to necessitate begging and paperwork and interviews and hassle, and you're not sure if you can bring yourself to go through all that.

It's easier to decide that you can't afford it, and that's that.

Don't know how to begin

The logistical difficulties of respite care are immense. Can somebody else do all the stuff you do for your piglet? Would they be reliable? How are you to set about locating somewhere for the piglet to go? How would you transport them? Pay? Sell the idea to the piglet?

It might well be different if someone turned up on your doorstep one morning and announced that respite care had been arranged. 'Here's how it's going to work,' they'd say, and all you and your piglet would have to do is go along with it.

But this is never going to happen, and you know it isn't. You also know you could research respite care, if you had the time and the energy. But somehow you haven't, so you don't.

All too difficult

Let's say you *have* done the research. You've found somewhere for your piglet to go for a week, and you think you know how it's going to be paid for. Now you turn your mind to the preparation period, when you have to face the piglet's worries and recriminations.

It's going to get really bad when the time comes to pack.

While they're away, will you check up on them? How often? What will happen if it goes wrong and they need to come home? Even if all goes well and they don't come back till the end of the respite period, what's it going to be like then? The situation might become worse then than it is now.

No, it's all too difficult. You cancel the whole thing.

Martyrdom

Of course you're not being a martyr – I know that. It's just that you're indispensable. When you say (to yourself or concerned friends): 'I can't possibly leave my piglet for more than five minutes,' it's no more than the truth.

Even so, feeling indispensable has its compensations. And martyrdom (which is what it looks like to other people) can be quite beguiling.

The problem with respite care is that it de-martyrs you. Hand your piglet over to someone else to look after, and where does that leave you? Feeling less important, that's where.

Now, I'm not saying this is why you haven't taken a break. In your case, I know, there are real problems and difficulties. All I'm saying is that some carers who could take a break don't, for the wrong reasons.

Guilt

All carers feel guilty. We may not be at all clear what we're guilty of, but we're sure there's something.

There are times when we know all too well that we've done something terrible, or thought something unthinkable. Then we even have a reason for feeling guilty. We may have given our piglet a slap or a push. Perhaps we shouted at them, or wilfully didn't do something we knew they wanted.

Suddenly, along comes the possibility of getting away from them for a week. But if we seize the opportunity, we'd feel really bad about ourselves. We may long to do it, but know we wouldn't be able to escape from the feeling of guilt if we did. So in the end we don't.

Tried, failed, won't go through that again

Maybe once you actually did arrange some respite care, and your piglet went away to a home. But it didn't work out at all well. In fact, it was awful. When you went to collect them, you found that they hadn't been given their medication, they'd been left to vegetate all day long, they were in a filthy condition, miserable and confused.

You got them back home, and it took days and days for them to recover. You swore you'd never put either them or yourself through that again.

So you haven't.

Choking the cat

There are more ways of killing a cat than choking it with cream. And there are other ways of achieving respite care besides sending your piglet away to a home.

You'd better look at all of them. Because it doesn't really

matter whether you've decided that a break is out of the question or not. The fact is, you've gotta have the break. It's like sleep. Deciding to do without it is not an option. Try to go without, and sooner or later something will give way. Your body, your mind, your spirit, your will to carry on. Something.

Friends

I've just written that sub-head, and now I'm not sure whether to go on with this paragraph. What I was going to say was that you might be able to persuade some, or even just one, of your friends to pop round to babysit. I was going to suggest that you could ask them to take over long enough for you to nip off somewhere, or even get your head down for a couple of hours of uninterrupted sleep.

But is that pie in the sky? I mean, if they haven't offered yet, are they going to come good now?

> 'You might be lucky, and get a friend to provide a bit of respite. But it's more usual for them to be suddenly busy or away when you need them.'
>
> *The Hon. Sec. of a multiple sclerosis support group.*

Give them their due, they always have excellent excuses. So should we just write them off as a lost cause, and look elsewhere?

I don't think so. What I've found is that Chaos Theory applies to respite care as much as it does to Officialdom (if that mystifies you, it's something I was saying back in Chapter 7). Order suddenly surprises you by emerging out of the chaos. Just when you've resigned yourself to bearing the load unaided, a friend will not only come up with an offer but even stand by it. And it'll usually be someone you haven't asked.

The level of respite care they can provide will depend as much on your piglet's needs as the friend's willingness. But it's not unknown (it almost is, but not quite) for someone to offer to move into your place and do everything you normally do, while you push off for a few days.

Don't believe me? Then who's being cynical now?

Day centres

The most common sort of respite care is the day centre. This is a place staffed by professional care-workers where your piglet can spend the day, or a good part of the day. It can be funded by Social Services, or a charity, or a support group. Some piglets attend their day centre regularly – say once or twice a week.

It's this very regularity which bestows the value. It provides the TGIF factor. In fact, if your piglet's day there is Friday, you can even say the words.

Then again, attending once a week becomes part of the routine, and therefore more acceptable to the piglet. A day centre really can be a blessing to both of you. A true gift of time.

Other places are day centres in disguise. Maybe your local community centre runs a disabled group which will provide care for a few hours under the guise of a coffee morning or a craft lesson.

Time to yourself in another room

You may be able to snatch some moments of respite without the aid of other people. Whether you can or not will depend on the nature of the disability and of your piglet's temperament. And of yours, come to that.

When I'm tapping away at my keyboard my piglet thinks I'm working. Which I'm not, of course. Sitting here writing to you hardly constitutes work. In fact, it's the reverse. It's respite. My theory is that she wouldn't let me get away with it if she didn't think it was work, and therefore important.

The arrangement we have is that while I'm working I'm not to be disturbed. She forgets a bit. Sometimes. And then she calls out that she needs this or that. But she's got better at leaving me alone. And I've got better at being deaf.

Hang on, what's that noise? No, I can't hear anything.

Catnapping

I've mentioned somewhere else in this book that single-handed sailing is a whole lot easier than caring, but that the two of them have things in common. In both, it's hard to take a break when you need it, but if you don't you can break something.

On board the boat, the difficulty is to snatch enough sleep. Stay unconscious for too long, and you could run into another vessel or aground. Even when you're not looking out, you may need to get up to reef the sails, or to adjust the self-steering.

At home with your piglet, it's rare for a ship to heave into view at 2 am. It's your piglet you need a rest from. You can't get off the yacht in mid-ocean to lie down on a hotel room bed. And you can't walk away from the piglet. In both cases, what you *can* do is catnap.

Catnapping for sailors means snatching sleep when and where you can. You don't have to get undressed, you don't even have to lie down. But nodding off for five minutes here, a quarter of an hour there, can keep you going. It's possible to go for weeks without sleeping for more than 30 minutes at a time. You may not be operating at maximum efficiency, but you'll be alert enough to be safe.

Catnapping for carers isn't about sleep so much as respite. What you do is leave home in your mind, for a quarter of an hour here, and half an hour there. You shut yourself off from your caring. You could be doing the ironing, cooking supper, even giving your piglet a bath. Wherever and whatever, you just take a mental break while you're doing it on autopilot. It doesn't sound very rewarding, but it could save your life.

255

Three conventional types of respite care

Catnapping is good, but a long night's sleep is better. And so with respite. A week's break, in which you get away completely from your caring role, is what you really need. Luckily for you, you don't have to wait till the voyage is over, unlike the single-handed sailor. There are three broad options:

Piglet goes away

This is mainstream respite care, in which the piglet goes into a home, hospital, or specialist care unit for a week, ten days or a fortnight. While they're there they'll be looked after by care-workers, and you can (in theory) stop not only doing things for them but thinking about them as well.

What you do with the time can, weirdly, be problematical, but the theory is that you can either stay at home and do un-carer-like things (like sleeping for nine hours at a stretch, eating when you feel like it, having fast and furious conversations with friends, having sex even, running and jumping, hanging out in pubs) or go off on holiday somewhere.

Pro:	*Con:*
You really want me to tell you what the advantages are? Come on!	George's daughter went into respite care in a specialist nursing home, but after three days he was asked to take her away. She was disruptive, he was told on the telephone. They couldn't do anything with her.
	When he got there, he said she was never like that normally, except sometimes while waiting

for her medication to kick in. 'What medication?' they enquired. Eventually they found it all, unused. Instructions about it were included in her notes, which apparently hadn't been read. None of the medication had been administered.*

She had also been left to feed herself, something she hadn't been able to do for years.

Piglet stays at home

In this version professional care-workers look after the piglet at home while you take yourself elsewhere.

Pro:	Con:
Your piglet isn't confronted by strange surroundings in addition to the trauma of being cared for by someone other than you.	It's hard to find helpers willing to care for mental health patients. The way it works is that the more care the piglet needs, the harder it is to find anyone to provide it.
	And there's always the danger that visiting care-workers will fall down on the job, or even that they won't turn up. This has been known.

* The other version of this scenario is that the piglet *is* given drugs, but ones which they don't normally have. These will probably be sedatives, administered in order that the staff can have an easy life.

You both go away together

There are a number of enlightened care centres which accept piglets and their carers together. The idea is that during the day you go off and do your own thing while the professional staff care for your piglet. When you get back each evening you might share a meal and even a bedroom with your piglet, and swap notes with one another.

Pro:	Con:
You go on holiday together – a much friendlier and more kindly prospect for the piglet.	It may not be much of a holiday for you, even though it's pretty well bound to be an expensive one. And your choice of location is strictly limited.

How would you like to pay?

This is the silly question they always ask you when you check into a conventional hotel. It's even sillier when you're talking about respite care. The answer is: extremely slowly. Or even: not at all.

The trouble is, you can't help comparing the amounts of money that paid care-workers expect with what you have to get by on. So the cost of respite care will seem absurdly high. So high that you may very well decide it's unaffordable.

Don't.

Don't conclude it's out of reach, that is. The funding will be out there somewhere. It may be available from Social Services, or if not from them then from a charity or perhaps your support group.

So before you shrug your shoulders and say: 'Oh well, I'd like a break but it turns out that I can't afford it; just have to soldier on, I suppose,' start asking around. If asking doesn't work, demand. Remember, it's break or break.

How to spend it

No, not the money. Your time off. It sounds crazy, but you forget.

Even though I've been preaching the Selfish Pig doctrine at you as loudly as I can, you probably haven't been nearly selfish enough. In fact, you've probably given so much to your caring that you've almost lost all sense of self. The result of this is that when you wake up on the first morning of respite and realise that your piglet isn't there, you won't be able to think of anything you want to do.

I can tell you what not to do.

- Do NOT clean the house.
- Do NOT tidy the piglet's cupboards.
- Do NOT tackle any Officialdom paperwork.
- Do NOT do anything at all connected with caring.

But can I call the shots on what you should do? This is harder. Of course, there's a chance that you may know exactly what you need. It might be something very simple but normally unattainable, like a long unbroken sleep. Or the ability to potter about in your own home without being at somebody else's beck and call.

Otherwise, the trick is very simple:

- Get selfish.

Re-entering the atmosphere

Are you reading this chapter before organising any respite care? In that case, skip this last bit for now. You can read it when the holiday is over and you've come back down to earth.

Okay? Welcome back. Feel as if the break has done you good? No?

It seems ironic, but when you get the break you've been longing for, you don't know how to make the best of it. And then, after it's all over, you're not sure if it was worth having. You might even feel more stressed than you did before the respite.

I think what happens is that we become accustomed to all the restrictions and routines of caring. Even though they rub and are uncomfortable, we develop calluses and become, to a certain extent, inured. When we put the load down for more than a few minutes, the protective skin begins to wear off. We remember what life used to be like, and experience what it could be again.

Then, just as you're getting used to being carefree, you're back in harness. And it chafes, badly.

You wonder whether the whole exercise was a waste of time. After all, the respite care was a real pain to set up; it didn't last very long; and now that it's over you don't feel any benefit (in fact, it seems to have made things even harder to put up with).

Luckily, these negative feelings are temporary. You'll find the break *did* do you good. Once you've re-grown your calluses, you'll cope more strongly. And you'll have learned one more lesson about how to be a carer. You'll have learned how to take a break without first breaking up.

CHAPTER 16

The independence catch

The independence catch

Piglets are, by definition, dependent. Which is not, on the whole, the way they would want it, given a choice.

It's your piglet's dependency which has turned you into a carer. And that, in its turn, is not exactly the way *you* would prefer it.

So, reasonably enough, you're probably keen to do what you can to make your piglet less dependent. Or, at least, to preserve for as long as possible such independence as they have. The more successful you are at this, the better life will be for the piglet. And the lighter your own load.

Except, needless to say, it's not quite as simple as that. There's not only a catch. There are several.

Catch 1

Today's the day of the assessment. You've applied to Officialdom for some help, and they're sending an expert round to check that your piglet is as disabled as you claim, and that you qualify for the help you say you need.

The assessor is due to turn up this morning. She made the appointment and specified the time, not you. You would have scheduled it for late afternoon. The trouble with mornings is that your piglet is always firing on twelve cylinders. Soon after lunch fatigue sets in, and then anyone can see how things are. But mornings . . . You're concerned.

The assessor is here. Clipboard on lap, brow slightly furrowed, gentle smile in place. She's asking the questions you expected, always directed at the piglet and not at you. And she's been getting the answers you dreaded. Here comes another one now. 'Do you need help going to the toilet?'

You think about what happened only an hour earlier. You trod in something squishy and didn't even need to look down to know what it was. That particular soft warm texture has become very familiar of late. At least you knew exactly how to deal with it. In the old days, when it wasn't such a usual occurrence, you were never sure which to clean up first: the piglet or the floor. If you tended to the piglet, you often trod in other, hitherto undiscovered, messes in the process. But if you tried to get the piglet to stay in one place while you cleaned up the surroundings, they somehow didn't, and the cleaning process became extended.

This morning it had all been relatively trouble-free. It hadn't taken more than half an hour, and the only remaining signs were a faint whiff of disinfectant.

'No, I can manage perfectly on my own.' This is your piglet speaking, sitting up straight, clearly articulating, holding the assessor's gaze with a look of controlled rationality.

The assessor makes a note, and you let out a low groan.

What should you do? To preserve your piglet's dignity, self-esteem and sense of independence (or appearance of independence, because you're never sure whether they're in denial, unaware, or just plain lying) you know you ought to hold your peace. But if you do, the chances of your being awarded the help you're looking for are zilch. It's the first independence catch.

Catch 2

This is the other side of Catch 1. You've got the assessor in your house, sitting on the sofa opposite, making notes. What's the point of letting her go away with the wrong impression? So you cough, wait for the assessor to look up at you, then hold the piglet's hand while you talk gently to them: 'Yes, you do need help sometimes,' you say, in a reminding kind of way. 'Shall we talk about what happened this morning?'

You're uncomfortable about confronting the truth. You don't want to belittle the piglet (which is how they're going to feel about it) because it's such an unkind thing to do. There will also be repercussions over the coming days, and you'll live to regret it.

Plus, you're worried about introducing a note of conflict into the assessment. Which one of you will the assessor believe? Suddenly you're overwhelmed by a rush of guilt for the lies which the assessor will probably think you're telling, but which you aren't.

Catch 3

Suppose your piglet has a touch of dementia. Officialdom has instructed you time and again to respect the piglet's wishes and independence. They haven't explained how you should do this – just that behind the dementia there's a human being.

The thing that the piglet hates more than anything else in the world is washing. At bath-time they cry, scratch, kick, and shout abuse. You almost never get them clean.

All right, then. The human being doesn't want to be scrubbed daily. So you stop insisting. Ever since, life has become much more easy-going for both of you. It's true there's an odd smell hanging about. But neither of you notices that sort of thing nowadays. And it's rare to receive visitors. Besides, it's not that you're neglecting the piglet. What you're doing is respecting their independence.

Next thing, someone is at your door. A relation, neighbour, or God forbid a representative of Officialdom. They come inside, notice, are careful where they put their hands, sniff delicately. And it's clear what they think about your ability to care.

Catch 4

There's nothing wrong with your piglet's reasoning processes (say). They're as sane as you are, maybe more so at times.

What they do is bully you. They should have been in the army. As long as they're awake, they're issuing orders, pausing only to shout out criticisms which you can hear even from the opposite end of the house.

'You've put my white pants in the same wash as the dark colours. They're ruined. You're always doing that. What's wrong with you? Look at them. I don't know how you can do that. I never used to do that when I did the washing. I'm going to take over from you. You don't seem to realise that you can't put my white pants in with dark colours. I don't know why you do it. You're always doing it.'

Okay, you're supposed to encourage their independence, aren't you? Well, then, they can bloody well do the washing themselves. Except, you remember, they can't. All right, then, they can find another pair of pants in the drawer and put them on all by themselves.

You stalk about, knowing that they can't do this either. Knowing they'll try, just to put you in your place. Knowing they'll still be trying an hour from now. Serve them right. Do them good.

All the while, you can't stop yourself thinking about what makes them so bloody-minded. You don't need to be told what the reason is. You've worked that one out long since. It's because they miss their independence. They hate having to rely on you for everything. Sometimes they even hate you because they're reliant on you.

And you're punishing them for that?

You storm into the room where a struggle to put the pants on is taking place. You help and they submit. Neither of you says anything because both your mouths are clamped shut, your lips in a thin tight line.

Catch 5

'I can do it' is a familiar cry in your house. Your heart sinks when you hear it, because you know it refers to something they really can't do.

This time it's about making the tea. But for once you just can't bear it.

'You go and sit down, and I'll do it,' you say, busying yourself with kettle and cups.

You're not being entirely selfish. The television programme they've been looking forward to all day starts in ten minutes, and it takes them at least half an hour to make tea – that's on the days when they can do it at all. If they come to grief with the tea AND miss the programme, they'll be sad.

And they'll be sure to make you sad, too.

So for both your sakes you make the tea, and rub your piglet's nose in their dependence.

Catch 6

Today you're feeling strong, and good, and generous. And time is on your side. So when they announce that they're going to make the tea, you say: 'Thank you. That would be really kind.'

You're at their side within a nano-second of the crash. It's not that you have the reflexes of a racing driver (though you do, now). It's that you were expecting something to happen, even though you weren't sure what it would be.

There's sugar all over the floor. You can hear it scrunch under your feet as you sprint into the kitchen. You can see at a glance that they dropped the big sugar container. Not the small unbreakable one that lives on the worktop, but the big heavy glass one that you keep on the top shelf out of their reach. Shards of glass are mixed with the sugar, and some of the sugar has a pink tinge to it, from the blood.

Despite the spectacular nature of the accident, you have it all cleaned up in seconds. You have to, to prevent further injury. At least, that's the main reason. Another part of the reason is to soften any sense of failure and inadequacy the piglet might suffer by seeing the mess. And yet another part is in case Officialdom comes to the door and suspects you of causing the injury.

Catch 7

'I want my slippers on.' It's a fair request. You have an idea that *you* wouldn't bother to pull your slippers on your own feet if you were rich enough to have a servant who would do it for you. I mean, come on, you have to ease your feet into them, and sometimes the backs won't slide up past your heels of their own accord. When this happens there's nothing for it but to bend down and stick your finger inside, then yank them up. It's hard work.

In the days when I had to wear a suit and tie, and when shoes had laces, I used to promise myself I'd have a servant – after I'd made my millions and had servants – whose sole job would be to iron my shoelaces and press my ties.

Your piglet isn't stupid. They haven't made any more money than you have, but they've got the servant. Why shouldn't they make use of you?

Now, you're well aware of the arguments. You've been through all this before. But today you do what they ask, and pull their slippers on for them. You know you're aiding and abetting their dependence. Speeding them towards total helplessness. Excising a few more molecules of self-worth.

What the hell? You're all for an easy life. You can't be expected to do the right thing every second of every day.

'There you are.' You stand up. 'Comfortable now?'

Catch 8

'I want my slippers on.' Only, this time, they're going to have to do it by themselves. They can, perfectly well. The only reason they like you to do it is because they're lazy, because you're there, and because they're used to having you do things for them. But it can't be good for them. They should be trying to be independent.

So this time, you don't pick their foot up. You put yours down.

'Try to do it yourself,' you say, 'and if you get stuck I'll help.' This is a cop-out, but you hope it'll persuade the piglet to do the job without any intervention from you.

It doesn't work.

In no time you've got a battle on your hands. It might not be about the slippers. It could be about something apparently unrelated. But you both know it was the slippers that caused it. And whatever it is, however ludicrous, it's endangering your entire day. You can feel the stress level building up. The deep breathing has no effect. You try the shouting.

Bugger it, next time you'll put the damn slippers on. To hell with the piglet's independence.

Catch 9

Who said it was the piglet who was the dependant in this relationship? It's YOU.

If it weren't for this disability, you wouldn't be a carer, and everything would be completely different. But your piglet *does* have the disability, and you *are* looking after them. Consequently your entire lifestyle is governed by your piglet and the disability.

In other words, you depend on your piglet just as much as the piglet depends on you. And sometimes you could do with an independence boost too.

Catch 10

The relationship between carer and piglet is about as intimate as it can get, physically. But somewhere along the line, honesty seems to have evaporated.

You've become a secret agent. You didn't mean to be, and you don't like it, but that's how it has to be. How can you read the leaflets about nursing homes in front of them? They might think you were planning to send them away, and be frightened. So you study them in private.

Ditto the medical prognosis, the fact sheets about the illness, the negotiations between you and Officialdom concerning respite and care-workers. Secrecy builds up, layer upon layer.

You let it happen because of your protective feelings towards the piglet. If they're to maintain a perception of at least *some* independence, they mustn't be made aware that you're doing practically everything for them. But there are times when you'd rather allow everything to come out into the open.

Catch 11

When you're with other people, someone sooner or later will wink at you, taking care that your piglet doesn't see. They're saying, silently: 'You and I, we're nice and normal, and aren't we good to be pretending your piglet is too, when we both know they're not?'

Sometimes you even go along with this, guiltily complicit, because you don't know how not to. They've put you in a position where you're either disloyal to your piglet or rude to your friend.

It seems that loyalty has gone out of the window, too.

Catch 12

This is the one where your piglet doesn't have an obvious disability – or, even if it's obvious to you, other people sometimes appear not to be aware of it. This would be empowering for your piglet if it were not for the fact that it can put the piglet in an awkward position.

Let's say you're having a meal in company with others, and somebody plonks a plate down in front of your piglet. It's laden with stuff which needs to be cut up, a manoeuvre thought by everyone there to be well within the piglet's capabilities, but which in fact is something they can no longer do.

You look into your piglet's face for a signal, but there isn't one. They're preparing to tackle the plate, as is expected of them. What you know, but nobody else does, is that this is going to lead with dreadful inevitability to a choking fit of life-threatening proportions. You can easily avert it. All you have to do is lean across and cut up the food into bite-sized chunks. But to do so will make it obvious to all that this is something the piglet needs to have done for them – and you know they would rather die than have their disability aired in public like dirty underwear.

Death by asphyxiation or shame. The piglet is the one who seems destined to suffer one of these fates, but you're the one who has to decide.

Catch 13

I didn't mean to fill this book with yachty stories, but I need to tell you about the time we sailed into Poole Harbour. It was at the very beginning of our nine-year cruise, before I was accustomed to the boat and to handling her on my own. My intention was to go alongside Poole Quay. I had prepared lines fore and aft, and hung out fenders, and was edging the boat towards a vacant space between a fishing boat and another yacht.

In that confined space our boat seemed unwieldy, and I wasn't sure how she'd respond. I really wanted my piglet up on the foredeck so that she could pass the line to whoever was standing on the dock. I knew that if the bow wasn't secured, it would be blown off by the wind, and in no time at all we'd be entangled with the fishing boat.

But my piglet, suspecting she might not be able to perform this task, was busying herself below with the washing-up. I stood at the wheel, trying to decide whether I would do more harm than good if I ran up to the foredeck, made the bow line fast, and then sprinted back aft to retrieve the stern line. But luckily, there was a watching man standing on the dock. I called out to him: 'Could you grab my bow line?'

He gazed back, interested. 'Are you on your own?'

I couldn't say yes, in case my piglet stuck her head up through the companionway. But if I said no, he might not help, thinking my crew would appear at any second. So I told him: 'My wife is disabled.'

It was the first time I had ever said such a thing. I had let the cat out of the bag to a complete stranger without even asking permission. A crashing wave of appalling guilt swept over me.

The man retrieved our bow line and made it fast to a ring on the quay. I secured the stern line. My piglet stayed below. And for the whole of the rest of the day I was conscious of having entered new territory. I had admitted publicly to the disability even though I knew it would be hurtful to my piglet to do so.

I could have gone on pretending that there was nothing wrong with her, as she did. But I told the truth, and it made me feel like a bastard.

Catch 14

Since I've broken my own rule and am now talking about myself instead of about you, I'll illustrate the next one with another story involving my piglet. (Then I'll stop.)

Our cruise is now over, and we're living ashore. One day a week my piglet goes to a day centre five miles away. She likes to get there on her own, by bus. The bus starts from near where we live, and drops her off right next to the day centre. The trip is relatively simple, though it takes an hour.

She could just as easily go by taxi. More easily, in fact, and also more cheaply since Social Services will pick up the cost. But she likes the adventure of going by bus. Taxis are nowhere near as much fun.

Coming back is more fraught. By then she's very tired, and she has to wait for the bus to come along. It might be late, and all the while she's standing by the side of the road. The list of things that could go wrong is quite extensive. She could

- fall over while waiting
- catch the wrong bus
- get wet
- get cold
- get lost
- get injured.

At the day centre, they're concerned, and sometimes they telephone me to ask whether they should put her in a taxi or let her take the bus. What's the correct decision?

The catch here is about the conflict between safety and independence. When we pushed off in our boat, heading across thousands of miles of ocean where there was no hope of rescue if we ran into trouble, we were sure that independence ought to win out over safety any day. Now, on dry land, and further into our disability, I'm not so sure.

It was our specialist doctor who gave me guidance on this one. She said to both of us: 'Life is all about risk. It can never be eliminated. If you want to take the bus but are concerned that something could go wrong, take the bus. If you are apprehensive that something may go wrong and consequently are frightened to take the bus, don't take the bus.'

Even so, it can be hard to tell right from wrong in questions like these. Friends don't help. They tell you: 'If something happens, so be it.' And you know what they mean is: 'Best thing, really.'

As always, you find yourself questioning your own motives. Are you encouraging them to be independent, or purposefully launching them into danger? Do you subconsciously want them not to take the bus, but to be run over by one?

Catch 15

Preserving your piglet's independence (or keeping total dependence at bay) means that you should care just enough, but no more. Exceed that amount of care, and it's unnecessary care. Self-defeating care. Wrongful care.

A good way of caring just enough is to be an SP. I may have mentioned this before. But how much of an SP should you be? Take it to its logical conclusion and you'd loll about in an armchair all day reading the racing pages, ignoring their shouts for help.

Okay, so that's going too far. But how do you find the right level of selfish piggery? Nobody will tell you. No-one will say '*Do* do this, but *don't* do that.' It's down to you to decide, and you have no means of knowing how. You're too close to your piglet, and together you go back too far for you to be wise. You're also too inexperienced. Unlike paid care-workers, you only have this one case history to draw on. The catch is that you understand the task – to limit their dependence – but you don't have the tools to do it.

Catch 16

Then there's the money trap. This is one of the complicated ones. You need to be at home, caring, but you can't because there isn't enough money. So you also need to be out generating money.

But if you work at something other than your caring job, there's less time available to care. What's more, the other job will deplete your supplies of energy as well as time. All in all you'll be less effective as a carer.

But caring has to be the most important job. So what do you do? The usual response is to go round and round in circles. But it's not a very useful one.

Catch 17

Imagine you're holding on to something that's important to you, but it's gradually slipping out of your grasp. Your natural response is to cling on even more tightly.

I guess that's what happens with piglets. The less they can do for themselves, the more they hang on to what they *can* do. But what they can do differs from day to day. So sooner or later you're going to be doing something for them that they want to do by themselves, without help from you. Which causes them to shout at you.

Next day, you may find yourself *not* doing something which they want to have done for them. And this also causes them to shout at you.

As their independence slips away, there'll be more and more occasions when orders are issued, demands shouted out, and criticisms voiced. If you didn't know better, you'd think the underlying reason was that the piglet was just being difficult.

You *do* know better, it goes without saying. But sometimes you forget.

Catch 18

Privacy figures large in the independence struggle. There are a number of items which the piglet ought to have about their person whenever they go out of the house: some money, front door key, notice explaining about their disability and listing telephone numbers to be contacted in case of emergency. The trouble is, these items tend to get left behind.

As a caring carer, your job is to go through the piglet's pockets or handbag to check that everything's in place. Like a thief or a spy.

You know you aren't really rifling their privacy. Even so, you can feel a bit shifty while you do it.

Catch 19

And then there's the one . . . ah, forget it. You've got the point.

In any case, you can probably think of plenty of other examples of the independence catch on your own.

Do you have one you think ought to be included? Try sending it to me* so that I can put it in next time. In the meantime, let's fast-forward to

Catch 22

> There was only one catch and that was Catch-22, which specified that a concern for one's safety in the face of dangers that were real and immediate was the process of a rational mind. Orr was crazy and could be grounded. All he had to do was ask; and as soon as he did, he would no longer be crazy and have to fly more missions. Orr would be crazy to fly more missions and sane if he didn't, but if he was sane he had to fly them. If he flew them he was crazy and didn't have to; but if he didn't want to he was sane and had to. Yossarian was moved very deeply by the absolute simplicity of this clause of Catch-22 and let out a respectful whistle.
>
> 'That's some catch, that Catch-22,' he observed.
> 'It's the best there is,' Doc Daneeka agreed.
>
> Catch-22, *by Joseph Heller*

---

* The publisher's address can be found in the front of this book.

That's the famous Catch 22. Ours is a bit different because we don't get grounded if we're crazy. All carers are crazy anyway (see Chapter 10).

Our Catch 22 is this. The more care we give, the higher the level of dependence we foist on our piglets; the more they depend, the harder the job of caring for them; the harder the job, the less likely it is that we'll do it well; the less well we do it, the worse we are at caring.

This is the independence catch.

And I reckon it's just as good as Doc Daneeka's.

CHAPTER 17

Is there anyone out there?

Imagine

Where are they?

Don't know you're there
Know you're there, but think you're doing okay
They're the wrong people

How do you find the right ones?

Clear the decks
Finding the replacements
    Other carers
    Cyberspace
    Telephone
    Support groups
        The specific ones
        General ones for carers

The general public

Is there anyone out there?

Carers are a sad bunch. Not tragic – but ludicrous, absurd, silly and ridiculous. We've got it into our heads that we're on our own – the lot of us. Whereas as soon as you write that down it's clear that it doesn't make any sense. How *can* we be all alone when there are so many of us?

But that's the way it seems. Promises are made and broken. Helping hands look as if they're being extended, but then are swiftly withdrawn. Most carers wouldn't even think of asking whether there was anybody out there, because they've become absolutely certain that there isn't.

Only it's not true. There are plenty of people out there. I'm not referring to *them*, the ones who can't understand, who get in the way, and make everything worse. I'm talking about people who do understand, who step forward to help, who lighten the load, and keep us going. They're there.

That isn't your experience? You haven't run across anybody who actually *does* anything for you? Anybody who contributes anything remotely helpful or useful?

While glancing through other parts of this book you perhaps nodded your head whenever you came to a bit about isolation. But you're shaking it now that I'm taking the other tack.

Well, here's what it is: you're a carer, so your perception has been distorted. You're under the impression that you're having to cope with this thing by yourself. That, whatever people say, you ARE on your own. That in your world there's just you, and of course your piglet.

> 'The worst thing about Alzheimer's is that there's nobody to share your memories with. And we have so many memories.'
>
> *Nancy Reagan*

It all starts with your piglet. Cooped up with them, the two of you form a microcosmic, slightly barmy, but self-contained unit. It doesn't matter whether they have Alzheimer's or something else. It doesn't even matter if they have all their wits about them or not. You spend so much time together doing piglet things and talking piglet talk that the rest of the world starts to take on the appearance of some other, more distant world. It's the carer's isolation syndrome. You feel as if you're alone (which you aren't) and going bonkers (which you probably are, a bit).

Imagine

Okay, now imagine some other carer out there who's going through precisely this experience. Take a look at them. They're desperate, they need help, it isn't forthcoming, they conclude they're on their own. Now imagine that you attract their attention. They notice you, and reach out to you for help.

Can you do anything for them? Yes, you can.

Are you willing to do anything for them? Yes, you are. Of *course*. You'll go out of your way, bend over backwards. Because you've been where they are, and you know what it's like. So not only can you help, not only are you willing to help, but you actually want to help.

There you are, then. If that's the way you feel about it, don't you admit that others probably do as well? Don't you agree that there must be people like you out there, who are in a position to lend a hand and would be more than happy to do it?

Where are they?

Out there. Somewhere.

And it stands to reason that if you're the one who needs the help, but you haven't found anybody prepared to step forward and be useful, the reason is *not* that there isn't anybody out there. It has to be that

- they don't know you're there

- they *do* know you're there, but they think you're doing okay

- the people you're talking to at the moment are the wrong ones.

Don't know you're there

How can they not know you're there, considering that you've been asking for help, pleading for help, yelling for help?

It's because they can't see you. You're invisible. They've been looking at your piglet, but they haven't spotted you.

Doctors are the worst culprits. They're geared up to patients, so they're focusing on the piglet, but not on you. Even if you do manage to persuade them to turn their attention to you, they're quite likely to convert you into a patient as well. Instead of listening while you pour your heart out, they'll prescribe tranquillisers, or begin manipulating your strained back. But they'll fail to see you as a carer who needs help to do the caring.

Know you're there, but think you're doing okay

This is what friends do. They think they know you, but the person they're thinking of, the one they're familiar with, is the old, pre-caring you. You've changed now, and everything has changed for you. But they don't appreciate that. They can't see the struggling carer; just the old, capable you.

They may say, behind your back, that you're a saint. But it doesn't really occur to them that you're in trouble. And it's no

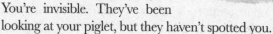

use pressing the point. They'll just decide that you need taking out of yourself, and try to get you to abandon your piglet and come on a pub crawl with them – or something else that (a) you can't do, (b) wouldn't help anyway, and (c) is more for their benefit than yours.

They're the wrong people

You would recognise a carer in distress. You've just said you would. Which means you'd be the right person to lend a hand. Conversely, if someone can't help, or doesn't help, they're the wrong person. A doctor who stares at his computer screen, taps out a prescription, and shouts, 'Next patient' when you've gone to them for help is the wrong doctor.

Anyone who says: 'I'll come round tomorrow and give you a hand,' but fails to turn up, is the wrong helper.

The friend you've tentatively asked to come round and cook a meal for your piglet because you're ill and feeling like death, but who only says: 'You don't look ill' is the wrong friend.

Anyone who constantly puts you in a position where you find yourself saying 'er, y-e-e-e-e-s' when you really mean no is the wrong anyone.

How do you find the right ones?

When you're getting nowhere in the matter of finding help, there's no point in shouting 'Sod the lot of them' and going back to coping, badly, on your own. The trick is to remember that the answer to the question 'Is there anybody out there?' is Yes.

Equally, there's no point in wasting time over the wrong ones. You've got the wrong doctor? This friend is the wrong friend? What are you going to do, work on them till they see the light of day?

No you're not. You're going to dump them. Chuck them out. Clear the decks.

Clear the decks

That sounds as if it can't be right. On the one hand you're feeling isolated, on the other hand what you should do is get rid of the few people you *do* talk to?

But it is right. They're in the way. They're not only not helping, but they're cluttering up your life. Your life as a carer. And you can't afford that.

It also sounds brutal. But it isn't. You don't have to go around taking out contracts on people, or issuing formal letters of dismissal. All you do is recognise that you're not stuck with them. If your doctor's a dud, ask to go on another doctor's list. If your social worker is always barking up the wrong tree, request that another one be allocated to you. In the case of friends who make your heart sink, be less compliant. They'll go away eventually, all by themselves.

And when they have, there'll be room for the right people to come through.

Before we get on to them, I ought to point out that it's not just people we're talking about here. It's other stuff as well. All that old stuff that's getting in the way and making life difficult. Kick that out too.

Like the day centre which is fully booked. Forget it. There are others.

And that wedding which you've been invited to attend. Part of you is keen to go; the rest of you knows it's going to be such hard work once you get there that you'd be better off out of it. If you accept and your piglet comes with you, you'll be too busy looking after them to enjoy the wedding. Alternatively, if you persuade a relief carer to stand in for you at home while you go to the reception, you'll pay for it later when the recriminations kick in.

Stuff like this could be enjoyable, if other people rallied round. But they don't. At least, hardly ever. And who can blame them? They haven't gone to the wedding to mooch around with your piglet. They've gone there to have a good time, to dance and drink champagne.

What you need to do is consign all this sort of thing to the dustbin. There's no point regretting the stuff which you'd like to do but can't, when there are plenty of other things you haven't considered yet but which you *can* do.

Finding the replacements

Once you've cleared the decks – a mental process – you're all set. There's now room in your life for more rewarding people and more possible things.

They don't all have to be new. Once you've stopped making room for the people who were getting in the way, you'll start to become aware of the ones who are left. They were there all along, but you didn't have time to notice them before. Now you do.

Ditto things. They don't all have to be new and different. But now that you've stopped worrying about the stuff you wanted to do but can't, it'll be easier to spot the stuff you can do.

When my piglet and I lived on our boat, shortly before the disability reached the point where it didn't make sense to carry on any longer, things we had got used to doing, and wanted to go on doing, started to become hard. Stuff like boat-to-boat visiting in crowded anchorages. It was how we conducted our social life, but it entailed getting in and out of dinghies, and hauling ourselves up on to other boats' decks. But though this sort of activity wasn't practical any longer, making long passages, even across oceans, posed no problem. At least, no problems connected with encroaching disability. We could still share our adventure together.

So what's this got to do with your predicament? Well, all I'm saying is that the adventure isn't necessarily over for any of us.

There's other stuff out there. You have to look for it, but that's a form of exploration. And when you explore, you discover things. Always.

I've done it again, haven't I? Digressed into philosophy. Okay, back to the question: where do you look for new people, and new things you can do?

Other carers. That's where you look.

Other carers

Carers understand. They know what the questions are, and they also know many of the answers. They've learned the ropes. They may be the only people who are in a position to give you the information and support you're looking for. Apart, of course, from those people who have been carers, even if they aren't any longer. In some ways these ones are even better able to help because they have more time.

I don't say you shouldn't talk to anyone who isn't, or hasn't been, a carer. I know plenty of people who don't have any direct experience of caring at all, but have been (and still are) amazing. But I still had to chuck out quite a bit of dead wood before I'd cleared enough space to concentrate on the good ones.

Do I know any carers I can't relate to, or who can't relate to me? I don't think so. Not really. Do I know any who whinge and complain about their lot? Surprisingly, no. This is what I thought they'd be doing, before I knew any. This is why I avoided other carers and piglets at first. It seemed to me then that it was hard enough shouldering my own load without having to witness the struggles of others. But it's not like that. They're not like that.

The assistance that carers can give each other is very wide-reaching. There's the obvious area of moral support, which is comforting. But there's also an enormous repository of solid information of the kind that you'd expect to come from Officialdom but doesn't. If you really want to find out about benefits, medical services, which doctor to go to, how to get your piglet on or off the toilet, where to go for respite care, how to afford an expensive gadget that you need, how to discover *which* expensive gadget you need,

ask a carer.

Even if a carer doesn't know the answer, they'll either know somebody who does, or they'll know how to set about finding the answer.

Carers are our most useful resource.*

The answer to the question: 'Is there anyone out there?' is really: 'Yes, and they're a carer.'

Cyberspace

Don't know any, or many, or enough, carers? You're surrounded by them, I assure you. Even if you live in the back of beyond so that you practically have to jump on an aeroplane in order to see another human face, there are still dozens of useful, knowledgeable, helpful, willing, wonderful carers within reach. They're all chatting away in cyberspace, exchanging information, propping each other up, on the message boards and in the chatrooms of carers' websites. Admittedly you need a computer connected to a

---

* It's kind of odd that Officialdom doesn't realise this, and make use of carers to provide advice, direct people to services, guide them through the official maze. But they don't. There may be a reason for this. On the other hand, there may not.

telephone line to meet up, and the basic skills necessary to operate them, but once you do you'll never again question whether there's anyone out there.

So important are computers to carers that there are various schemes in place to make them available to carers, in some cases even free of charge.

I'm tempted to list some websites here, but will resist because carers' groups come and go, and because it's easy to find a good one just by searching for 'carers'. On the other hand, maybe this is a good place for me to give credit to The Princess Royal Trust for Carers' website (www.carers.org) which has proved so helpful to me both in my caring and in researching this book.

Telephone

In the UK, the BBC started an initiative to enable carers to get in touch with one another by telephone. It's called Ring Around Carers, and provides a meeting place on the phone, which is both confidential and free.

*

But in neither of those two forums can you actually touch or see the other person. If this doesn't seem like an advantage to you (it will to some), then you really ought to consider joining, or attending, a support group.

Support groups
They come in two shapes:

- Specific support group for your piglet's disability
- General support group for carers.

Both can be international, national, regional or local, and all have something to offer.

The specific ones
I suspect there isn't a disability that doesn't have its own support group even if the disability is nothing more or less than old age. Assuming that there is one for you and your piglet, it'll offer advice, support, news and information some of which will be comforting, some interesting, and some vital.

The only specific support group I've had dealings with is the Huntington's Disease Association, which has been almost literally a life-saver. I have no idea if the HDA is outstanding in the sense of being markedly better than all the others. It's certainly been brilliant, but then so will yours be, probably.

The help I've received from the HDA includes:

- Stress counselling (without which I might not be sitting here bashing the keyboard right now)
- Advice that we were eligible for a reduction of council tax by 25% (this fact had been withheld by all other sources, and was even denied by the local council at first)
- Ongoing information about treatment, and progress towards a cure
- Purchase at their expense of a bath lift
- Training (of me)

- Training (of Social Service care-workers in the peculiarities of Huntington's Disease).

Our local branch also organises regular events and gatherings for all of us, piglets and carers alike. It's hard to say exactly why these are so soothing, but they are. I think it's got something to do with the fact that everyone attending them is in the same boat (though not literally). We all understand one another perfectly. Nobody is asked to do anything that makes them uncomfortable. Anything can be, and is, discussed openly. There are no secrets. We're not a family, exactly. We're closer than that.

General ones for carers

Just as the disability-specific support groups (like the HDA) are focused on people affected by the disability, carer support groups are focused on the carers. In the company of the people attending these, we can sound off about our piglets, and the problems arising from our handling of their care.

Whatever is currently driving you to distraction, you can bet that there'll be somebody else there who has experienced the very same problem, and can tell you how they solved it.

I personally have reason to thank both the carers' groups I've come into contact with. The national one is The Princess Royal Trust for Carers, and the local one is Carers Together. They, along with the HDA, have fully answered my previously shouted question: Is there anybody out there?

This is where they are.

The general public

It's an odd thing, but in the short term you can sometimes find more support and understanding among strangers than from people you know well, or from Officialdom, who ought to know better. And not necessarily just strangers: anyone out there.

According to my friend Mary, when her husband fell over and she needed help to get him on his feet again, she used to run down to the butcher's shop where she could always be sure of finding a pair of willing, beefy hands that would happily be placed at her disposal.

The thing about the world at large is that it keeps its distance, but out of a reluctance to interfere rather than indifference. And probably out of uncertainty as to how best to help, rather than unwillingness to get involved.

The disadvantage of appealing to the world at large for help is that you have to go to them. They're too sensitive to make the first move.

The advantage is that there are an awful lot of them.

Is there anybody out there?

There certainly is.

CHAPTER 18

The messy stuff

A topic that's hard to grasp

Time

Altered relationship

Adapting to the new relationship

Alter your mind
Alter your understanding

Potty training

Can it be prevented?

Minimise it

The piglet's clothing
Their diet
Modifying your house

Those dreadful nights

Bathing

Washing clothes

Doing the housework

Eating

Your piglet's mind

Your mind

The messy stuff

Have you looked at the chapter on sex yet? I only ask because I think this chapter comes into the same category as that one. They're both parts of the book you only need to read if you're having problems with the subject.

Sensible people (I'm not one of them, unfortunately) won't even know what I'm talking about. Messy stuff? What does he mean, and what's it got to do with caring? It's quite possible that you've only checked in here out of curiosity, to find out the answer to this question. If that's the case, go somewhere else. This bit has got nothing to do with you.

So, what is it about? Principally, it's about what the care community calls 'toileting'. Or not getting there in time. Or getting there in time, and what to do about it immediately afterwards. Or never getting there at all.

I may be the only person in the world to have been psyched out by all this stuff. In that case, and with any luck, this means that I'm now talking to myself. Good. Even *I'm* not bothered any more. I can remember what it was like, though, to squirm and go 'Ugh' at the very thought of getting my hands dirty in this way. I suspect I'm not unique. If I once felt like that, I'm prepared to bet somebody else does now. You?

Just now I said that this sort of thing didn't bother me any more. And yet, now that I'm confronting it in these pages I find I'm not at all clear what terms to use. The subject is riddled with

- euphemisms (poo)
- slang (crap)
- techno-medico terms that aren't normally used at home (faeces)
- techno-medico terms that are used in homes where caring goes on (incontinence).

It seems to me that when we have trouble finding words for something it's quite likely because we have trouble thinking about it.

A topic that's hard to grasp

Sorry, I couldn't resist that.

Anyway, we're going to grasp it, if only because when I set out to write this book I wanted to include all the things I wished I'd been told about. And shit – this is the word that comes to my mind, so it's the one I'm going to use (if you're uncomfortable with it, just translate it in your mind to something more congenial) – is one of them.

Incidentally, the term 'incontinent' is often used to describe a person who pees inadvertently in their pants or bed. When it's messier than that, and they also shit in their pants or bed, the phrase is 'doubly incontinent'. I'll get to the peeing bit later on in this section. But let's deal with the serious stuff first.

It may be that because I'm a man I'm not genetically programmed to wipe other people's bottoms. Or perhaps my middle-class upbringing conferred on me a sad and quite unjustifiable fastidiousness. Who knows?

What I do know is that at a point in my life as a carer when I was finding it quite hard to come to terms with coping with somebody else's shit, I wrote about it. I think perhaps I was in search of sympathy. Or possibly just recognition of one of the things that went on behind the closed doors of places where carers look after their piglets. Whatever it was, my brother-in-law, who proof-read the copy for me, rapped me over the knuckles. 'I found the scatological references deeply offensive,' he said.

I didn't publish it. He made me feel ashamed. Even now I'm reluctant to talk about something that is going to cause offence, deep or otherwise.

I'm going to, though, this time. And the reason is that I know a bit more about it now, and what I've discovered might just be welcome news. It's this: if you too are finding it hard to come to terms with this aspect of caring, it's going to get better for you as a result of one of the things that makes most aspects of caring more difficult: time.

Time

It's time which produces the squeeze effect of stress, and leads ultimately to burnout.

When your caring goes on and on and on and on and on and on until you either take a break or suffer a breakdown, the chief culprit is time.

When your piglet does something over and over and over and over and over and over again till you feel like pushing them down the stairs, the problem is not that they do it, or say it, but that they keep on doing it, or saying it. It's time.

BUT, strangely, when you have to cope with shit again and again, it gets easier. Instead of thinking 'If I have to do this one more time I'll go berserk,' you almost stop thinking about it at all. It becomes routine. Except for sleep: see later under 'Those dreadful nights'.

It's when the whole business is new to you that it's so hard to cope with. At least, without scrunching your eyes half-shut and wearing rubber gloves.

So if you haven't had to come to grips with shit yet, but know you *will* have to and are dreading it, don't panic. It will become easier than you dare to hope.

Or have you already discovered, to your intense surprise, that there's nothing much to it after all? Aha! You're becoming a professional.

Why did the prospect ever make you squirm in the first place, do you think?

Altered relationship

One of the things which separates us from paid care-workers is that almost all of us had a different relationship with our piglets once. The person that paid care-workers mop up is a stranger. Or it's someone they've only ever known as a patient. Whereas we're wiping the behind of a parent, a spouse, a partner, a neighbour. At any rate, someone we knew in a different life.

For some reason this altered relationship makes it awkward for us. Perhaps it's because we suspect we'd hate it if our child, or spouse, or partner, or neighbour, performed the same duty on us. We're conscious of what we suppose must be an indignity, and are uncomfortable by proxy. Which is all nonsense, needless to say. If and when you can't do this for yourself you're probably going to be all too happy for somebody else to do it for you. And if it's someone who cares about you, as opposed to someone who does it for a living, so much the better. All right, there's a chance that you'll hate it. But what you'll be unhappy about is the fact of your dependence and loss of ability rather than the fact of having your bottom wiped by someone you know.

Even parents of disabled children face the same altered relationship syndrome, I suspect. Changing your baby's nappy is simply no problem. It just isn't. Well, not usually, anyway. But if the baby grows up and still has to have her nappy changed, there's a changed relationship there, and what didn't use to be a problem can become one.

Take a parent. One moment they're telling you to eat up your greens and do your homework. Next thing, you're changing their nappies. It's a quantum leap in relationships, so no wonder it's psychologically fraught.

Take a lover. In one phase of your life together you're doing all those amazing things to one another, and in the next you're wiping their bottom. Admittedly both acts are very physical, very intimate, and totally secret. But they're as different from one another as passionate kissing is from a session with the dentist.

The reason it becomes easier is that we adapt. It's what we humans are astonishingly good at.

Adapting to the new relationship

I discovered how adaptable we (humans, I mean) are when we (my piglet and I) moved out of our house and on board our boat for the first time. Within days the boat's accommodation had ceased to seem small and cramped, even though by comparison with the smallest flat it certainly was.

It's an old naval signal – it means 'who gives a sh...'

And then there was the trip from Guatemala to Colombia – almost 1,000 miles against strong winds and an adverse current. For the first twenty-four hours we both felt ill as the boat reared and plunged and smashed and reeled, and we thought of giving up. We felt ill for the next two days, but progressively less so even though the weather was just as bad. By the fourth day we were able to sit and read down below without discomfort. And after that (the trip took nine days, incidentally) I was able to work on the boat quite happily, doing jobs like servicing the engine and mending the toilet.

It wasn't that we were in the least hardy or determined or unusual. It's just that human beings can get used to more or less anything. It doesn't even take that long. But as far as the messy aspect of caring is concerned, there are things you can do to speed up the adaptation process.

Alter your mind

Not in the sense of shifting your opinion. Change your mindset is more what I mean. If your piglet is your mother, so long as you continue to think of her as the person she used to be it's going to be hard to bring yourself to wipe her bottom. But as soon as you change that perception of her, and think of her as your piglet, everything becomes simpler. If she had always been your piglet and never your mother, there probably would never have been a problem in the first place.

Alter your understanding

Incontinence is widespread – look, you're going to have to ignore the double entendres; they seem to be inserting themselves into this chapter despite all my efforts to the contrary. What I intended to say is that it's commonplace. Just because you may not have encountered it before doesn't mean it's anything special. In fact, it's so commonplace that books have been written about it, research departments set up to investigate it, websites designed to provide information about it, and specialists paid to help you deal with it.

Potty training

Training for carers is something that is strangely hard to come by. Usually. Enquire about it, ask for it, plead, shout – the result is hardly ever much more than a few surface-scratching leaflets or some vague advice which doesn't seem to apply to you. But not on the subject of incontinence.

I don't say you'll get all the information you're looking for in one hit. You may find that your doctor throws a bit of light on the subject, the district nurse rather more, your support group an even better-focused and closer look at the whole business, and Social Services some practical information about gadgets. However it comes, the information is out there and it *will* come so long as you press for it.

The great thing about training is not that it turns you into an instant expert, but that it removes the unknown. It makes you feel more familiar and therefore more comfortable with the subject. Ignorance is fear, and fear of the messy stuff can seriously spoil your day if you're a carer. Feeling comfortable with it, on the other hand, can convert it from being a nightmare into just another job you have to do.

What training does is to take the taboo out of turds. Something else it might possibly do (no promises, mind) is to reduce or even stop it altogether.

Can it be prevented?

It has to be said that, if your piglet is peeing and/or shitting where and when they shouldn't, they almost certainly can't help it and it's highly unlikely that they can be prevented from doing it. But it's not impossible.

The first thing to do is get medical advice. Your piglet's doctor, or even more to the point the specialist, may have something useful to say on this. Incontinence is sometimes the result of a treatable condition, and therefore curable. For example, let's say the piglet is on a daily diet of drugs. One of them could be reducing mental awareness or muscular control. Cutting down on that particular drug could clean up the problem. Of course, it could also introduce others.

Or the piglet could be suffering from an ailment quite separate from the primary disability or illness. For instance, someone with Alzheimer's might also be suffering from prostate trouble. Treatment for that won't do anything for the Alzheimer's, but it could dry up the dribbling.

Or yet again, you might (if you haven't yet received any training) be giving them too little to drink, and actually causing the incontinence yourself.

So yes, there is a possibility that it can be prevented, or reduced, or postponed. Don't assume the worst at first.

Minimise it

Suppose the medical consensus is that your piglet's incontinence isn't treatable (which is what it probably will be if there's any mental confusion or dementia), what then? Grin and bear it? Not necessarily. Not yet.

This is where the potty training comes in. Not theirs; yours. You won't be able to train your piglet to stop – as the books say – 'soiling the sheets' at night. They would if they could. But the training will show you ways of minimising the problem. Actually, you already know what these methods are. It's just that you aren't putting them into practice.

For example, taking them to the toilet and sitting them on it every two hours, and last thing at night. Or encouraging them to go on the commode you've got on permanent loan from the Red Cross. Or cutting out coffee and tea in the afternoons and evenings. Or getting them up twice a night.

They're all obvious. You may have thought of them but not got round to implementing them. You may not even have thought of them because you haven't been thinking clearly. And you may not have been thinking clearly because you've found the whole business disgusting and unthinkable-about.

Training. Don't forget. It might even tell you things you didn't know before, however obvious they might seem with hindsight.

The piglet's clothing

If they go to the loo by themselves, or try to, complicated clothing equipped with stubborn zippers and fiddly buttons won't help. Elastic waists and Velcro fasteners can work wonders. There are even pants or trousers that are split at the back to allow easier access where it counts, yet preserve dignity at the front.

That's not the problem? They don't even think of going to the loo? O they may think of it, but get caught short long before getting there? Or don't even know what they're doing? Nappies may be the answer here.

Only they're not called nappies. Or even diapers. But when you come across a range of products under the heading 'incontinence pants' or 'incontinence pads', that's the job they do.

Training will put you right on these and other aids.

Their diet

Here's what the books say: make sure your piglet eats plenty of vegetables, fruit, cereals, and foods with lots of fibre. Yeah, yeah. What the books don't seem to understand is that you've probably got your work cut out with all those other considerations, such as what the piglet likes or can be persuaded to take in. OF COURSE you're giving them a balanced diet within those constraints.

Even so, when you find yourself once again searching for ideas on what to cook for supper, have a think about bowel effects while you're at it.

Modifying your house

I'm not talking about modifications to help your piglet here. That's all covered in Chapter 19. In this bit I'm really thinking about alterations you can make which will help *you*. It goes without saying that if they help you, they'll also help the piglet.

The sort of thing I'm thinking of is the special toilet which squirts a jet of water upwards to clean the bottom that's sitting on it. This saves you from having to use toilet paper on the bottom, and is much more painless and effective, not to say dignified.

But forget about the toilet itself for a moment. Let's think about other places which you find yourself constantly and complainingly cleaning. Can they be modified so that the cleaning process becomes swift and easy? Suppose, for example, there's a fitted carpet in the bathroom or bedroom. Cleaning shit off that involves knees, a stiff scrubbing brush, special cleaning fluid, disinfectant and time. Were you to pull the carpet up and chuck it away (no-one will buy it now so don't even think about trying to sell it) and replace it with cork tiling or linoleum, the shit might not go away but the problem certainly will.

It gets on the wallpaper too? You can see the stains now, even though you've tried to wash them off? Try gloss paint on the walls.

There are all kinds of cunning sheets and cushions which absorb moisture, are easy to clean and don't smell. You may not know what's available, but there'll be somebody near you who does. Training is what you need.

Those dreadful nights

> *And still she slept an azure-lidded sleep*
> *In blanched linen, smooth and lavendered,*
> *While he from forth the closet brought a heap**

Accidents during the night are really hard to bear. There you were, lost to the world in your blanched linen, and the next moment you're up to your arms in it. It's at moments like these that the worst side of your nature comes to the fore. Carers have been known to swear at their piglets in the middle of the night, even though it never does any good, never did, and never will.

This is one of the reasons why it can be a better bet to set your alarm to go off twice a night, and to wake your piglet for a loo break. Once it has become routine for both of you, their bodies may respond in the way you hope, and you'll be able to carry out the chore in your sleep, almost. A half-hour rest during the day is easily enough to compensate for the sleep lost during the night.

I learned about this on our boat. I almost never got an unbroken night's sleep when we were at sea, and I could go for weeks at a time without losing efficiency.

---

* This is from 'The Eve of St Agnes' by John Keats, and admittedly the verse goes on:

  'Of candied apple, quince, and plum, and gourd;
  With jellies soother than the creamy curd,
  And lucent syrops, tinct with cinnamon.'

But I was thinking of something rather different.

Bathing

Piglets tend to be less mobile than non-piglets, as well as messier. So, small but important manoeuvres like cleaning between the legs can become logistical brainteasers. A piglet in the bath will be sitting on the very part that needs to be washed. Getting at it may be impossible.

Showers are easier in theory, but it's still hard to clean a bottom whose buttocks are clamped together.

What you will have discovered the hard way (if you haven't yet, you will) is that partial bottom-wiping combined with partial washing produces a very distinctive smell. It's one that the lucky piglet won't be able to detect, but you certainly will.

It's a solvable problem. Whether the cure involves a special toilet, or a different technique for bottom-wiping, or wet-wipes, or what, depends on your particular circumstances. Training is what you need. It's only a problem at the moment because it's a new one to you.

Washing clothes

He didn't want a bath today, and for once I agreed because it was easier not to have a battle, and anyway it would give me a break. But he sat on the loo as usual. I wiped his bottom for him afterwards, and I'm certain I did it properly.

Then, when getting him dressed I sat him down on the bed to pull his pants over his feet, and when I pulled him up there was a lump of shit on the sheet. It could have been that I didn't wipe him properly, or maybe he crapped a little bit afterwards.

Anyway, instead of taking his pants down and cleaning him up a second time, I merely dabbed at the sheet, then finished dressing him. He didn't notice anything amiss, and I didn't say anything.

Am I getting better or worse at caring?

Query from a worried carer

Well, I don't know the answer to this one. I have an idea that a lowering of standards is probably a good thing. Cleanliness, as far as piglets are concerned, may not be next to godliness after all.

It wouldn't do to lose sight of the fact that looking nice and feeling clean may boost the piglet's sense of well-being and even their sense of self-worth. But it can be taken too far.

You could be changing their clothes and washing them all day and all night, but what does that achieve? Impressing the neighbours shouldn't be a concern for carers. For anyone.

Doing the housework

If shit needs to be scraped off the walls or a urine-soaked chair washed and dried, there's no question that it's got to be done. But ordinary housework may not need to be done to such high-falutin' standards as in non-piglet houses. I'm not preaching a policy of deliberate squalor. All I'm saying is that caring means caring for the piglet, not the house.

When it comes to a choice between catching up on some of the sleep you missed last night, and polishing the handle of the front door, forget the front door.

Eating

For some piglets, eating can be a messy business. But it's clean mess, compared with the other kind. So you may be far more relaxed about mopping it up.

And quite right too. What's the point of becoming stressed out by gobs of yoghurt on the floor, if they're an inevitable by-product of meal times? There may be virtue in being house-proud and fastidious, but not under these circumstances. At least, not till you tread in it.

Or do you justify your pernicketiness on the grounds that it's demeaning for your piglet? Fair enough, if the piglet notices.

But if they're unaware that it's a problem, then it *isn't* a problem. On the other hand, should the piglet be embarrassed about, though unable to avoid, making a mess, how about worrying more about the embarrassment than the mess? A big wrap-around apron might answer. It offers more protection than a napkin and is easier to wash, but its real advantage is that there's no stigma attached. Cooks wear aprons. Aprons are in. Having a napkin tied round your neck may make you look helpless or silly. But an apron can be worn with pride.

There are other items of equipment which can help here too. Straws may make drinking easier, wet-wipes may be better for cleaning up. But you'll learn what's good for you and your piglet.

The trick is to keep your mind open, try different things, and not mind. The real messy stuff is not what's in the bed, or the toilet, or the dining room. It's what's in your and your piglet's minds.

Your piglet's mind

A piglet who is aware that the mess they make is the result of a loss of control is reminded many times each day of their disability. It can make them feel desperate, embarrassed, ashamed and frightened.

I said at the beginning of the book that the focus of attention would be on you, and not the piglet. And I've said repeatedly throughout it that you probably need to be more of an SP, not less of one. But it's no good rubbing the piglet's nose (either literally or figuratively) in their disability by making a fuss about the messy stuff.

Take it as a matter of course and they'll feel better about themselves. Which in turn should make your job easier.

Your mind

Why is wiping a small child's bottom painless, and yet doing the same thing for your mother difficult if not unthinkable? It's not the size of the bottom. It's what goes on in your mind, and possibly in the mind of the piglet too, that messes everything up.

And it certainly does mess things up. It can have you screaming with frustration. You start to believe they're doing it on purpose, out of spite. And the problem is, they keep at it. No sooner have you cleared up one mess than they've done another.

I haven't any idea what the incidence of pushing-down-the-stairs is following inadvertent mess-making. But I bet it's significant.

Isolation makes it worse. Caring takes place behind closed doors, out of sight and out of mind. And as like as not it'll drive you out of *your* mind from time to time.

You may know very well how to come to terms with the messy stuff, yet be unable to do it. The answer almost certainly lies in sharing the problem – with professionals, in the form of training, or with anyone you can discuss it with.

You can't discuss it? It's taboo? Disgusting? You can't bear it but you can't talk about it either?

Rubbish. What do you think we've been doing for the last half hour?

CHAPTER 19

Getting information

Sources

The medical profession
Social Services
Occupational therapist
Citizens Advice Bureau
Specialist support group
Carers' support group
Internet

Categories

Benefits
Caring techniques
Gadgets and equipment
Grants
Home help
Modifications to the home
Moving and handling
Respite care
Toileting
Transport
   Car
   Taxi
   Passes for bus and rail

The ARSE factor

Getting information

You may have picked this book up in the expectation of being given a detailed map to help you find your way round the bewildering maze of grants, benefits, gadgets, techniques, home modifications, short breaks, long-term residential care, home help, toileting, moving and handling, you name it. And you're probably fed up that you haven't found it here.

I'm sorry. I just couldn't think how to include all this stuff in such a way that it would be up-to-date, accurate for the part of the world where you live, and relevant to your circumstances and your piglet's disability. Correction: I *did* think of a way, but the answer wasn't in the form of a book. It was a website, into which you would enter all your personal details, and which would come up with a comprehensive dossier of detailed information specifically for you. A team of researchers worldwide would keep it current on a daily basis. Then, any time your circumstances changed, you could just go back into it and extract any new information you needed.

If there is such a website already in existence, I haven't discovered it. There's certainly a need for one. Maybe this could be a project for you, if you're computer-literate and a dab hand at research?

Meantime, what this book can do is help you find all the information you need, in ways which are currently available.

First, let's look at the possible sources. And after that I'll just run through some of the areas on which you might need information, and suggest where you should go to get that information.

Sources

In the absence of the website I was talking about back there, there is no single source of information. Nor is there any (all right then, much) training available. So you're going to have to reconcile yourself to an awful lot of groping around in the dark, in the hope of eventually piecing together all the strands of information you need.

The places where you'll be groping are:

The medical profession

A whole book could probably be written on how to find your way around here. Medicine is a bit like religion: it's a huge and complex edifice composed of mysteries, hierarchy, arcane terminology, history, divisions and subdivisions (frequently at war with one another), and faith.

In your search for information you'll start with your doctor, who'll be a general practitioner. Because of this (ie, because they're generalists) you're quite likely to discover that you know more about your piglet's particular problems than they do. If so, don't panic. Within the temple walls lies all the information you're looking for. And even if your GP doesn't have that information, they'll have the key to getting it. They'll be able to locate the people who do have it, and arrange for you to see them.

For example, somewhere in your area there will be a doctor who specialises in your piglet's disability. You need to talk to them, and not just for your piglet's sake. They'll be able to help you understand what's happening inside your piglet, and maybe even give you a clue as to what's going to happen next. Their knowledge, if they share it with you, can go a long way to helping you care.

The GP is also the route to hospital, and to a district nurse. Both can provide you with information, as well as administering medical care to your piglet.

Note that I don't say they will, only that they can. The problem is, they may choose not to. The medical profession has for centuries liked to keep its patients in the dark. In recent years there has been a marked movement towards openness, but it seems to be suffering a setback, possibly brought about by the fear of litigation. What with that, and the fact that they're all overworked – so may not have the time to educate you in addition to treating your piglet – you may have to fight quite hard to extract the information you're looking for.

I've known carers who have given up on the whole of the medical profession in disgust. There are others, and I'm one of them, who feel that they've been well served. For all of us carers, though, the trick is to be aware that the medical information you need is in there somewhere; that your doctor's job is not necessarily to provide it, but it *is* to guide you to it; and your job is to winkle it out once you get there.

Social Services

Are you a carer who's in denial? What I mean is, someone who, though they care for a piglet, thinks of themselves not as a carer but only as a parent, child, neighbour, spouse or partner? Because if you are, then it's quite possible that you either won't have thought of making yourself known to Social Services, or that you haven't done so out of a belief that they'll interfere.

Well, it's a mistake. Social Services are there not just to take action on your behalf (and you may decidedly not want them to take action) but also to give you guidance and information. You do need them, believe me. And they can help.

Areas in which Social Services can assist are: benefits, occupational therapy, respite care, home help . . . now that I come to think of it, almost all aspects of caring come under Social Services, somewhere or other.

I know they are the arch-representatives of Officialdom, but let's not get into that here. We've covered all that negative stuff in Chapter 7. Here we're looking at sources of information, and Social Services is one of the main providers.

Occupational therapist

The OT person in your area knows not only about handrails in the bathroom, stairlifts and wheelchair ramps. They have also received a thorough training, and are in a position to pass on a good chunk of this training to you.

For some reason which I can't put my finger on, OTs also tend to be friendly, helpful, willing, unpretentious, open and straightforward. That is a terrible generalisation, I know, and I apologise for it. Even so, in my experience it has to be worth making an appointment to see an OT with a view to getting information on handling your piglet.

In my area, occupational therapy comes under Social Services. In yours it may come under the Department of Health, who knows? Your GP or social worker will point you in the right direction.

Citizens Advice Bureau

The Citizens Advice Bureau is a curious mixture of Officialdom and charity. It is a charity and it's reliant on volunteers, but it's also a professional national agency in the UK. It offers free, confidential, impartial and independent advice on matters which are central to many people's lives (not just carers'), such as debt and consumer issues, benefits, housing, legal matters, employment, and immigration.

Advisers can help fill out forms, write letters, negotiate, and represent clients at court or tribunal.

They may not have at their fingertips the information you're looking for. But they'll do their best to find it out for you.

Specialist support group

There'll be a support group specialising in your piglet's disability, and by extension it will also specialise in your caring. You may be one of those who have steered clear of such organisations because you're not sure that you need, or can face, tea and sympathy. I used to be one of them myself. But your support group will also be home to a huge store of relevant specialist information that you'd be crazy not to take advantage of.

Most support groups of this kind comprise

- a national base organisation that publishes a regular newsletter, holds an annual conference, and perhaps employs care advisers

- regional branches that hold regular meetings and raise funds. I have found that some of the best information of all comes out of the get-togethers organised by the local branch, because it's there that you can quietly chat to other carers in exactly the same boat as you, and learn from each other.

Carers' support group

These exist to prop up carers regardless of their piglets' problems. There will almost certainly be one near you. It will have been created as a result of Officialdom's inability to provide all the support and information you need. It'll probably be a charity, and run by volunteers, and it may not have much money to publicise its existence. To draw attention to itself, it may rely on leaflets put out in doctors' surgeries, which you may not have seen if you haven't scanned the notice boards there. In any case, the receptionist in charge of the surgery probably took it down if it was looking a bit dog-eared.

But it's worth searching for this support group (via the local newspaper, local radio, Yellow Pages, Social Services, the Internet) because it could just be in a position to provide you with information you haven't been able to get anywhere else. And unlike some of the other potential sources of information, this one is keen to meet you, and to help.

Internet

If you have a computer at home and are online, skip this paragraph. If you haven't and aren't, DO NOT SKIP. I don't care whether you think computers are a pain and an irrelevance. For accessing information, the Internet is a necessary and unique tool, and you must take advantage of it. Doesn't mean you've got to buy a computer and learn how to use it. All you need is to find someone who can use a computer, and who can be armtwisted into doing some research for you.

They don't even need to have a computer at home, as there'll be one nearby which they can access, in the public library or a cyber cafe.

Ask them to carry out a search for

- carers in your country
- carers in your locality
- your piglet's disability.

Either sit there with them while they do it, or get them to print out the results so that you can study them at home.

Categories

Now let's whip through some of the topics about which you might have been hoping for detailed information in this book. I haven't been able to provide that information, but maybe I can help you get your hands on it.

Benefits

What financial aid you're entitled to is going to depend on your financial circumstances, so not everyone at your support group, or in your street, is going to qualify for the same benefits. But the support group, and the street, are good places to start asking. They'll give you an idea of what's available and what other people are getting.

Next, you should ask Social Services. Then the Citizens Advice Bureau. And finally check through the government's websites.

Benefits are woven into a spider's web, in which one strand leads to another, and this one crosses that and makes it untenable. If money is a problem for you, it's worth following each strand to its conclusion. If you don't feel it's worth the effort, then probably you don't really need the help.

But remember, there are millions of people who don't claim the benefits they're eligible for, and not all of them are so rich they couldn't use them. They're just defeated by the difficulty of acquiring the information. Don't be one of them.

- Support group ☞
- Social Services ☞
- Citizens Advice Bureau ☞
- Government websites ☞
- Any other carers you can think of ☞

Caring techniques

Caring is a skill that can be acquired, and ought to be passed on to us through training, but isn't.

Make the mistake of believing that it's all just a matter of common sense and you could end up damaging your back or dropping your piglet. So it's worth chasing up any information on this subject.

One way is by asking Social Services for an assessment, and making clear at the interview that you want some training in caring techniques. They'll probably arrange for a visit from the occupational therapist, or a physiotherapist, or someone from a neurological rehabilitation group.

Another way is to seek help through the specialist support group for your piglet's disability. It's possible that the GP can help here, too, by arranging for the district nurse to show you a few ropes.

- Social Services ☞
- Support group ☞
- District nurse ☞

Gadgets and equipment

This is the realm of the occupational therapist. The OT may even be able to provide some bits, free of charge. Others they may only be able to advise on. But they know what's out there, they can tell what's appropriate for your piglet, and they have direct experience of most of it.

There are specialist shops selling (and installing) this kind of stuff, but if you're using your own money to buy it you may want to obtain some independent advice first. In my local hospital there's a unit (Aid and Equipment) which stocks all this kind of thing, but doesn't sell it. Their advice is informed, up-to-the-minute, impartial, and invaluable. But you need to be referred there by the doctor or OT.

> • Occupational therapist ☞
> • Doctor ☞

Grants

If you need to buy something that you can't afford (I'm talking about something for your piglet, or something to help you in your caring, you fool), you may be eligible for a grant to cover the cost or contribute towards it. Your occupational therapist is a good starting point; or failing that, the local carers' support group.

> • Occupational therapist ☞
> • Support group ☞

Home help

This is about people who come in to help care for your piglet. They might deal with bathing and toileting, help the piglet get dressed and undressed, cook or provide meals, do the shopping, or just keep the piglet company while you whiz out for a couple of hours.

Social Services may provide home helpers, or show you how to organise your own. They may pay, or contribute towards the cost.

There are specialist agencies which supply home help, and you can approach them direct. But Social Services are the best starting point for information.

> • Social Services ☞

Modifications to the home

Installation of lifts, hoists and ramps, and widening of doors all come under the heading of modifications rather than gadgets. OT is the starting point. But in my area there also exists an agency offering technical support with building works and adaptations. It's a voluntary body, but it's funded by Officialdom. I don't know whether there's a comparable agency where you are, but it's worth finding out through Social Services.

> • Occupational therapist ☞
> • Social Services ☞

Moving and handling

This is all about heaving your piglet up from chairs, on to the toilet, into and out of bed, what to do when they fall over or get stuck in the bath, and so on. It's a thoroughly dangerous business, and because carers get no training, it does actually result in all manner of health problems for carers.

The book *Moving and Lifting: a Handbook for Professional Carers*, by Martin Hutchinson, is full of diagrams and descriptions, and could provide the basis for some self-training. So could any of the several books on back troubles, such as *The Back, Problems and Prevention*, by Vivian Grisogono. Your OT will have been trained, and can pass much of this on. Your specialist support group will have lots to say on the subject as well.

> • Occupational therapist ☞
> • Support group ☞
> • Public library ☞

Respite care

For regular short-term respite care, what you need is a day centre (likely to be organised through Social Services) or a group activity for the disabled (which could be organised by a local voluntary organisation such as the community centre). For longerterm respite care, such as an annual holiday, there are special centres with staff and facilities. Social Services will have a directory, and may be able to contribute to the cost. Your specialist support group may also have a list of places which cater for your piglet's disability. There are also charities which specialise in respite care.

- Crossroads ☞
- The Winged Fellowship ☞
- Social Services ☞
- Local community centre ☞
- Support group ☞

Toileting

Lots of people know all about this. It's one of the strange subjects in which there are many answers to questions which nobody is asking. Try

- Doctor ☞
- District nurse ☞
- Support group ☞
- Occupational therapist ☞
- Social Services ☞
- The Internet ☞

Transport

Transport for carers and piglets can be a business so fraught, expensive, complicated, difficult and necessary that you might have expected information to be hard to come by. In fact, there's a lot, just as there's a lot of help available. Let's break it down a bit:

Car

If your piglet has a car or the use of one, they may be exempt from car tax. The Driver and Vehicle Licensing Agency has an application form for this.

> • Social Services ☞
> • DVLA ☞

Help towards buying or contract-hiring a car is available (or may be) through a specialist charity.

> • Motability ☞
> • The Internet ☞

Help with parking is available through the international Blue Badge scheme. For information on that, start with

> • Social Services ☞

Taxi

Whether or not you have a car, there may be times when a taxi is the best or only option. Some taxi firms specialise in vehicles suitable for the disabled. Help with fares may well be obtainable.

> • Social Services ☞

Passes for bus and rail

Most bus and rail companies offer concessions for piglets and carers.

> • The Internet ☞
> • Social Services ☞

The ARSE factor

This chapter has been devoted to the acquisition of information. The trouble is, whenever you ask advice on any topic (come to that, whenever you're given advice whether you've asked for it or not), the ARSE factor comes into play. Since we carers desperately need advice and information, I feel slightly bad about drawing attention to the ARSE factor here, as it implies a lack of gratitude and respect.

But you need to be aware of it, so I'll tell you very quietly:

Not all advice can be relied on. In fact, quite a lot of the stuff you'll be told will be complete balderdash. So there's a need to be able to distinguish between the solid gold and the unadulterated rubbish. I have looked, on your behalf, for a formula that will provide an indication as to how seriously you should take any advice. I've called it the Advice Reliability Statistical Evaluation factor. Here's how it works.

The reliability of any given piece of advice is in inverse ratio to the degree of emphasis with which it is given. Got that? What it means is that if somebody tells you something with utter confidence, in a very loud voice, it's probably not at all reliable. On the other hand, if they say that they believe something or other to be true but they'll have to check first, then it almost certainly will turn out to be true.

I don't claim that the ARSE factor itself is always one hundred per cent reliable. Just that it's a good indicator, and one which I have often used to good effect. For example, when I wanted to know whether my piglet qualified for the higher level of the care section of Disability Living Allowance, I called the Benefits Office to find out. The person I spoke to told me it almost certainly wouldn't be worth our while to apply. She said that it would mean our case would be re-evaluated, and that my piglet stood as much chance of losing the benefits she was currently receiving as of obtaining a higher benefit. In other words, she did her best to put me off. It was as if she was being asked to dish out her own money, rather than the State's money, which is the same thing as our money. She was so emphatic about it that I applied the ARSE factor, and obtained a low reading – low reliability, that is. I went ahead and applied for the increased benefit, and got it.

It's my belief that the ARSE factor should be borne in mind by all carers because we're easily outfaced by Officialdom, and we have no other means of testing the accuracy of what they tell us.

Sometimes we're in no position to assess the advice we're given, regardless of where it comes from. I'm thinking of those times when we've had it up to here and just can't think straight any more. When I was in that situation (I'm not any more), two people advised me to push my piglet down the stairs. This was quite separate and independent advice. They didn't know one another, and neither one was aware that somebody else was saying the same thing. The advice wasn't absolute or explicit. It was hedged about with phrases like 'Nobody would blame you' and 'It would be much the best thing all round'. But there was no mistaking the substance of the advice: 'Push. Now.'

I didn't take it. I may or may not have wanted to; that's not something for discussion here. But ever since, when I'm tempted to comply with a piece of advice that's likely to have momentous consequences, I take the ARSE factor down from the shelf where it lives, dust it off, plug it in, and pay close and respectful attention to its meter reading.

CHAPTER 20

Tips which the experts don't give you

Ask another carer

Develop a thick skin

Don't want what you can't have

Share

Start talking

Keep asking

Keep piglet time

Wear a special uniform

Living will

Be an SP

Tips which the experts don't give you

Maybe the heading of this chapter ought to be 'Tips Which The Experts Never Gave Me'. I don't know why they didn't, because every one of them is blazingly obvious. Perhaps that's why they didn't. Maybe these things are so obvious that nobody thinks they're worth drawing attention to. But being a carer can be deeply confusing, and stuff which is obvious to the outside world, particularly the expert segment of the outside world, may be all but invisible to carers until they've been at it for a reasonable length of time. Say, ten years or so.

Most of these items have cropped up elsewhere in the book – but not all. None of them is mandatory. That's to say, you won't come to a sticky end if you don't follow them. But I've found every one of them makes a difference out of all proportion to its apparent significance.

Anyway, see what you think. Here goes.

Ask another carer

Looking back at the help I received and the information I acquired, I now see that almost all of it came from other carers. Carers are the ultimate pundits on caring. You could go round in circles looking for a piece of information, but where you're most likely to get it is from another carer.

So when stymied, or even before you're stymied, ask another carer. Ask them first.

They'll know.

Develop a thick skin

Carers have to be like double glazing salesmen: thoroughly accustomed to rejection, and totally resilient to it. I've never actually sold replacement windows, but I've often been on the receiving end of a salesman's attempt to persuade me to buy. And each time I've said no I've felt sorry (a bit) for the poor old salesperson. How can they bear it? I suspect the reason they don't go home and hang themselves has less to do with the lack of any convenient hook to attach the rope to than with their training. They're taught how to cope with rejection. They're shown how to bounce back.

And they know from experience that sooner or later some punter or other will say yes.

Needless to say, nobody ever tells *us* how to keep on knocking at Officialdom's door without becoming suicidal in the process. Yet it's something we have to find out. All those comforting comments about 'Always being here when you need us' and 'Help is available; all you need do is apply' lead inevitably to disillusionment the moment you do apply. But give up and you get nowhere. You won't get the grant or benefit you need, you'll miss out on the respite care, your piglet will have to do without the aids and gadgets that they need. No, you have to persist. And it can be a debilitating process.

Rejection techniques enable you – so I'm told – not to take it personally. To understand that rejection is not a reflection on you or the justice of your cause. It's just something that happens to everyone. I expect there are courses you can attend. I also

expect that they're expensive and time-consuming, and held somewhere where you aren't. They'll be full of aspiring salespeople, too, which could be a drawback. Perhaps there are correspondence courses?

Anyway, if they can develop a thick skin, so can you. You're a selfish pig, aren't you? So you're covered in impenetrable rind. Be glad. You're going to need it.

Don't want what you can't have

As you've discovered, caring can clip your wings. Things which you used to do, or which you yearn to do now, or which you feel you ought to be doing, you can't. At least, you can't so long as you're giving your piglet the care they need. This can be deeply depressing and frustrating. It can get in the way not only of your caring, but of your life.

The trick is not to want those things. I'd like to give a couple of examples, one of something fundamental and the other one something trivial. The trouble is, we're all so different that the things I want to do are almost certainly not at all what you want to do. I'll sketch out two of mine, anyway, if only to give you an idea.

Yesterday my piglet and I received an invitation to a party that's being thrown by a couple who have just built the most amazing house. It would be the first opportunity for us or any of our friends to see inside this house which is reputed to be stuffed full of expensive computer-operated gadgetry and marvellous works of art. Everybody will be there, and the invitation mentioned music, magic and champagne.

I would have wanted to go (if I hadn't remembered this tip). But I knew that the evening would be a nightmare if we did. Dressing my piglet in her finery would be a complicated and fraught affair. We wouldn't be able to park outside the door, so we'd need the wheelchair which my piglet doesn't like to be seen in. Once inside I wouldn't be able to circulate, because it's certain that nobody would breathe into my ear that they'd look after my piglet while I whizzed round the house. The end result would be an evening of hard and unrewarding work surrounded by friends having a wonderful time.

Now, if I did, really badly, want to go, I'd be faced with a difficult decision. Accept, and I would be guaranteed a wretched time. Decline, and I'd be in danger of feeling seriously sorry for myself. What I did instead was to decide that I didn't want to go.

I happily refused the invitation, and instead my piglet and I will have a party of our own, at home, doing stuff which we *are* able to do, in our own place and at our own pace. It wasn't a case of making the best of the situation. I simply didn't want to go, so didn't. That's the trivial example.

The fundamental one is all about sailing (I told you it wouldn't be your cup of tea). When my piglet and I set out to live on a boat for years on end, we weren't after adventure. We wanted to live out a dream. Usually, dreams fall short of expectations, but this one didn't. We had stumbled on a way of life which we both loved and wanted to continue for ever. It came to an end when my piglet's disability prevented her from taking part any more. After we had moved ashore, well-meaning people constantly asked me whether I missed sailing and our old life. I always told them that I didn't, though the truth is that it almost killed me – to begin with. But then I learned not to want the old life back. I came almost to believe it. I certainly believed it enough to be able to live with myself, my piglet, and our new roles with equanimity and even enjoyment.

Not wanting what you can't have is a trick of the trade. It's not something that comes naturally, but it can be learned. It's worth learning.

Share

There's a difficulty about allocating the disability to your piglet, and keeping the caring role for yourself. Well, not so much a difficulty as a wedge. Something that separates you, and can drive you apart.

Far better to think of the disability as something that you share. Something that unites you. I know that the piglet is the one who has it, clinically speaking; but it's affected you nearly as much. Perhaps just as much, though in a different way.

It isn't your piglet who has wrought this cataclysmic change in your life. It's the disability. So you both share it.

And since you share the disability, it's okay to share the caring. One moment their needs are paramount, and the next yours are.

Share and share alike.

Start talking

We carers feel isolated. This is not good for us, it's not good for our caring, and it's not good for our piglets. That's what it's not. What it *is* is our own fault. This tip is about not suffering in silence. It's about talking to anyone who'll listen, and even to those who won't.

It's about unpenning your emotions. About harassing Officialdom, sharing with other carers, coming clean with friends. It's about getting things straight between you and your piglet. It's about straight talking to yourself.

Carers are traditionally terrible about talking. And look where it's got us. Well, no more. Start talking now.

Keep asking

It doesn't really matter what you're asking for (information, support, equipment, whatever). The chances are you'll get

- no answer
- an incorrect answer
- a 'there, there, dear' answer.

rather than the sort of answer you are seeking, need and deserve. Since many of these answers originate in Officialdom, the natural course of action is to retreat, nursing a sense of powerlessness.

But if you keep on asking, you stand a very real chance of getting.

And don't forget the first tip listed in this chapter.

Keep piglet time

Shall I say this again? Well, you can easily skip if you're fed up with it. But whenever you become frustrated at the pace of living imposed by caring, it's highly likely that you're operating within your old time frame, or the time frame of your friends and colleagues. Slow down and start to live at your piglet's pace, and much of the frustration will fade peacefully away.

Wear a special uniform

I don't say you ought to wear a white coat while doing your caring. At least, not literally. But some carers do, and the rest of us can at least wear metaphorical uniforms to achieve the same result.

Ever tried to teach someone to drive – someone you're close to? And all they do is criticise you for the way you're doing it? But turn them over to a driving instructor, and they (a) believe what the instructor tells them, whereas they never believed you, and (b) do what they're told. It's the same thing with caring. If they're stroppy with you and won't co-operate, it's because it's you. If the district nurse were to come in and order them about, they'd as likely as not fall straight into line.

You could try putting on the district nurse's uniform, but the chances are they'd see straight through it (if you see what I mean). But what you *could* do is adopt a professional persona when you're carrying out tasks like bathing or feeding. This persona is different and distinct from your persona as your piglet's partner or child or parent. It will carry the authority of a uniform, and might persuade them to pay attention to what you say. Just for a short time.

Living will

It's not just the law which is an ass. It's medical science. And as a result any one of us could find ourselves being kept alive by technology when we'd be far better off dead. It could happen to me, it could happen to you, and it could happen to our piglets.

Is it part of a good carer's job to minimise the chance of its happening to the piglet? Probably.

Is talking about it in advance, let alone taking pre-emptive action, something that's virtually unthinkable? Or if not unthinkable, then at least undo-able? Possibly.

But the thing is, this could be your final act of caring, and one of the most significant contributions you can make to their quality of life. Conversely, if you do nothing, your inaction could be your most telling failure on their behalf.

It may be that your piglet, when fully competent mentally, gives clear instructions as to what they do and don't want to happen to them when they're close to death. In that case, there's no problem. What you need to do is have a 'living will' drawn up, in which the piglet's wishes are clearly set out. It should be properly phrased, signed and witnessed just like any other legal document. A lawyer will help, or you can download sample living wills from the Internet. It should set out the circumstances under which the piglet would not want to receive life-prolonging medical treatment.

But what if the piglet doesn't broach the subject? Should you bring it up? If so, how? Yes, this is a tough one. And I have no clue what the answer is. Of course, it doesn't mean that they're automatically doomed to spend years on a life-support machine.

Or that their final days will drag painfully and unnecessarily simply because you didn't have the moral courage to get them to face the problem while they could. But it might.

Or what if the piglet is mentally impaired, so that it's out of the question to think in terms of living wills? Can you get round the difficulty by discussing their case with their doctor in advance, and relying on the doctor to see that what happens at the end is what is right rather than merely what is possible?

Again, not necessarily. But you might.

Be an SP

This one has cropped up repeatedly throughout the book. I wondered whether to repeat it here, on the grounds that it's the single most important trick of the carer's trade. But then I started to have second thoughts. Am I strolling into a minefield by advising all carers to be selfish pigs, if they aren't already?

I may be. It certainly sounds a bit suspect. On the other hand I'm not sure if I know any carers who are truly selfish. There are plenty of SPs around the place, but they're not carers. So I think I'm safe. Anyway, to cover myself I'd like to emphasise that I don't want you to think only of yourself so that your piglet suffers. I just want you to be a bit less altruistic than you almost certainly are.

The first duty of any commercial organisation, so it's said, is to stay in business. Not to go bust. Well, the first duty of a carer is to go on caring. Caring is long-term. It's physically tough, emotionally draining, and financially difficult. It's all too easy to run out of energy, and to burn out. When that happens, you stop caring.

Unluckily for you, you're not a saint, or a paragon, and if you let the hardships of caring get you down, you won't be able to last the course. The way to last the course is to recognise how crucially, vitally important you are. Take your own needs into account.

Being a proper SP doesn't mean neglecting your piglet. That's not what it's about at all. What it's about is not neglecting yourself. Which I bet you have been doing.

CHAPTER 21

Young carers

What makes you different?

Difficulties you might have

At school
Getting there on time
Attending regularly
Bullying
Not being able to concentrate
Leaving early

At home
Taking the decisions
The messy stuff
Social life
Homework

It isn't fair

Losing out
Education
Friends
Your body
Your future

How did you get into this situation?

Is there anything you can do about it?

Family
Friends
Officialdom
   Teachers
   The doctor
   Social worker

Why you're stuck

Don't want to stop
Scared to
Can't

Anyway, isn't this what families are for?

No need to be a single-hander

Talking
Who to?

Young carers

This is a chapter for teenagers. Is that what you are? If so, it's highly unlikely that you'll have looked at any other parts of this book. Which is just as well, really, because I have to admit I wasn't thinking about you when I wrote those sections. To be honest, I had no idea there were so many of you. It turns out that there are more than 1½ million young carers in the USA and UK.

That's my excuse for writing the book the way I have, and for sticking this chapter at the back. As excuses go, this one's sad, I have to admit. You deserve a bit more help than that. No, that's not true. You deserve a LOT more help than that. Almost all carers have a hard time, but you get the rawest deal of the lot. And make the least fuss.

So how come you're reading this at all? Probably because somebody lent you the book, and marked the chapter with a yellow post-it note. They must have thought there was something in it for you. I don't know whether I've got anything useful to say or not. But I'm going to try.

What makes you different?

I don't mean different from other carers. I mean different from other people of your age. Actually, though, you *are* different from carers of my age as well, in that you're even more invisible. I said in the first paragraph that I didn't know there were so many carers in your age group. Well, nor did most people, not very long ago. As far as the general public was concerned, you were just a bunch of kids helping out at home. It's beginning to change now, though. With every month that goes by there's more awareness of people like you.

But how aware are *you*? Do you think of yourself as a carer? Or is it possible that you haven't given yourself that label? Maybe you see it this way: that there just happens to be

someone (or maybe more than one person) in your family who can't do things for themselves. It could be a parent. Or a grandparent. Or a brother or sister. And you just happen to do a lot of those things for them, because you just happen to be there. And there's no-one else who can do them. Or at least, no-one else who does do them.

What sort of stuff? Well:

- Washing
- Dressing and undressing
- Shopping
- Cooking
- Feeding
- Toileting (this is what it's called in the trade, and if you do it you'll know what it means)
- Making the beds, washing up, washing clothes, cleaning the house
- Planning all the above
- Or just being there for them instead of going out.

It may be that you don't do all of those things. But it's certain that you *do* do a lot of stuff that other people in your age group don't have to do. So you're different from them.

You're also different from a carer like me because you've probably got nothing to compare your life with. I can look back at a time when I wasn't a carer, and look ahead to one when I won't be. But you may always have been a carer, even though you didn't know that's what you were. And now that you know, maybe you feel that you always will be.

Being different is bad news. It can lead to all manner of difficulties.

Difficulties you might have

Most of the other parts of this book are about how hard it can be to care for somebody else. They're about stress and depression and having no time for yourself and not being able to do things which you'd much rather be doing or things which you feel you ought to be doing. It's about feeling bad that you sometimes have horrible thoughts. It's about the whole complicated business which all carers go through.

Well, teenagers face pressures and strains that adults don't. And now a load of other problems have been piled on to you as well. To be frank, it's asking too much of you. You're caught between a rock and a hard place. And it probably isn't doing you any good.

For example:

At school

At school they can tell you're different, but they may not understand that this is because you're a carer. You may have tried to explain, but got nowhere. Or it's just as likely that you haven't explained at all. If you never realised till now that you were a carer, then no wonder you couldn't tell anyone else.

So you're not exactly flavour of the month with either the teachers or the other people of your own age.

Getting there on time

If you have to get your piglet* up and washed and toileted, and give them their breakfast, and help them get dressed, it's bound to be difficult for you (all right, then, impossible) to get to school on time every day.

Attending regularly

There are going to be days when you can't get to school at all. For instance, when your piglet has a fall, or is just in a bad mood, or when the things that have got to be done at home are so pressing that you have to deal with them. This is when you need to be two people, one who can stay at home and another who can go to school. But you can't split yourself, so you do what seems to be the most important.

Bullying

Anyone who's different is a target for bullying, so you're going to be a target automatically.

Not being able to concentrate

When you're at school your mind isn't really on it. It can be hard to concentrate on lessons, or your friends, if you think something more important could be happening at home.

Leaving early

Sometimes you may be so worried about what's going on at home that you have to rush back early.

---

* This is short for *Person I Give Love and Endless Therapy* to, and it's the name I've given to the person who's looked after by adult selfish pigs. You are definitely NOT a selfish pig, but I'll stick to piglet anyway for the person you care for because the name is short and convenient.

At home

Then, while you're at home, a whole load of different problems are waiting for you.

Taking the decisions

If you're the one who has to do the cooking, you'll know that this is the easy part. It's working out what to get that takes the concentration and the time.

The messy stuff

Dealing with the mess caused by piglets who can't go to the toilet on their own is hard for pretty well all carers. But if you're having to do this for a parent, then it's seriously hard – maybe for both of you.

There's a chapter on this whole topic (Chapter 18) a bit earlier on. In it I said that carers can get a lot of help from being shown how to cope by nurses and specialists. You can be helped, too, though this isn't what I want for you. You see, I don't think you should be doing this at all. I don't think it's right for either you or your piglet.

Social life

Carers get cut off from the outside world. It's what happens to almost all of us. So it's probably happening to you too. When you're home, you're busy doing caring jobs. Which means you don't get to do the things that other people of your age do. Which means in turn that you don't get to do those things with them. So your friendships suffer. And the trouble with this is that having friends isn't just quite nice. It's important.

Homework

Equally, it's going to be hard if not impossible to find time for homework when your work's cut out looking after your piglet. And this is all wrong, as well.

It isn't fair

No it's not. But you may not feel too badly about it. For one thing, you aren't like those other people who don't have piglets. This may have been your way of life so long that it seems natural to you. Tough at times, admittedly. But natural, and so probably right.

For another thing, your family comes first for you. Certainly before the other people at school, or the ones who live nearby.

So though you know you're different, and there are times when you admit that it isn't fair, you put up with it. You might even put up with it gladly. Which is fantastic – for your piglet. And in some ways it's a good thing for you too, to have this bond. And to have passed this test of responsibility.

> The road is long
> With many a winding turn
> That leads us to who knows where
> But I'm strong
> Strong enough to carry him
> He ain't heavy, he's my brother.
>
> *Words by B. Scott and B. Russell*

But there are other ways in which it's distinctly bad for you. After all, you have needs too. And they're not less important than your piglet's. But they *are* different.

You have to be allowed to get educated. Anything that interferes with this is wrong.

You have to be allowed to grow up – which means spending time with your own age group.

If your piglet is your parent, you should not have to be responsible for their medical treatment, or for performing intimate tasks such as bathing them or dealing with their toilet functions.

You may do it because it has to be done and there's nobody else to do it. You may do it because 'he ain't heavy, he's my brother'. You may do it because you can't remember why you do it, but you just do. Whatever the circumstances, the chances are that you're losing out.

Losing out

I don't just mean that you're losing out on something more enjoyable that you could be doing today. What I mean is that your whole future is at risk. Overdramatic? I know it sounds like it. But the fact of the matter is that your caring role now can have long-term repercussions on your emotional development and aspirations.

You're not thinking that far ahead – of course you're not. What all carers do is get through each day as it comes, and this is what you're doing. Other people ought to be thinking ahead for you, and doing something about it. The trouble is, they probably aren't. So, because you're being a good carer and an unselfish pig, you're missing out on:

Education
Education is your right. It's also a necessity for your future. You shouldn't be made to feel that you're needed somewhere else.

Friends
Carers become isolated from their friends by

- the demands of caring
- the attitude of the piglet who may not want you to go out
- feelings of guilt or loyalty
- attitudes of friends.

The sort of thing that can happen is this: you can't stay out late because of the demands of caring, so your friends learn to do without you, and eventually you're no longer part of that circle of friends. If you hate that and so do go out, you feel guilty, and think twice before going out again. Let's say you decide to go out again anyway, it's quite likely that your piglet will feel neglected and will find a way of causing you more work just to make sure you stay by their side.

Your body

If your piglet is bigger and heavier than you are (which is more than likely if they're your parent), it's not only hard for you to lug them about, heaving them on to the toilet or back into bed or even up the stairs, but it could be dangerous for you.

And when I say dangerous, I'm not just thinking about a possible injury or strain today. I'm thinking about a long-term effect which could be with you for the rest of your life.

There are some young carers who heave their parents about, as a matter of routine, in a way that professional care-workers are prohibited from doing. Why are the professionals prohibited? Because it's dangerous for them. And they could be strong men. Yet you're doing it, and nobody's trying to stop you.

Your future

So you see, the things you're doing today for your piglet, out of the best possible motives, could be putting your whole future at risk. And even if other people aren't showing much concern about this, I am. And so should you be.

How did you get into this situation?

Silly question, I expect. It probably just happened. Perhaps you've been a carer for as long as you can remember. Or maybe you know exactly when it started, but can't begin to imagine what else you could have done.

And it's true, you probably couldn't have done anything about it. But the fact remains that you shouldn't really be having to shoulder all this responsibility; and since you are, it's almost certainly because somebody has foisted it on to you. In other words, somebody is exploiting you. Who?

All those people who know what's going on, and are in a position to rescue you but aren't. It could be other members of your family, who don't want to take on the responsibility themselves so are happy for you to let them off the hook. They may know very well that it's not right for you to be doing this caring job, but are turning a blind eye because they're worried that they'd end up doing the work themselves if they stopped you.

Or it might be neighbours. People who live close by, see you missing school, watch you coming home with the shopping, know that your piglet is housebound – and look the other way.

It might even be what I call Officialdom. Adults who are paid to look after you and/or your piglet, but perhaps aren't. Or at least, aren't doing as much about it as they really should. The teachers, for example. Have they noticed you're not putting in as much time at school as some of the others? Have they discovered why? And if so, are they doing anything to lift the load from you?

Or how about social workers? And the doctor? All these people have certain powers which could make your life better. If you're a young carer, the chances are that Officialdom isn't doing what it could and should.

One thing you should know: all carers, young and old, are overcome by great waves of guilt from time to time. And it's almost always unfounded. So if you should ever feel it's your fault that you're in this situation, forget it. It's certainly somebody's fault, and somebody's responsibility. But it isn't yours.

Is there anything you can do about it?

I'd like to say yes. I *do* say that there probably is. But you'll have to fight for it. Which isn't going to be easy, seeing as how you're fully stretched as it is.

What you have to do is turn to those people I mentioned in the previous section, the ones who represent Officialdom, and get them involved. If they're turning a blind eye, make them see you. If they're pretending they're too busy, make a nuisance of yourself till they're forced to pay attention.

You won't win with every single one of them. But if you get just one person to step in and help out, you'll be in a better position than you are now.

Family

Even in big families, most of the caring responsibility tends to fall on one child. It doesn't get shared out, or not much. The ones that don't help are probably too angry or scared or even lazy. Or maybe you're the oldest, and everyone else is too young to help.

So it probably won't do any good for you to appeal to the other people in the family. Even if they could help, ask one of them and they'll come up with all manner of reasons why they can't. They need to pop out to see someone, they've got a job to do round the corner. Whatever.

Or they may agree, and promise to be there. But fail to turn up. And next day they'll say it slipped their mind.

The trouble with all this is that your hopes get raised, and then smashed. It's also disrupting and time-consuming. In the end you could be excused for believing that it's easier just to get on with the job yourself.

Caring is hard enough without having to put up with disappointment and rejection as well. Or so you reason. Well, keep on asking, but don't keep on hoping. Something could happen. Whereas if you never ask, you'll never get.

Friends

Friends and neighbours can carry on in much the same way as family. They can be too busy with their own problems to help you with yours.

348

This is fine, except that yours are more important than theirs. They really are. You've GOT to get help. So don't be too sympathetic to their excuses. Keep asking. One of them will come good, sooner or later.

Officialdom

This is where help is most likely to come from – hard as it is to believe. In another part of this book (Chapter 7), I've said that Officialdom is really on your side even though it doesn't look like that. Officialdom is not only paid to help you, but it actually wants to. The trouble is, they're too busy, and they're hedged about by too many rules and restrictions.

So what you have to do is make them see that you're in trouble. Hanging back is pointless. You have to jump up and down so that they notice you, and then you have to make them aware of what your life, as a carer, is like.

It's no good letting them either ignore you or bully you. *You* have to bully *them*.

Oh yeah? I'm telling you, a teenager, to bully the doctor and head teacher and social worker? Yes, that is exactly what I'm telling you to do.

You've already tried, and got nowhere.	I know, it can be like this. The big problem with Officialdom is that it's divided up into boxes. A teacher's job is to teach, and if you haven't had time to do your homework the teacher may be unwilling to step out of the teaching box to find out why you haven't. Or, if you explain to the teacher what's going on at home, they may decide that your home life is outside their area of responsibility. They may say this is a matter for the social worker.

	But the social worker may see that you're doing a fantastic job for your piglet, and decide that if this doesn't leave you enough time to do your homework, then that's a matter for the school and not for Social Services. Well, what you have to keep sight of is that they're wrong, and you're right. You need help, and it's their job to provide it.
They won't listen?	As far as they're concerned, you're just a kid, whereas they are adults, and professionals, and they know best. Yes, well there's a lot of this about. But not all members of Officialdom are the same. Find one who can and will listen.
They don't understand.	They may be professionals, but they're not carers. They have no idea what you're going through. They live in a different world. Again, not all members of Officialdom are the same. Find one who can understand.
You haven't even tried to get help from Officialdom, because you're afraid to do so.	I'll come to that bit further along. Keep reading.

350

Meantime, let's have a look at the separate boxes of Officialdom, and see what approach you could take with them.

Teachers

I'm thinking here of all your teachers, including the head. A lot of young carers find that teachers are hostile and antagonistic to them. But this is because they don't understand what's going on.

If you tell them, and if they believe you (which they may not), they may respond by not giving you such a hard time. But this isn't the same as helping you solve your problem. Turning a blind eye to the fact that you've bunked off school, or turned up late without your homework, isn't being kind and understanding. It's adding to the problem that you're missing out on your education because you're a carer.

Another response they can have is showing kindness, but in an inappropriate way. One young carer finally got through to her teacher that she was looking after her mum all hours of the day and night, and the teacher organised the rest of the class to buy a plant for her mum.

But school isn't some kind of obstacle put in your path by Officialdom. It's your right, and it's your future. Teachers have a million problems of their own, but they do have a duty to educate you. And they have more power than you do to take some of the caring load off your shoulders.

Some schools have a counsellor or a youth worker you can talk to. And all schools have a nurse. They may be a better bet than a teacher, so try them. Try all of them. Keep at them.

The doctor

Doctors are other members of Officialdom who have the power to help you, but may not come through with the goods. This is

- partly because they don't have enough time to listen to your explanation of what goes on at home

- partly because their knee-jerk reaction to any symptom of any of their patients is to prescribe some medicine or tablets

- mainly because they're concerned with ill people, so focus on your piglet and not on you.

Other health professionals, like district nurses, may be no more useful. For instance a visiting nurse told Claire not to lift her mum, but didn't tell her what she should do instead. She didn't even tell her how to lift her mum properly. All she said was: 'Don't do it.'

What can you do about this? Well, you can write them off as useless, and carry on with your caring. But that's not very clever. Better to recognise that doctors and nurses have powers which you haven't got, but which *can* help, if only indirectly.

What I mean is that their job is often not to solve a problem, but to redirect it to someone who can solve it. For instance, a patient goes to the doctor with back pain, and the doctor sends them to a physiotherapist or other specialist. If you go to see your doctor, not about your piglet but about your problems, the doctor can send out cries for help in many different directions. And as they come from the doctor, they're more likely to result in some action.

Social worker

Your social worker (if you have one) may appear to be more concerned about your piglet than about you. But that's only the way it seems. Social workers *must* concern themselves with the needs of carers as well.

Is this what bothers you? You're worried that the social worker will announce that you mustn't be allowed to look after your piglet and will either put you into care or send your piglet away? Well, those are certainly possibilities. But only if someone is harming you and everything else has been tried. Social workers have other options, too.

For example, they can leave both you and your piglet at home, but send in helpers to do a lot of the tasks you have to cope with at the moment. Especially the ones you hate or find hard.

Want to know why Officialdom would prefer to send in help rather than take one of you away? It's because it's cheaper. So it's government policy to keep carers and piglets together, and if they need help, to provide it.

Young carers all over the place are avoiding social workers, or being rude to them, or ignoring them, for reasons that are wrong. Understandable, but wrong.

Your social worker can change your life. For the better. But you have to give them a try.

Why you're stuck

Let's suppose you're stuck with being a carer, and it's getting in the way of your social life, education, everything. But the reason is not any of those I've suggested so far. What else could it be?

Don't want to stop

Maybe you don't want to come out into the open, and admit to all the things you do as a carer. Perhaps you

- feel more comfortable hiding

- believe it's better not to rock the boat

- don't want to think about the future, but just about today

- haven't thought of yourself as a carer – just someone helping a family member who needs help

- want to keep things in the family.

If your piglet has a disability which you think you might be in line for some day (like one that's passed on through the genes), you may feel that it's only right and proper for you to look after them, and that it would be wrong of you to offload the problem on to someone else.

Well, in 20 years' time you're almost certainly going to look back at what you did today with all the best intentions in the world, and decide some of it was a mistake.

You've been amazingly strong. You *are* being amazingly strong. But now's the time to be strong in a completely different way.

Scared to

You're scared that one of you will be put into care if you draw attention to what you have to do at home. You're frightened that the family will get split up, and that it'll all be your fault.

Well, as I said just now, you're probably worrying unnecessarily about this. The family is more likely to be split up if you don't get some help in.

Can't

You can't stop caring because your piglet needs you, and there's no-one else, and you haven't got the power to change things or the time to try, and this is how life is for you so you're just getting on with it.

Anyway, isn't this what families are for?

Yes, it is. Of course it is. In a way. But you're a member of the family too. And who's looking after you?

Maybe you don't need looking after. Your piglet does, so it's right and proper that you should look after them. Is that what you think?

The trouble is that you didn't really reach that decision. You just found yourself doing the caring because it needed to be done, and you were there. Adult carers get to choose whether they take on this sort of responsibility. But you never had any choice in the matter.

The first two chapters of this book (which you haven't read) are all about deciding whether to care or not. Somewhere else in the book (I can't remember where exactly) it says there may be cases where it's right *not* to care. And in fact some people do choose not to.

But you, you're doing it because you have to. Even though it's preventing you doing other things which, at your age, you really ought to be doing. Even though it might be harming you, emotionally or physically or economically or socially.

What if, knowing all that, you would still choose to care for your piglet? In that case, I'd like to think you would do it in a different way – ie, with help. Because, though it's great that you're caring, it's not great that you're losing out in the process.

It would be better if you carried on showing love and support, but not at the expense of school, friends, going out, listening to music, etc. And it would be much, much better if you didn't have to do stuff which is horrendous, like emptying colostomy bags or clearing up shit, or seeing your mum naked, or anything else that you don't like and can't talk about.

And the fact is that you shouldn't have to do these things. I don't mean that it's a pity you have to do them, and it would be nice if you didn't. No, I mean that you shouldn't be doing them, and in fact you don't have to.

So who's going to take them on?

No need to be a single-hander

Help is out there. There is an alternative. You haven't found it yet, and you almost certainly don't believe me. But there is. There always is, even though nobody tells you what it is, or where to find it.

And the alternative doesn't have to mean you being separated from the person you look after, or one or the other of you being put away. It means help coming in to take some of the load off your shoulders.

Where from? Probably not from the people who *ought* to provide it, like other family members, friends and neighbours. It'll come from the people who *have* to provide it, which means Officialdom. I don't say that these professional care-workers will do as good a job as you. Or that they'll be as reliable. No, there'll be days when they turn up late, or don't turn up at all. They'll do the bare minimum whereas you do much more than that. But the thing is, they'll ease the load for you. And you'll be able to get at least some of your life back.

It's important that you demand proper, ongoing help, as opposed to what's on offer. The support that's on offer is crisis support. People come in when your piglet falls over and you can't get them up again, or when they're even more ill than usual, or when you're ill. But as soon as you begin to be able to manage again, it all disappears.

The other time when professionals step in is when the law has been broken – eg if you don't attend school.

But what you and your piglet both need, and CAN GET, is regular help, every single day, from professional care-workers.

I don't want to be patronising, or to belittle you. But it's a fact that children feel responsible for all sorts of things that happen in their lives which in reality they're not responsible for. In your caring role you're not behaving childishly at all. Caring is an adult role. But thinking that you can or should do it on your own, this is something that comes from the child's belief that it's all their fault, all their responsibility.

You're already doing an adult's job. Now do it the adult way, and get help. You can begin by

- admitting to yourself that you're a carer

- recognising that it's hard to do it on your own

- understanding that you're as important as the person you're caring for

- telling other people, including your teachers, social worker and doctor

- believing in your right to get help

- fighting for it.

How do you set about getting help? Simple. By:

Talking

You have to talk to other people about what you're doing. This isn't disloyal to your piglet. It isn't dangerous, and liable to lead to the breaking up of the family. It's the key to your problems.

There's probably a Young Carers Project near you. If there is, you'll be able to talk to someone who knows a lot about what young carers go through, and who will understand. They'll give you information or advice if you want it. And they'll keep what you say private (unless they think you're in danger or that someone is hurting you, in which case they'll explain that they have to tell someone like a social worker).

There may be a young carers' club that you could visit. If there is, you really should give it a try, because talking to other people of your age group who are in a similar situation to you can be a brilliant experience.

If you're one of the unlucky ones who can't get to a Young Carers Project or club, you can still talk by phoning Childline (0800 1111). This is also a good option if you want to be absolutely sure that what you say won't be told to anyone else, no matter what. You can give them a made-up name, or no name at all. You won't have to tell them where you live, or anything else that you don't want to. And their number won't show up on most phone bills because it's free.

Who to?

What if you haven't talked to anyone before about any of this? What if you understand what I've been on about in this chapter, and agree there may be something in it – but still find it hard to know where to begin?

And one more thing: what if you're not much of a talker, and are scared that you won't be able to get your message across?

Don't worry about it. It's not a problem. Take this book, with the bit of paper marking the chapter, and show it to all those people who have the power to make things happen: your teacher, doctor, social worker, for example. Or if not them, then someone else who you think might start the ball rolling for you.

Help is there, I promise you. And it's time you got it.

CHAPTER 22

Afterwards

Don't even think about it

How it can come about
Piglet recovers
Somebody else takes over your job
Piglet dies

Grieving

Adjusting

The rest of your life

Afterwards

When I set out to do this book I was really thinking of you as someone who was new, or fairly new, to caring. Someone who was struggling to come to terms with it. Someone who was fighting against the injustice of having their own life taken away from them.

If that is indeed where you are, the prospect of an afterwards may seem distant and, at the moment, irrelevant. What's more, for some carers there may never be an afterwards at all. If you're the parent of a disabled child, for instance. For you, caring could be a project for life. Again, if you're already old, or very ill yourself, it's a fair possibility that your piglet will outlive you.

Of course, it's nonsense to say there won't be an afterwards in those circumstances. All I mean is that there won't be an afterwards for *you*. If you die first, your piglet will still be here, and will still need to be looked after.* The business of dependence, being cared for, battling on, will continue for them. But as for you, you'll be out of it.

However, this book is for selfish pigs, not for piglets. So this chapter isn't about what might happen to the piglet after you've popped your clogs. It's about you and the as yet hypothetical time in the future when you find that you're no longer a carer.

Don't even think about it

The big question is: should we even contemplate a time when our caring days will be over? Is it right? Is it helpful? Is it possible, even? I suspect most of us find that we can't see round the

---

* Incidentally, just in case you should be run over by a bus while out shopping, having left your piglet at home, it might be a bright idea to keep a note in your wallet or handbag saying something like this:

  'I am a carer. The person I care for [name] may be at [address] and in need of help. Please contact X.'

next corner, and that the only thing we can do, whether we like it or not, is plod on, taking each day as it comes.

On the other hand, you may find that you *do* think about the future. And when you do, it's with mixed emotions. There may be times (I'm thinking of those terrible times in which terrible thoughts assail you) when you find yourself guiltily yearning to be released. At other, happier moments, you may regard it with dread. Whether you do either of these things, or never think about it at all, what I believe I've learned is that it will come as a shock when it does come.

So maybe there is a case for looking ahead. Perhaps, when the time arrives, you'll be better equipped to cope if you've thought about it first.

You see, according to the books, it's important not to let caring take over your whole life. If you fall into that trap, they say, you'll be less effective as a carer and you'll bugger up your chances of having a life afterwards. And that's what we're really talking about here: your life afterwards.

The trouble is, caring *is* your whole life, while you're doing it. How can it not be considering the nature of the job, the hours you put in, and the way it has revolutionised absolutely everything? So the odds are that, when and if your caring role ceases, you'll see it less as a blessed release for you than the end of everything you've come to know.

That may be hard to believe right now. At a time in your caring life when you constantly lift your eyes heavenward and mutter (or scream) 'Give me a break,' the last thing you expect a permanent break to be is the end of your life.

So, how can you engineer it in such a way that, far from being the end of everything, it turns out to be a new beginning? Or rather, how can you think of it from the perspective of now, without feeling guilty that you're thinking about it at all, in such a way that you're less likely to have the rug pulled out from under your feet when it happens?

How it can come about

There are several ways in which your caring days could finish.
For example:

Piglet recovers

Or stabilises and becomes more independent. You'll know
instantly whether to go on with this paragraph or not. Obviously
I realise you won't have picked up a book about the difficulties
of being a carer if you're nursing somebody through mumps.
Whatever the disabilities our piglets suffer from, they're not the
sort that suddenly disappear. Even so, not all piglets remain
dependent. Some – and I'm not talking about miracles –
improve enough for you to turn your attention to other matters.
In which case it's either a respite or a happy ending to your
caring story, and one which may not pose too many difficulties
for afterwards.

Somebody else takes over your job

Perhaps another member of the family will step in and relieve
you. No, don't say 'fat chance' so dismissively. What if you got so
dangerously close to burnout that it became impossible for you to
carry on? Or if you became physically incapacitated yourself?

Officialdom could decree that you mustn't continue to bear
the burden of caring, either because you're too young and it's
spoiling your life, or because you're making a cock-up of the job
and it's decreed that the piglet needs to be removed for their
own good.

The most likely circumstance in which you hand over the job
to somebody else is when your piglet goes into full-time residential care. In other words, a care-home, or special hospital, or
nursing home. This will almost certainly be a really hard decision and a difficult time for both of you. But if it's what happens

you won't actually turn into an ex-carer overnight. So I don't count this situation as coming under the heading of afterwards.

What it'll mean is that you stop being a full-time carer and turn into a carer-by-remote-control. You'll visit the piglet, have consultations with the care-home staff, and go on liaising with the doctor. True, you'll have much more time to yourself, but what you aren't going to feel like is an ex-carer.

But ex-caring is the situation which you need to think about here. The point when you get your life back. And I'm sorry to say it, but this really means when your piglet dies.

Piglet dies

I'm now looking at a place I haven't visited. All I have done is think about it, which is what I'm suggesting we all should do. Not all the time, of course. Not much, even. But beforehand, sometimes, if possible.

What we're told is that the death of a piglet, whether anticipated or not, always come as a sudden shock. And that the time it takes to get over it is always long.

When you became a carer, you may have had to adapt quickly. For instance, if your previously healthy piglet suffered a stroke, you will have been landed straight in it. Alternatively, you may have spent years even coming to a state of recognition that you were in fact a carer – for example, if the person you live with was almost imperceptibly slipping into dependence. Well, this time you've got to face both processes at the same time but in reverse.

One day you're a carer and the next day you're not. But next year, or the year after that, you may still not quite have remembered who you used to be. What it's like to have a life of your own. What techniques there are for putting yourself first.

> 'I lost my best friend, my lover, my husband. Everyone told me that now I'd be able to do anything I wanted, go where I liked. But all I wanted to do was what I'd been doing before, and look after him.'
>
> *Mary, on the death of her piglet*

It's not that Mary, or you, or anyone else, is unable to change. It's shock. And grief.

Grieving

It seems to me that probably all grief is intolerable, unique, and incapable of being managed. And that the grief of a bereaved carer may very well be among the hardest of all to bear. You and your piglet will have shared a disability. You will have sailed together through the same sea, and during the voyage you will have become interdependent. Joint piglets. In some ways almost interchangeable. So now you're only half of a previous whole. You're one hand clapping. Except that you won't want to clap.

> *He first deceased; she for a little tried*
> *To live without him: liked it not, and died.*
>
> *Henry Wotton, 1568–1639, upon the death of a widow*

But you won't die. You'll go on. And for an unspecified time, you'll grieve.

This book, and this author, can offer no help. I wish we could. What I can do is recommend Virginia Ironside's book *You'll Get Over It* (published by Penguin Books) because it tells it the way I suspect it is, and because it helped a friend of mine.

I found that a lot of what Virginia Ironside had to offer rang bells. For example: 'The only single truth about bereavement that I can come up with is that it is something that has to be endured alone. True, people on the sidelines can give encouraging waves; other travellers might be able to help over rocky patches; but though our emotional experiences may be similar, none of them are ever the same.'

If that's true, then your time after caring is going to resemble, painfully, the time you spent as a carer. You're on your own in your caring, and it looks as though you're going to be just as much on your own in your grieving afterwards. But knowing that it is so could lend you some of the strength you'll need to live through it.

How long will it take to recover? Quoting V. I. again: 'Recovery implies that after a certain time you return to your natural state, but nothing, after a big bereavement, can ever be the same again. Recovery of what? Does recovery mean being able to go back to work? Even if it does, you will not be the same person as you were beforehand, that's for sure.'

And again: 'My own instinctive feeling is that you *do not work through bereavement. It works through you.*'

Finally: 'How long does it last? For ever, I would say. But the actual period when you feel utterly screwed up could be anything from six months to six years.'

Adjusting

The reason I started on this chapter, and probably the reason you're reading it, is to think ahead about what to do after caring, when you get your life back. Well, it looks as though there's going to be no sudden transition between being a carer and not being a carer. It looks as though there'll be a period in which you're no longer a carer but haven't yet regained what, before, you would have called normality.

If this is the way it works out, and yet you haven't expected it, you could find yourself asking: 'What's wrong with me?' But there won't be anything wrong with you.

> 'People said: "It must be marvellous for you to have your freedom back." But it wasn't. For a long time. And then suddenly it was. And then I was like a child in a sweet shop.'
>
> *Mary, on having stopped being a carer*

To begin with, Mary clung to some of the old routines which had been established during her caring days. She cooked and ate the same sort of meals that she had cooked for her piglet. She even ate at the same times throughout the day, and as before never varied from them.

Though she knew she could now do anything and go anywhere, she didn't. Instead she built restrictions around herself, this time based on her dog.

Every morning she would eye with apprehension the day stretching before her, a day bereft not only of her piglet but of all the tasks which had previously occupied her. Now she didn't know how to fill the hours. She told me: 'In a way, life seemed pointless because I no longer had this job to do.'

When her piglet had suffered his first stroke, it affected his speech, so he and Mary had communicated through gestures and, it seemed, by thought, almost. After he died, she found she was constantly called on to use words; lots of them. She wasn't used to this, and found it tiring.

Another thing she found was that her self-confidence was at a low ebb. She attributes this to the effects of her caring when (as the rest of us have found out for ourselves) there is no recognition, no outside reward. So, with low self-esteem, but forced to confront a now alien world, she faltered and progressed in tiny steps.

But after 18 months, she said, 'I was beginning to feel like a separate person, instead of half of a joined-up one.' She still hadn't decided how to shape her new life. But she was almost ready to start.

The rest of your life

Perhaps you already know what you're going to do with your life when you get it back. I sometimes think I do. But at other times I'm not so sure. The problem is that caring changes you. So it may not be realistic to assume that the person you will be can simply pick up at the point where the person you used to be left off.

It seems to me that you'll be at a T-junction. You'll be able to choose to go one way or the other, but not both. If you go in one direction, you'll move right away from everything to do with caring. You'll feel that you've been there, done that, and now it's time for something completely different. You'll want to explore some of those areas which were out of bounds to you before. You may even have made plans while you were still caring. If so, now's the time to see if you can make them happen.

The road leading in the opposite direction will take you to places which you couldn't have visited before you became a carer. Go down this road and you'll be acknowledging the changes that have overtaken you. Perhaps utilising them as well.

I know some ex-carers who, aware of how little they knew when they started out and how much valuable information they have stored away since, decided to place this experience at the disposal of newcomers to caring. Also of those, not necessarily newcomers, who were in trouble. And I have reason to be grateful to them.

Which way will I go? I don't know. Some days I dream of sailing down to Cape Horn, up to Alaska via Tahiti and Hawaii, then back by way of California, the Panama Canal, Bermuda and the Azores. Other days I plan schemes to provide training for carers, helping them to avoid being driven to distraction by this demanding job, breaking them out of their solitary confinement.

I even play around with thoughts of trying to achieve both. Then I'm brought up short by the realisation that I may never even reach the T-junction. Or that if I do I might be too old to achieve anything very much.

If that's how it works out for me, will I mind? Once, I thought I would, and oscillated between bitterness and a determination not to be cheated out of the life that ought to have been mine.

Now, as time goes on, I'm not so sure. It's true there are things I wanted to do, and haven't done. But then, there are things I've learned, things I didn't know before, and would never have discovered otherwise. I never incorporated them into any of my plans. I never thought they were important. But looking back, I find I think they are.

What will I do when I get my life back? What will you do? Who knows? All those decisions are round the corner, where none of us can see. Meantime, we have our piglets to look after.

THE END

Glossary

Advocacy

A technical term in the world of caring. It means: speaking up on behalf of a piglet or carer to try to ensure that their voice is heard, that they get the services they want and need, that they know their rights, and have the information to make informed choices.

Care in the Community

Officialdom's phrase for the mix of help, support and care which allows people to go on living in their own home rather than having to move into a residential home. The same as Community Care.

Caregiver

Someone who cares for a person who is disabled, sick or elderly, usually a relation, neighbour or friend, and is not paid for doing so. The same as a Carer.

Carer

Someone who cares for a person who is disabled, sick or elderly, usually a relation, neighbour or friend, and is not paid for doing so. The same as Caregiver

Care-worker

Someone who is paid to care for another person. As opposed to a Carer, or Informal Carer, who is unpaid, and usually a relation, friend or neighbour.

Community Care	Officialdom's phrase for the mix of help, support and care which allows people to go on living in their own home rather than having to move into a residential home. The same as Care in the Community.
Day Centre	A place, properly equipped and staffed, where piglets can go during the day.
Direct Payments	A scheme by which Social Services give you money to buy the services you need, instead of providing the services themselves. The idea is that you then have greater choice, control and flexibility in managing the services you get.
Independent Living Advocacy (ILA)	An independent formal advocacy service managed by disabled people. Independent Living Advocacy promotes the empowerment of disabled people. Empowerment is the process of supporting disabled people to take control for themselves.
Informal Carer	Officialdom's word for a Carer, ie someone who cares for a person who is disabled, sick or elderly, usually a relation or neighbour, and is not paid for doing so.
Occupational Therapy	Occupational therapists (OTs) help piglets improve their ability to perform tasks in their daily living and working environments. They work with piglets

who have conditions that are mentally, physically, developmentally, or emotionally disabling, and with their carers. They help piglets develop, recover, or maintain daily living and work skills. OTs try not only to help clients improve basic motor functions and reasoning abilities, but also compensate for permanent loss of function. Their goal is to help clients have independent, productive, and satisfying lives.

Outreach	A service that reaches out to people outside the normal operating area of an organisation.
Respite Care	Care for the Carers: in which the piglet is looked after for anything from a few hours to a few weeks while you have a break.
Social Services	The arm of local government responsible for the support of piglets and Carers.
Speech and Language Therapist (S&LT)	If you have trouble understanding your piglet because of problems with swallowing or speaking, the S&LT may help you cope by giving you a better understanding of what's going on.
Triage	Allocation of treatment to patients according to the urgency of their medical needs.

Sources

Backs – Injury Prevention, by Leonard Ring
Care for the Carer, by Christine Orton
Carers, Research and Practice, by Julia Twigg
Carers' Companion, by Richard Corney
Carers Awareness Programme – a series of seminars by Carers Together, a carers' support charity in Hampshire, UK
Caring for the Carers, by Christine Ledger
Caring for the Carers, by Valerie Barden
Children Who Care, by Jo Aldridge and Saul Becker
Counselling and Helping Carers, by Alastair McDonald and Mitchell Noon
Helping Yourself Help Others: A Book for Caregivers, by Rosalynn Carter, with Susan Golant
Mental Health of Carers, by Nicola Singleton
Moving and Lifting: a Handbook for Professional Carers, by Martin Hutchinson
The Princess Royal Trust for Carers, a charitable trust and carers' support group
Safer Handling of People in the Community, produced by Back Care, co-ordinating author Ron Steed
Staying Sane, by Tanya Arroba and Lesley Bell
The 36-Hour Day, by Nancy Mace, Peter Rabins, Beverly Castleton, Evelyn McEwen and Barbara Meredith
The Back, Problems and Prevention, by Vivian Grisogono
The Comfort of Home: An Illustrated Step-by-Step Guide for Caregivers, by Maria M. Meyer with Paula Derr
The Which? Guide to Managing Back Trouble, by Dr Harry Brown, revised by Dr Jeremy Soper
Understanding Caring, from the Carers National Association
Who Cares – Looking After People at Home, by Cherril Hicks
Working With Carers, by Rosie Bell

Young Carers, by Andrew Bibby
Young Carers, by Chris Dearden
You'll Get Over It – the Rage of Bereavement, by Virginia Ironside

Index

THE STEP-PARENTS' PARACHUTE

Flora McEvedy

In a society where one in three marriages now ends in divorce, the traditional model of the nuclear family unit is losing relevance. A startling one in every six children is a stepchild. Yet this phenomenon is hopelessly uncharted territory, where the image of the wicked stepmother still presides.

Flora McEvedy could find nothing to help her when she became a stepmother at the age of twenty-eight and the unique passion and energy of this book stems from her experiences. Neatly organised, easy to use, practical and positive, this is an inspirational book that gives the reader sound advice and practical help from someone who has experienced the difficulties of step-parenting herself.

The Step-parents' Parachute sets out sound principles – which the author divides into four key cornerstones – that include the importance of teamwork between partners to overcome jealousy, and keeping rejection at arm's length if the step-parent/child relationship is initially hostile. These cornerstones offer a path through a subject riven with negative assumptions and enable the transformation of the stepfamily into a happy, rewarding and stable unit.

THE MIND GYM:
WAKE YOUR MIND UP

In much of our lives, our minds operate on autopilot.

Rather like the tourist who repeats the same words louder each time the local doesn't understand, we tend to continue thinking and behaving in similar ways, even if this isn't getting us what we want.

However, once we can spot these mental habits, we can change them.

As a result, we are more likely to

• achieve more in less time

• gain energy and have less negative stress

• resolve difficult challenges

• win people round to our point of view

• enjoy life

Over 100,000 people have taken part in and recommended *The Mind Gym*'s workouts. Now, for the first time, hundreds of these practical tips and techniques based on applied psychology are packed into this book and, with your free personal membership number, at *The Mind Gym Online*.

THE MIND GYM:
GIVE ME TIME

I haven't got time to read this book

The problem of not having enough time is as old as time itself, and so are most of the proposed cures. The trouble is, they don't seem to work.

The Mind Gym: Give Me Time proposes a radically different approach to time and how we use it.

Combining extensive psychological research with five years of testing amongst The Mind Gym's 100,000 members, this book offers practical solutions that will make you feel great about how your time is spent.

The Mind Gym: Give Me Time is packed with techniques including

• how to achieve more by slowing down

• tiny time investments that deliver massive returns

• how to say 'no' and be loved for it

• simple ways to get other people to do your work for you

• how to get time with people who haven't got time for you

And there's no need to read this book from cover to cover. The questionnaire at the start guides you directly to the chapters that will help you most.

Find time, inside.

YOUNGER NEXT YEAR

Henry S. Lodge, M.D. and Chris Crowley

Younger Next Year is for men who want to turn back their biological clocks. It explains how men can become functionally younger every year for years to come, and continue to live with vitality and grace into their eighties and beyond. Harry's Seven Rules – Harry being Henry S. Lodge, M.D. – can help to reverse the typical path of ageing. Exercise six days a week for the rest of your life. Quit eating crap. Connect and commit. And to prove it works is his star patient, the no-punches-pulled Chris Crowley, a seventy-year-old who left the slippery slope of retirement and turned his life around. Harry tells you what to do. Chris shows you how. And their argument is irresistible.

Marrying science and reality, *Younger Next Year* is a convincing and passionate argument that if you train for the Next Third of your life, you'll have a ball. Follow its simple rules and you'll find yourself in the best shape – in mind, body and spirit – of your life.

Chris Crowley is a former lawyer who retired in 1990 to write, ski, sail, windsurf, cook and spend time with his wife. Henry S. Lodge runs a world-renowned practice in Manhattan. Both authors live in New York.

Other bestselling Time Warner Books titles available by mail: